WITCHBLADE: DISTINCTIONS
ISBN: **1-58240-199-3**

Published by Image Comics™

WITCHBLADE: DISTINCTIONS VOL. #1, APRIL 2001. FIRST
PRINTING. Published by Image Comics Inc. Office of Publication:
1071 N. Botavia St. Suite A Orange CA 92867. $14.95 US / $23.80 in
Canada. Collecting Tales of the Witchblade issues 1-6. Witchblade®
its logo and all related characters ®, ™ & © 2001 Top Cow
Productions Inc. ALL RIGHTS RESERVED. T
this book are ™ & © 2001 Top Cow Product
to persons living or dead is purely coinciden
of artwork used for review purposes, none of
may be reprinted in any form without the exp
Marc Silvestri or Top Cow Productions Inc.

PRINTED IN CANADA

Other Witchblade books available from
Top Cow Productions & Image Comics:

WITCHBLADE DELUXE COLLECTED EDITION (ISBN: **1-887279-15-2**)
WITCHBLADE REVELATIONS (ISBN: 1-58240-161-6)
WITCHBLADE: PREVAILING (ISBN: 1-58240-175-6)
MEDIEVAL SPAWN/ WITCHBLADE (ISBN: 1-887279-44-x)
WITCHBLADE/ DARKNESS: FAMILY TIES (ISBN: 1-58240-030-x)

Also available from Top Cow Productions & Image Comics:

RISING STARS: BORN IN FIRE (ISBN: 1-58240-172-1)
THE DARKNESS DELUXE COLLECTED EDITION (ISBN: 1-58240-032-6)
THE DARKNESS: SPEAR OF DESTINY (ISBN: 1-58240-147-0)
CYBERFORCE: ASSAULT WITH A DEADLY WOMAN (ISBN: 1-887279-04-0)
CYBERFORCE: TIN MEN OF WAR (ISBN: 1-58240-190-x)
TOMB RAIDER: SAGA OF THE MEDUSA MASK (ISBN: 1-58240-164-0)
TOMB RAIDER: MYSTIC ARTIFACTS (ISBN: 1-58240-202-7)

To order telephone 1-888-TOPCOW1 (1-888-867-2691)

What did you think of this book? We love to hear from our readers.
Please email us at: witchblade@topcow.com.
or write to us at:
Witchblade c/o.
Top Cow Productions Inc.
10390 Santa Monica Blvd. Suite 110
Los Angeles, CA. 90025

visit us on the web at
www.topcow.com

FOR image COMICS
JIM VALENTINO
publisher

for

WITCHBLADE
DISTINCTIONS

Original Series Editor:	DAVID WOHL
Original Series Assistant Editors:	MARY BUXTON, MICHAEL MANCZAREK
Design:	JASON MEDLEY & -EL-
Art Direction:	PETER STEIGERWALD
Collected Editions Editor:	PETER STEIGERWALD
Managing Editor:	RENAE GEERLINGS
Editorial Assistants:	JASON ROSS, STEVE HALVERSON & SINA GRACE
Editor In Chief:	DAVID WOHL
Production:	NICK CHUN, ALVIN COATS, & BETH SOTELO
Cover:	RANDY GREEN, D-TRON & STEVE FIRCHOW

TOP COW is

MARC SILVESTRI_chief executive officer
MATT HAWKINS_president of publishing
DAVID WOHL_president of creative affairs/editor in chief
PETER STEIGERWALD_vp of publishing and design/art director
RENAE GEERLINGS_managing editor

FRANK MASTROMAURO_director of sales and marketing
NICHOLAS CHUN_production manager
VINCE HERNANDEZ_direct sales manager
ALVIN COATS_special projects coordinator

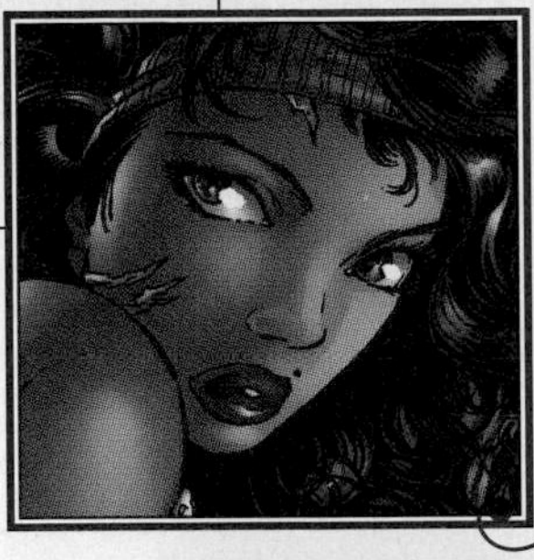

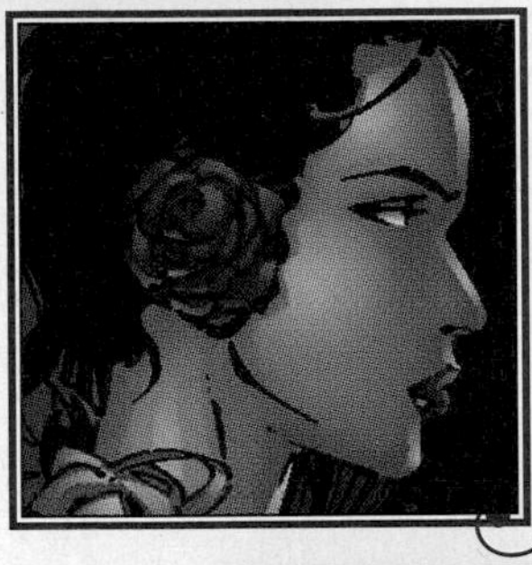

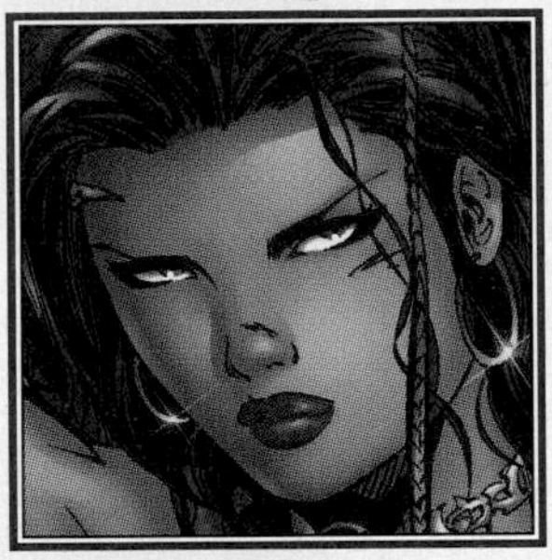

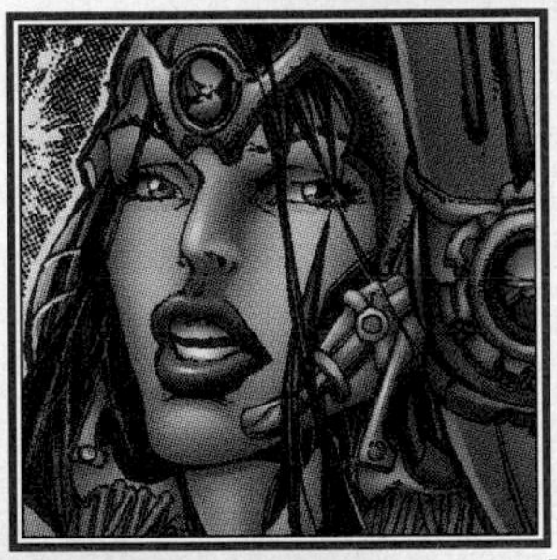

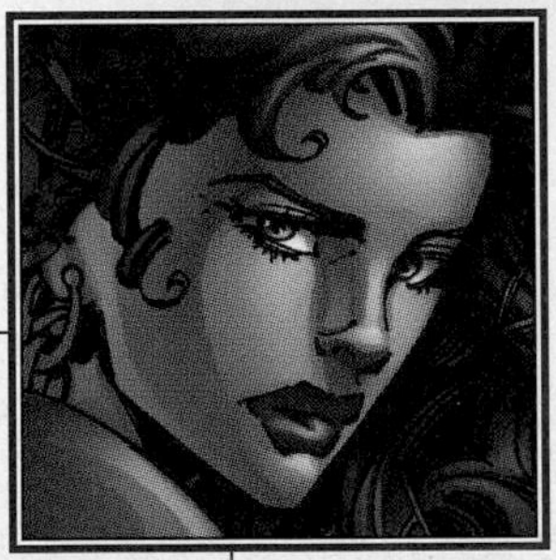

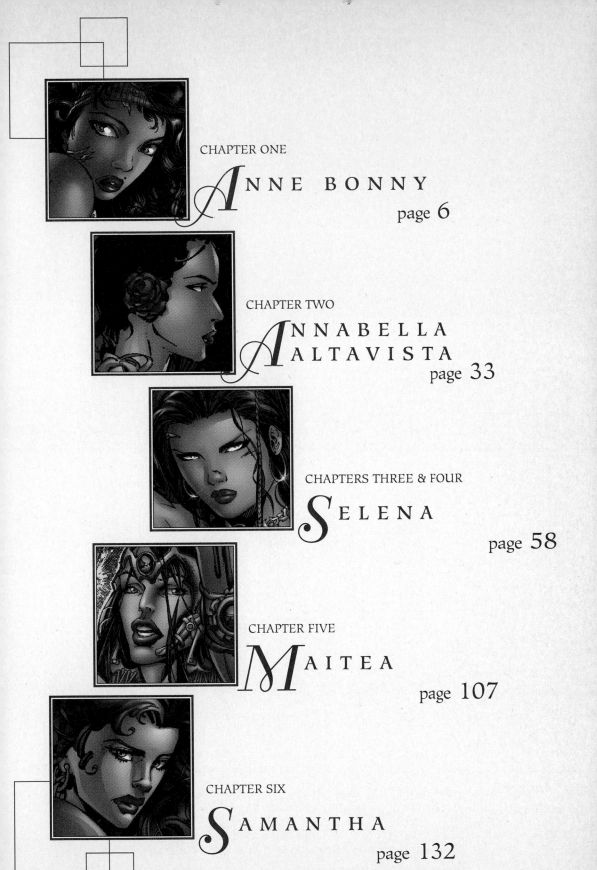

Witchblade Created by: MARC SILVESTRI, DAVID WOHL, BRIAN HABERLIN AND MICHAEL TURNER

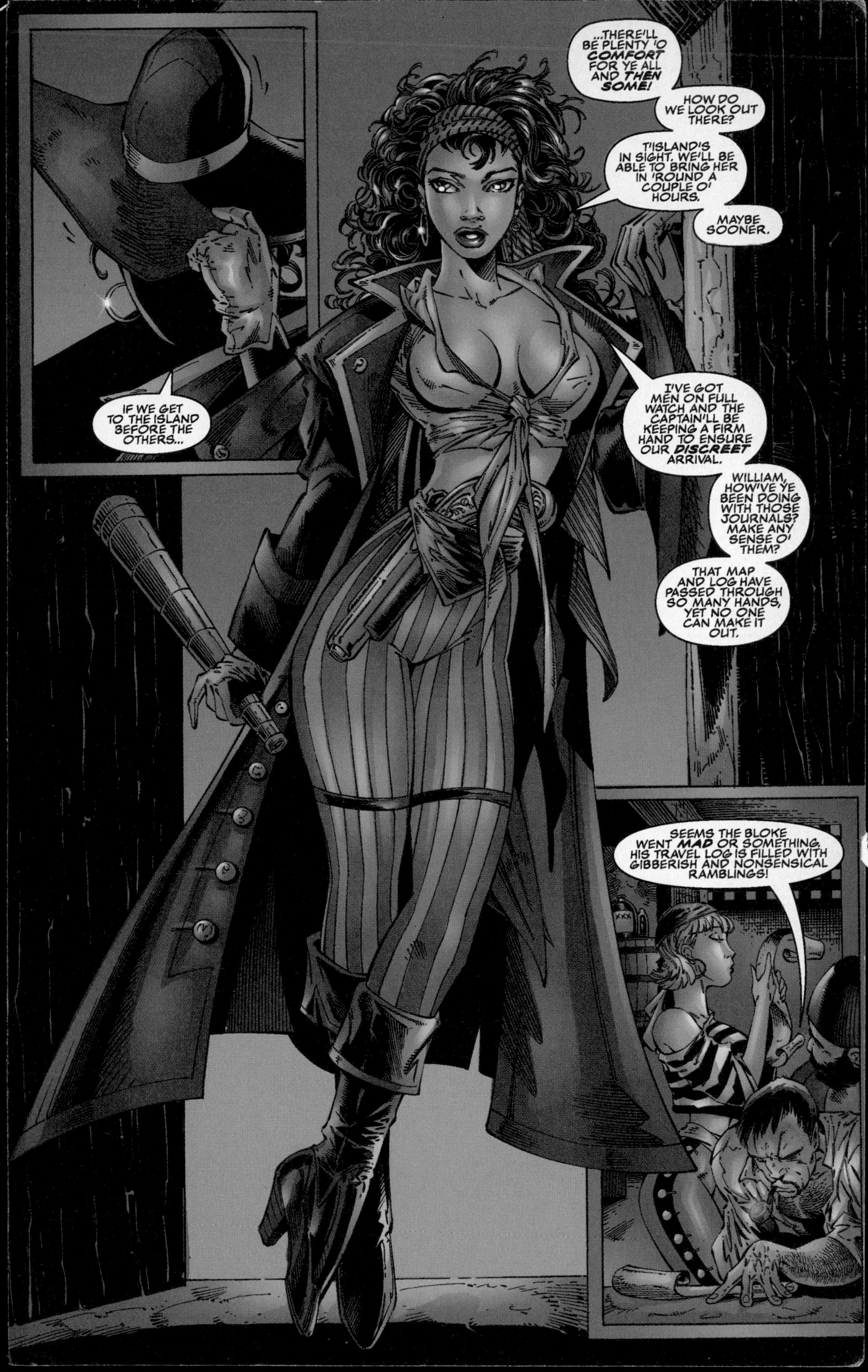
...THERE'LL BE PLENTY 'O COMFORT FOR YE ALL AND THEN SOME!
IF WE GET TO THE ISLAND BEFORE THE OTHERS...
HOW DO WE LOOK OUT THERE?
T'ISLAND'S IN SIGHT. WE'LL BE ABLE TO BRING HER IN 'ROUND A COUPLE O' HOURS.
MAYBE SOONER.
I'VE GOT MEN ON FULL WATCH AND THE CAPTAIN'LL BE KEEPING A FIRM HAND TO ENSURE OUR DISCREET ARRIVAL.
WILLIAM, HOW'VE YE BEEN DOING WITH THOSE JOURNALS? MAKE ANY SENSE O' THEM?
THAT MAP AND LOG HAVE PASSED THROUGH SO MANY HANDS, YET NO ONE CAN MAKE IT OUT.
SEEMS THE BLOKE WENT MAD OR SOMETHING. HIS TRAVEL LOG IS FILLED WITH GIBBERISH AND NONSENSICAL RAMBLINGS!

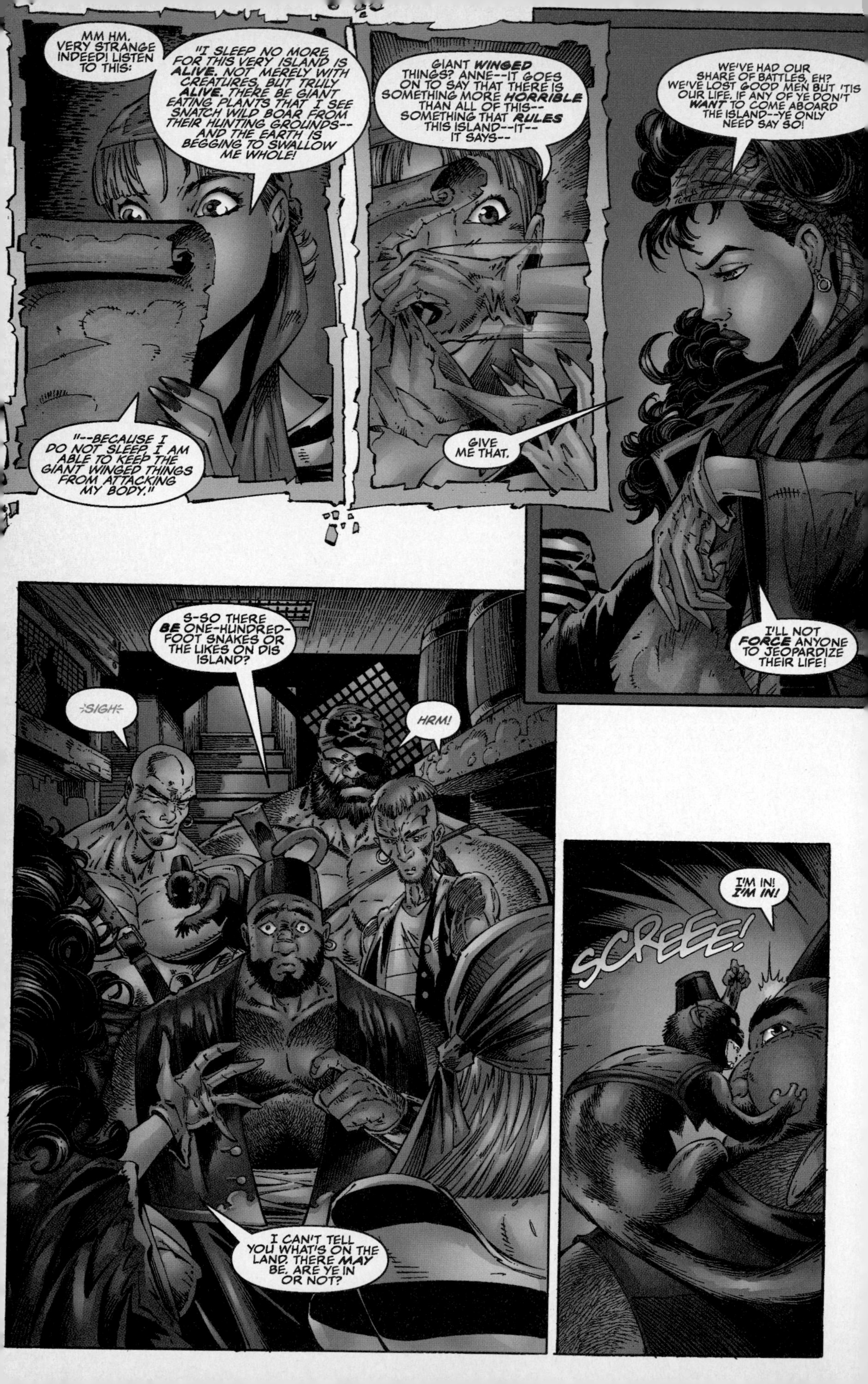
MM HM. VERY STRANGE INDEED! LISTEN TO THIS:
"I SLEEP NO MORE, FOR THIS VERY ISLAND IS ALIVE. NOT MERELY WITH CREATURES, BUT TRULY ALIVE. THERE BE GIANT EATING PLANTS THAT I SEE SNATCH WILD BOAR FROM THEIR HUNTING GROUNDS--AND THE EARTH IS BEGGING TO SWALLOW ME WHOLE!
"--BECAUSE I DO NOT SLEEP I AM ABLE TO KEEP THE GIANT WINGED THINGS FROM ATTACKING MY BODY."
GIANT WINGED THINGS? ANNE--IT GOES ON TO SAY THAT THERE IS SOMETHING MORE HORRIBLE THAN ALL OF THIS--SOMETHING THAT RULES THIS ISLAND--IT--IT SAYS--
GIVE ME THAT.
WE'VE HAD OUR SHARE OF BATTLES, EH? WE'VE LOST GOOD MEN BUT 'TIS OUR LIFE. IF ANY OF YE DON'T WANT TO COME ABOARD THE ISLAND--YE ONLY NEED SAY SO!
I'LL NOT FORCE ANYONE TO JEOPARDIZE THEIR LIFE!
S-SO THERE BE ONE-HUNDRED-FOOT SNAKES OR THE LIKES ON DIS ISLAND?
:SIGH:
HRM!
I CAN'T TELL YOU WHAT'S ON THE LAND. THERE MAY BE. ARE YE IN OR NOT?
I'M IN! I'M IN!
SCREEEE!

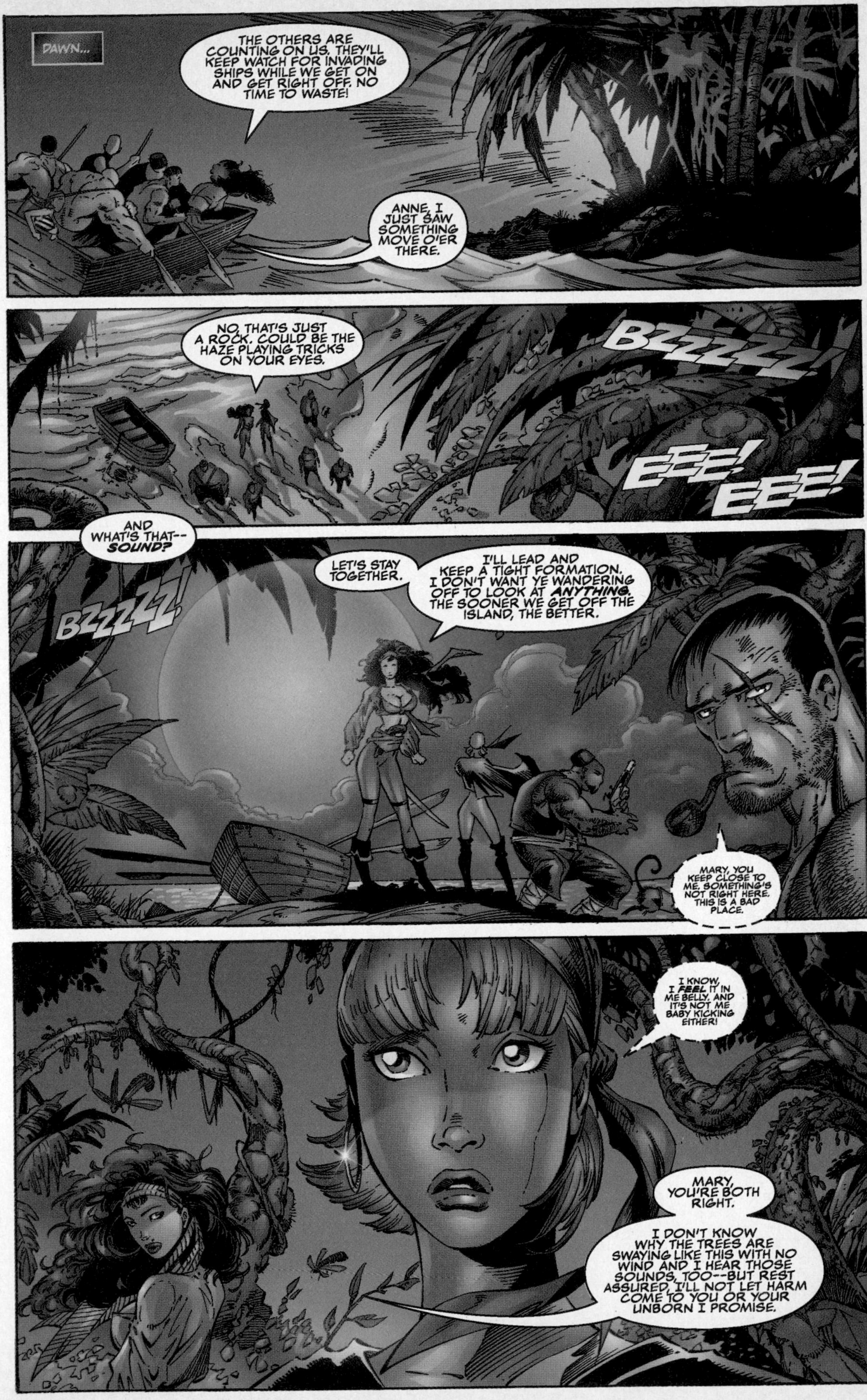
DAWN...
THE OTHERS ARE COUNTING ON US. THEY'LL KEEP WATCH FOR INVADING SHIPS WHILE WE GET ON AND GET RIGHT OFF. NO TIME TO WASTE!
ANNE, I JUST SAW SOMETHING MOVE O'ER THERE.
NO, THAT'S JUST A ROCK. COULD BE THE HAZE PLAYING TRICKS ON YOUR EYES.
BZZZZZ!
EEEE! EEEE!
AND WHAT'S THAT-- SOUND?
BZZZZZ!
LET'S STAY TOGETHER.
I'LL LEAD AND KEEP A TIGHT FORMATION. I DON'T WANT YE WANDERING OFF TO LOOK AT ANYTHING. THE SOONER WE GET OFF THE ISLAND, THE BETTER.
MARY, YOU KEEP CLOSE TO ME. SOMETHING'S NOT RIGHT HERE. THIS IS A BAD PLACE.
I KNOW, I FEEL IT IN ME BELLY, AND IT'S NOT ME BABY KICKING EITHER!
MARY, YOU'RE BOTH RIGHT.
I DON'T KNOW WHY THE TREES ARE SWAYING LIKE THIS WITH NO WIND AND I HEAR THOSE SOUNDS, TOO--BUT REST ASSURED, I'LL NOT LET HARM COME TO YOU OR YOUR UNBORN I PROMISE.

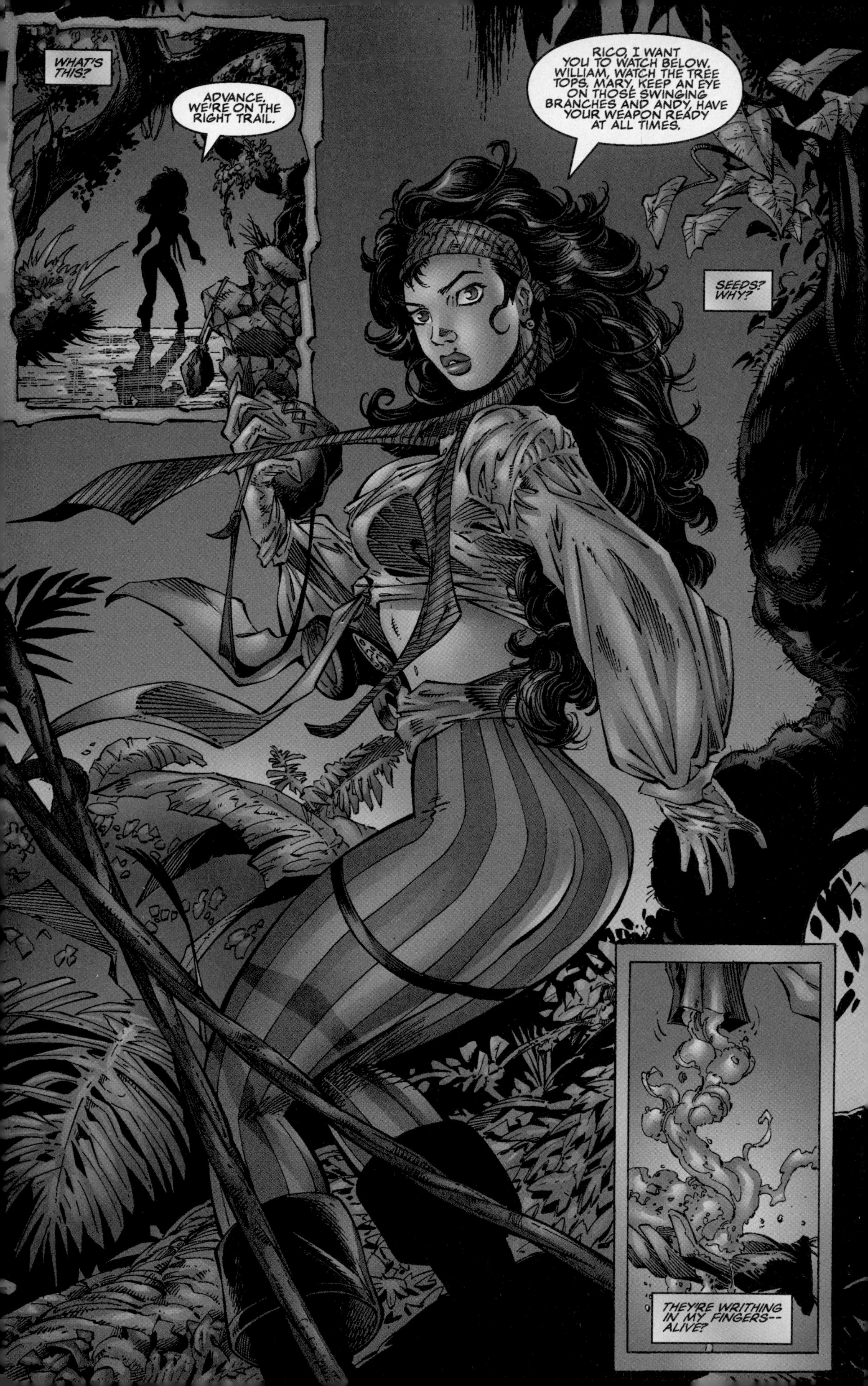
WHAT'S THIS?
ADVANCE. WE'RE ON THE RIGHT TRAIL.
RICO, I WANT YOU TO WATCH BELOW. WILLIAM, WATCH THE TREE TOPS. MARY, KEEP AN EYE ON THOSE SWINGING BRANCHES AND ANDY, HAVE YOUR WEAPON READY AT ALL TIMES.
SEEDS? WHY?
THEY'RE WRITHING IN MY FINGERS-- ALIVE?

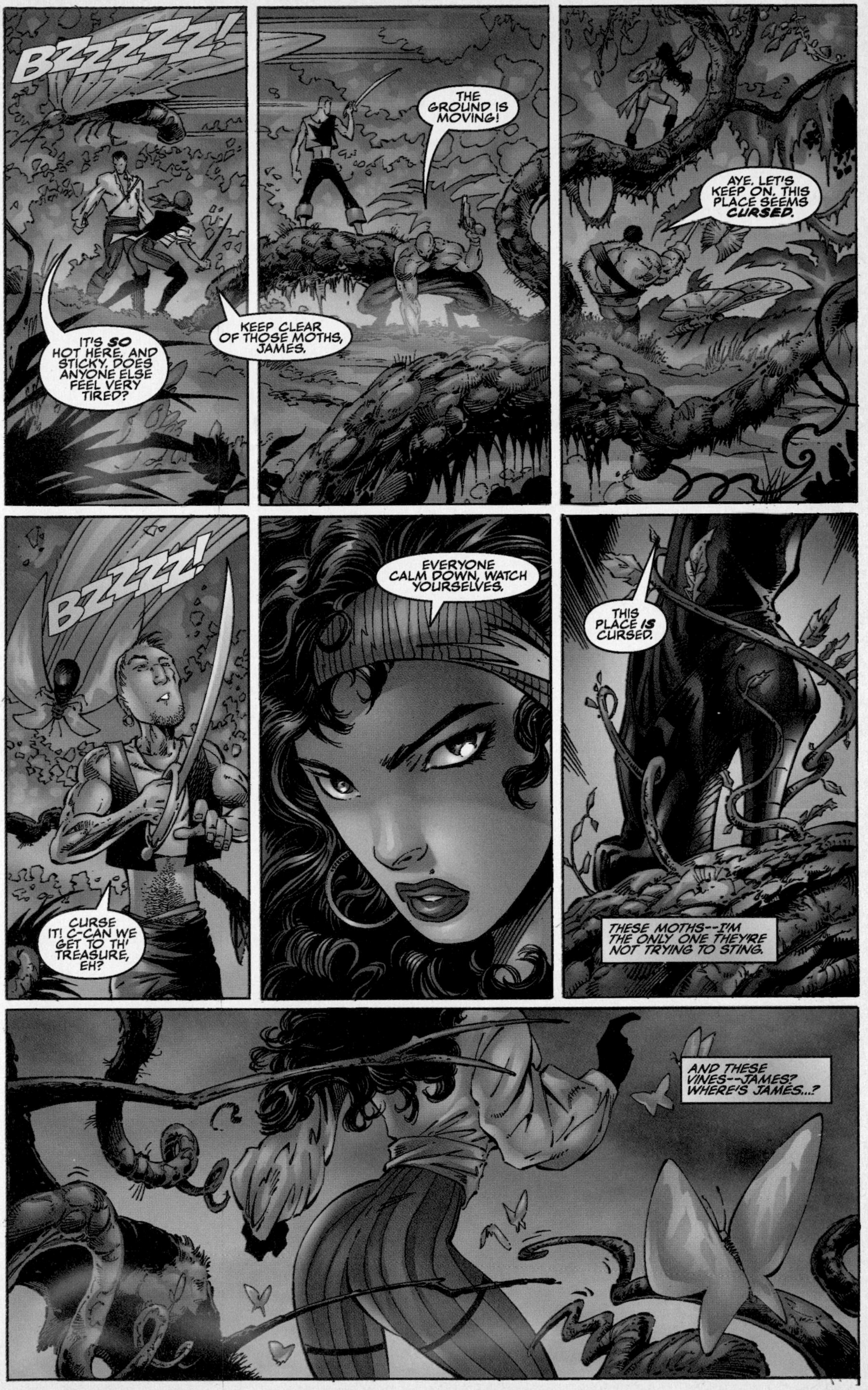
BZZZZZ!
IT'S SO HOT HERE, AND STICKY. DOES ANYONE ELSE FEEL VERY TIRED?
KEEP CLEAR OF THOSE MOTHS, JAMES.
THE GROUND IS MOVING!
AYE. LET'S KEEP ON. THIS PLACE SEEMS CURSED.
BZZZZ!
CURSE IT! C-CAN WE GET TO TH' TREASURE, EH?
EVERYONE CALM DOWN. WATCH YOURSELVES.
THIS PLACE IS CURSED.
THESE MOTHS--I'M THE ONLY ONE THEY'RE NOT TRYING TO STING.
AND THESE VINES--JAMES? WHERE'S JAMES...?

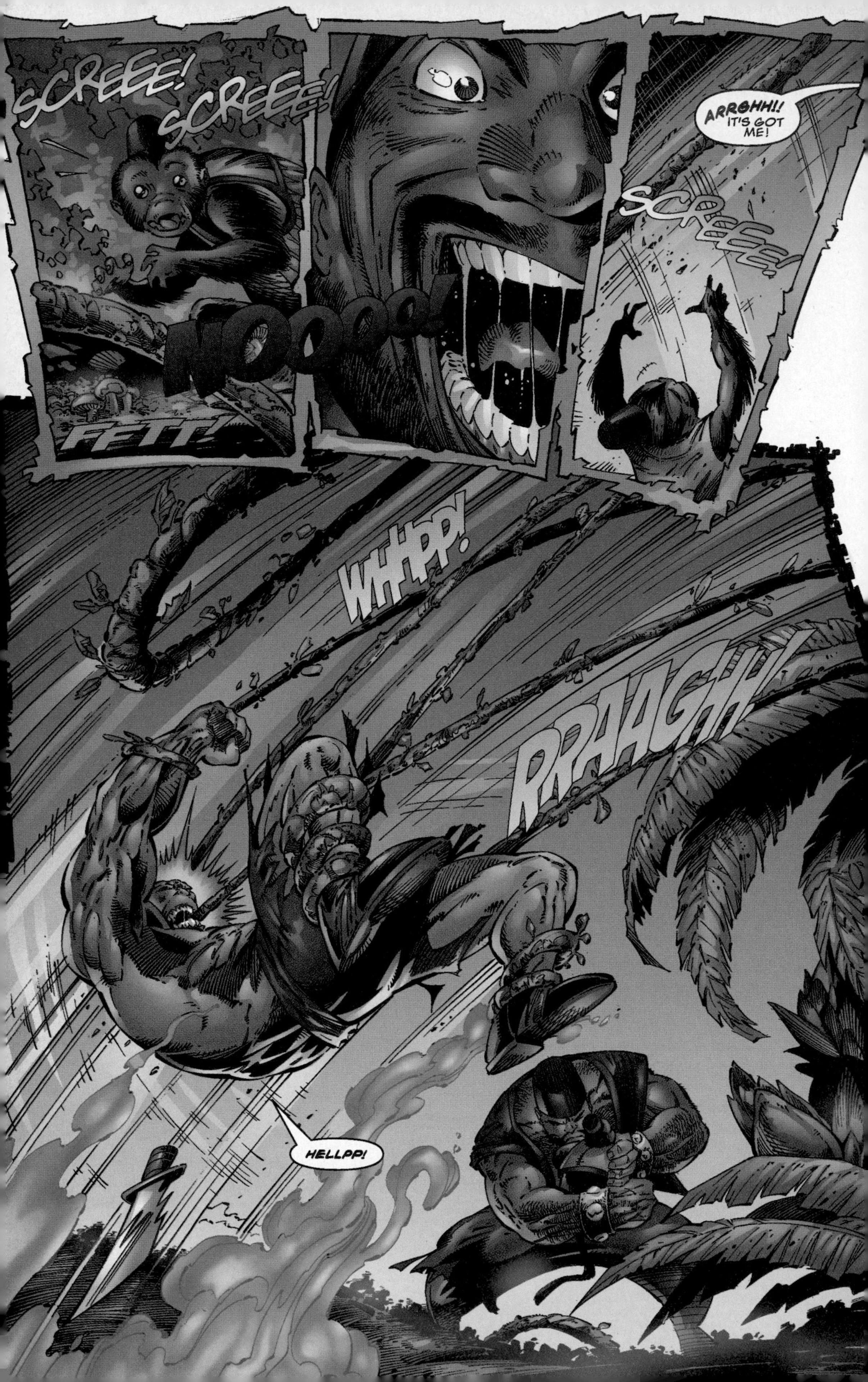
SCREEEE! SCREEEE!
FFTT!
NOOOOOO!
ARRGHH!! IT'S GOT ME!
SCREEEE!
WHHPP!
RRAAGH!
HELLPP!

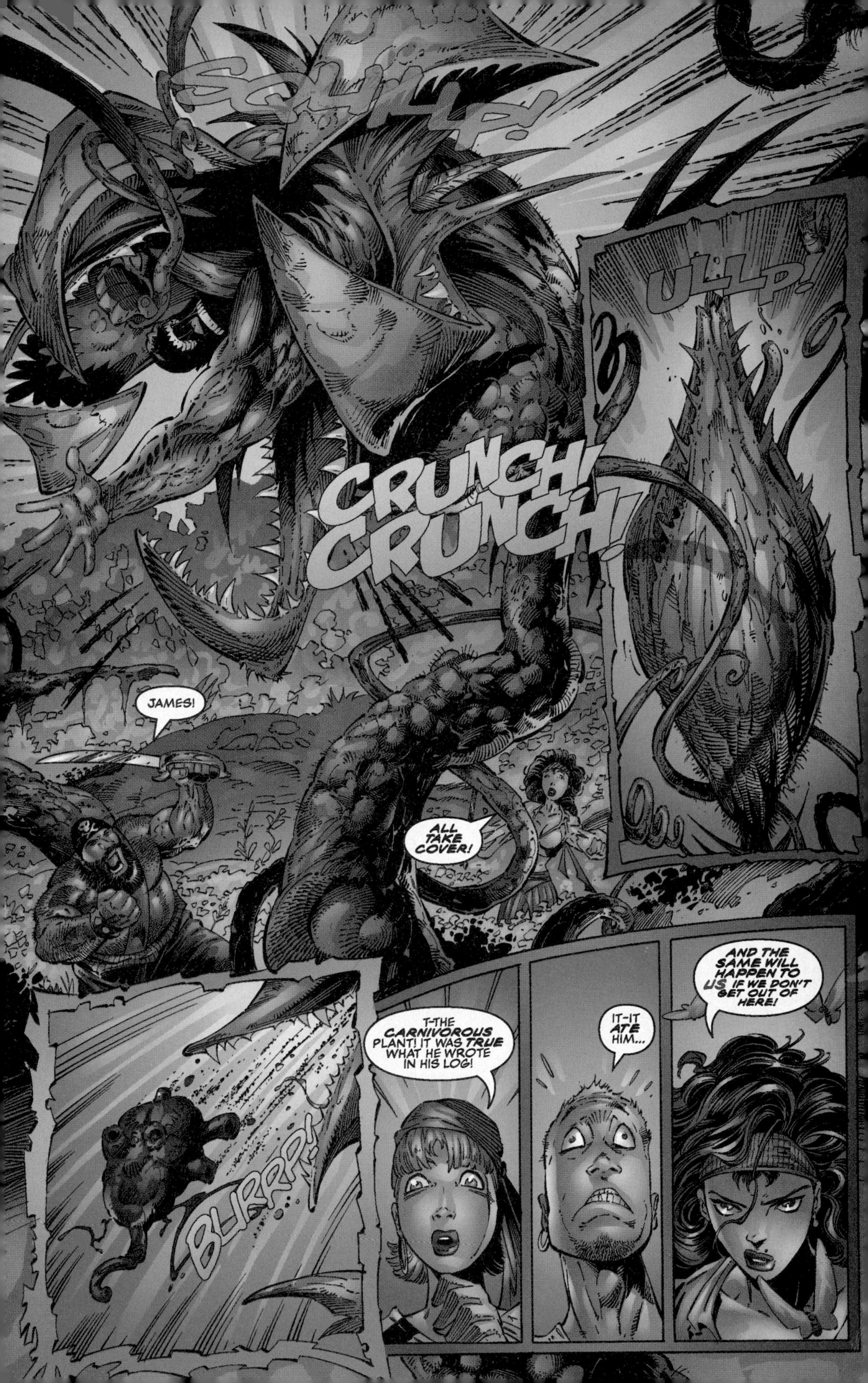
SCHLLP!
ULLP!
CRUNCH! CRUNCH!
JAMES!
ALL TAKE COVER!
BURRP!
T-THE CARNIVOROUS PLANT! IT WAS TRUE WHAT HE WROTE IN HIS LOG!
IT-IT ATE HIM...
AND THE SAME WILL HAPPEN TO US IF WE DON'T GET OUT OF HERE!

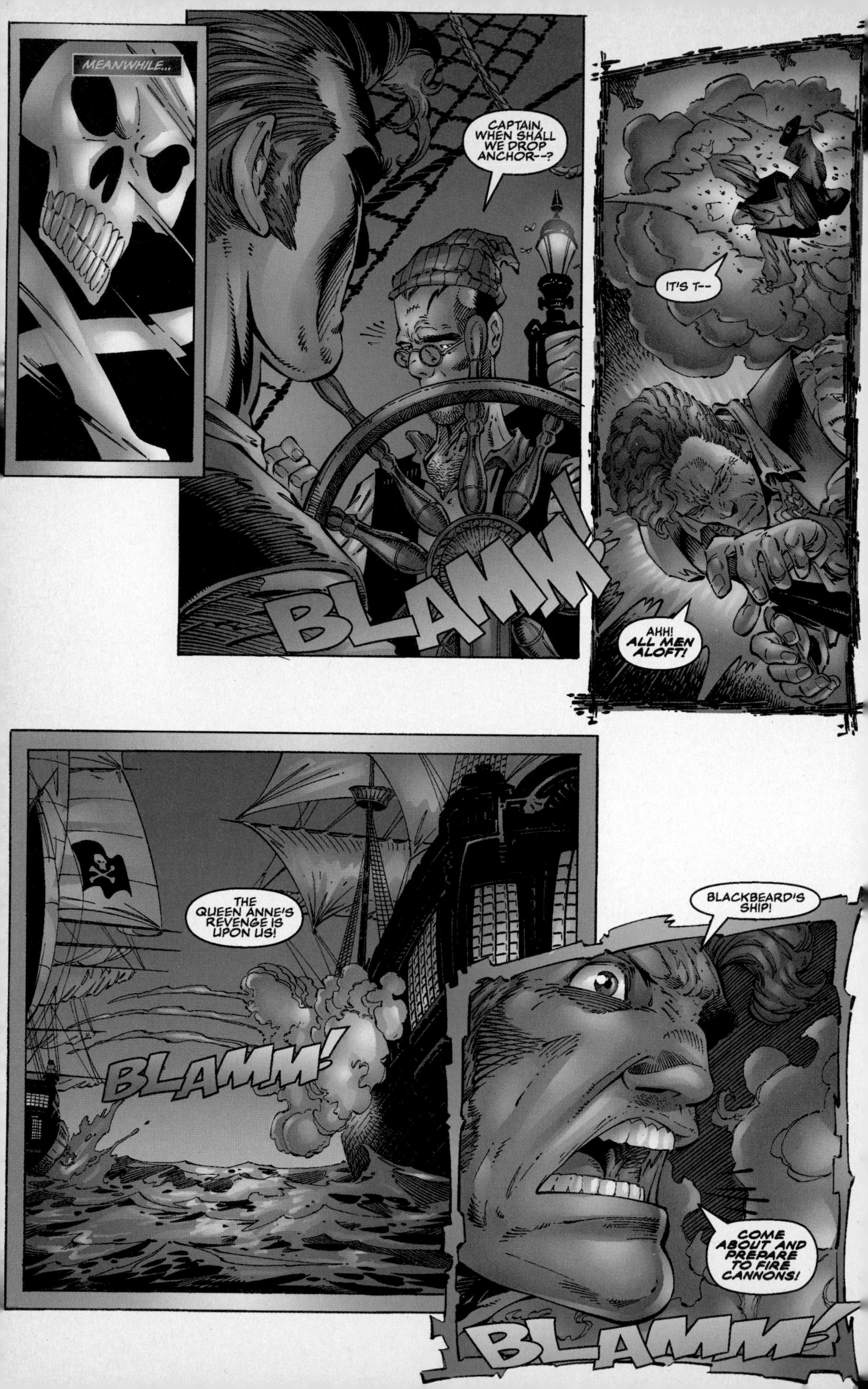
MEANWHILE...
CAPTAIN, WHEN SHALL WE DROP ANCHOR--?
BLAMM!
IT'S T--
AHH! ALL MEN ALOFT!
THE QUEEN ANNE'S REVENGE IS UPON US!
BLAMM!
BLACKBEARD'S SHIP!
COME ABOUT AND PREPARE TO FIRE CANNONS!
BLAMM!

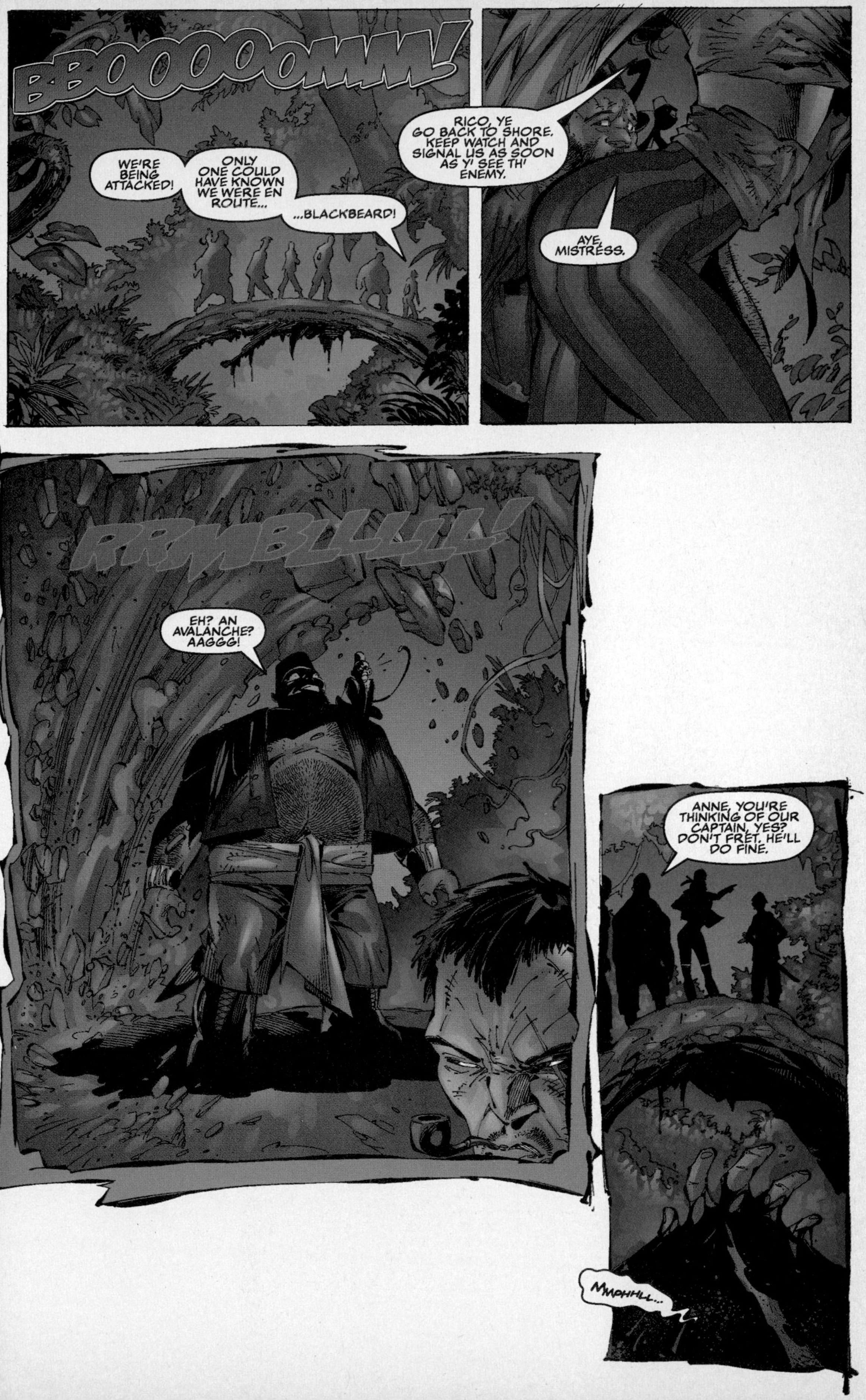
BBOOOOOMM!
WE'RE BEING ATTACKED!
ONLY ONE COULD HAVE KNOWN WE WERE EN ROUTE...
...BLACKBEARD!
RICO, YE GO BACK TO SHORE. KEEP WATCH AND SIGNAL US AS SOON AS Y' SEE TH' ENEMY.
AYE, MISTRESS.
RRMBLLLL!
EH? AN AVALANCHE? AAGGG!
ANNE, YOU'RE THINKING OF OUR CAPTAIN, YES? DON'T FRET. HE'LL DO FINE.
MMPHHLL...

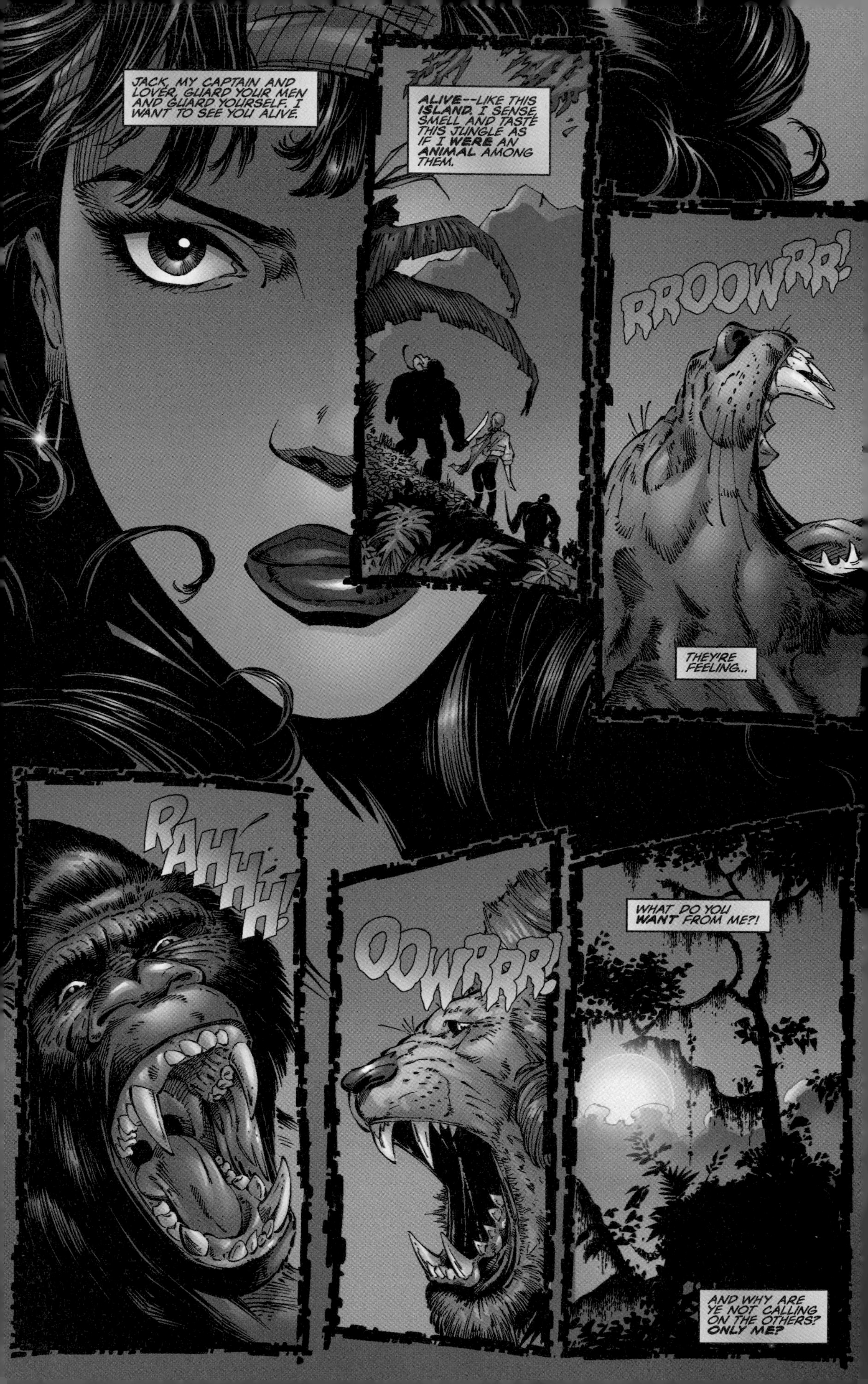
JACK, MY CAPTAIN AND LOVER, GUARD YOUR MEN AND GUARD YOURSELF. I WANT TO SEE YOU ALIVE.
ALIVE--LIKE THIS ISLAND, I SENSE, SMELL AND TASTE THIS JUNGLE AS IF I WERE AN ANIMAL AMONG THEM.
RROOWRR!
THEY'RE FEELING...
RAHHHH!
OOWRRR!
WHAT DO YOU WANT FROM ME?!
AND WHY ARE YE NOT CALLING ON THE OTHERS? ONLY ME?

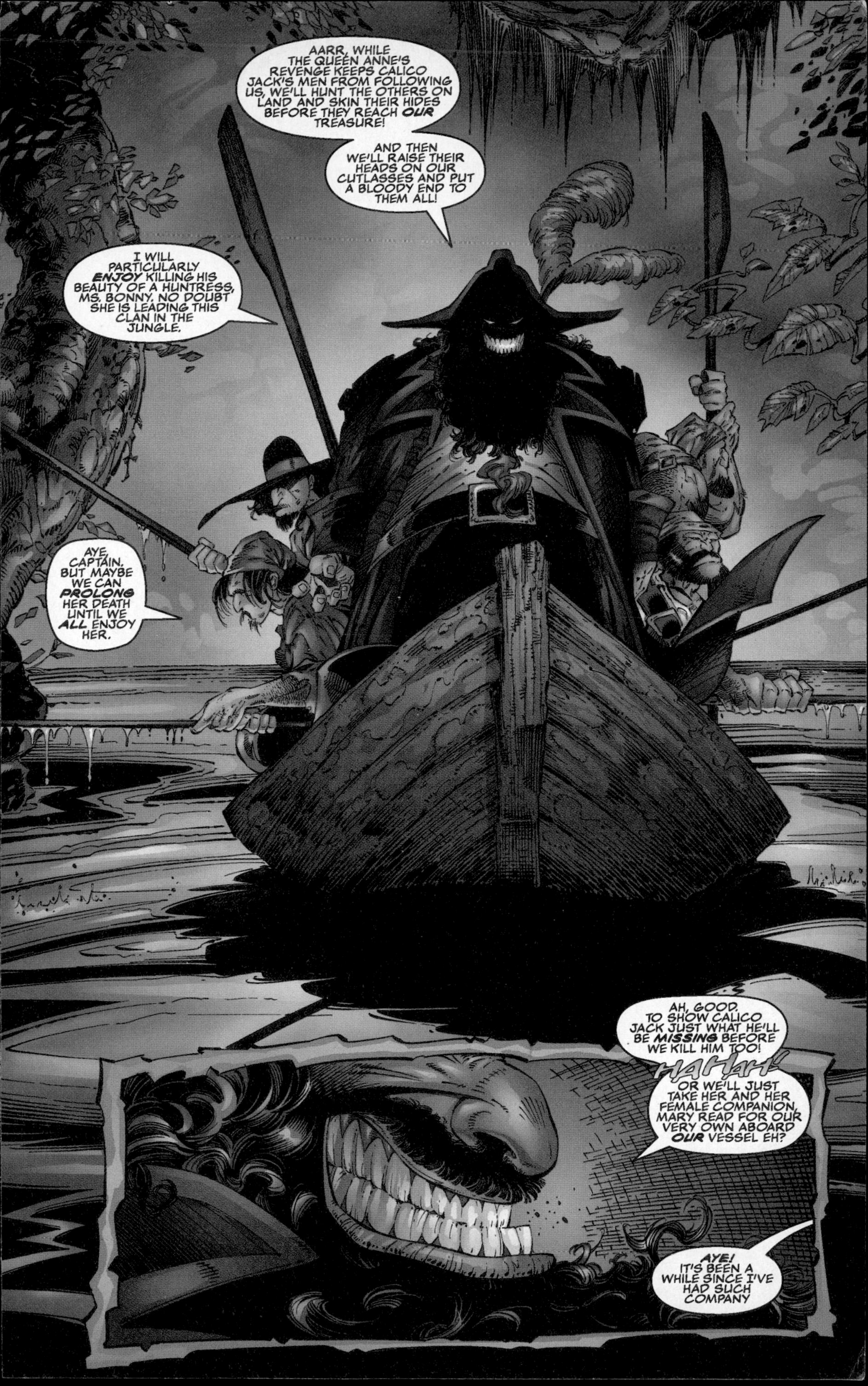
AARR, WHILE THE QUEEN ANNE'S REVENGE KEEPS CALICO JACK'S MEN FROM FOLLOWING US, WE'LL HUNT THE OTHERS ON LAND AND SKIN THEIR HIDES BEFORE THEY REACH OUR TREASURE!
AND THEN WE'LL RAISE THEIR HEADS ON OUR CUTLASSES AND PUT A BLOODY END TO THEM ALL!
I WILL PARTICULARLY ENJOY KILLING HIS BEAUTY OF A HUNTRESS, MS. BONNY. NO DOUBT SHE IS LEADING THIS CLAN IN THE JUNGLE.
AYE, CAPTAIN. BUT MAYBE WE CAN PROLONG HER DEATH UNTIL WE ALL ENJOY HER.
AH, GOOD. TO SHOW CALICO JACK JUST WHAT HE'LL BE MISSING BEFORE WE KILL HIM TOO!
HA HAR!
OR WE'LL JUST TAKE HER AND HER FEMALE COMPANION, MARY READ FOR OUR VERY OWN ABOARD OUR VESSEL EH?
AYE! IT'S BEEN A WHILE SINCE I'VE HAD SUCH COMPANY

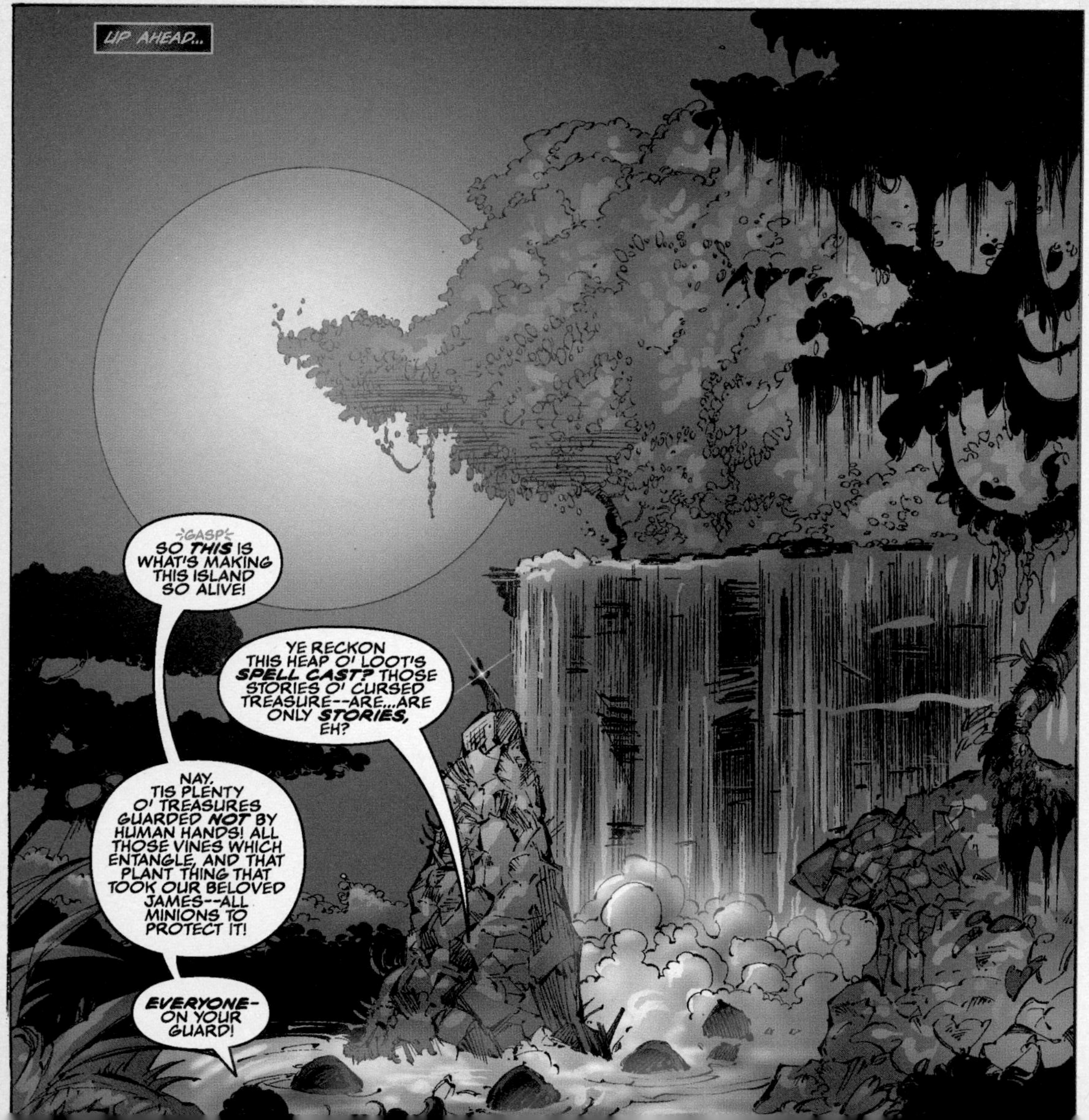
UP AHEAD...
GASP
SO THIS IS WHAT'S MAKING THIS ISLAND SO ALIVE!
YE RECKON THIS HEAP O' LOOT'S SPELL CAST? THOSE STORIES O' CURSED TREASURE--ARE...ARE ONLY STORIES, EH?
NAY. TIS PLENTY O' TREASURES GUARDED NOT BY HUMAN HANDS! ALL THOSE VINES WHICH ENTANGLE, AND THAT PLANT THING THAT TOOK OUR BELOVED JAMES--ALL MINIONS TO PROTECT IT!
EVERYONE-ON YOUR GUARD!

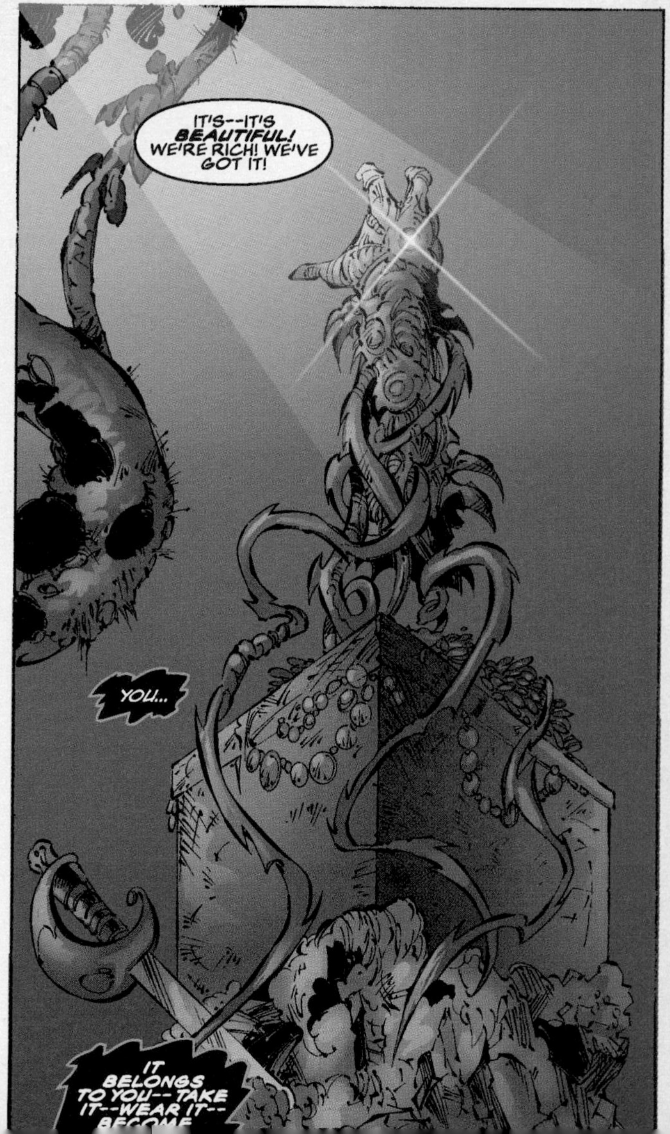
IT'S--IT'S BEAUTIFUL! WE'RE RICH! WE'VE GOT IT!
YOU...
IT BELONGS TO YOU--TAKE IT--WEAR IT--

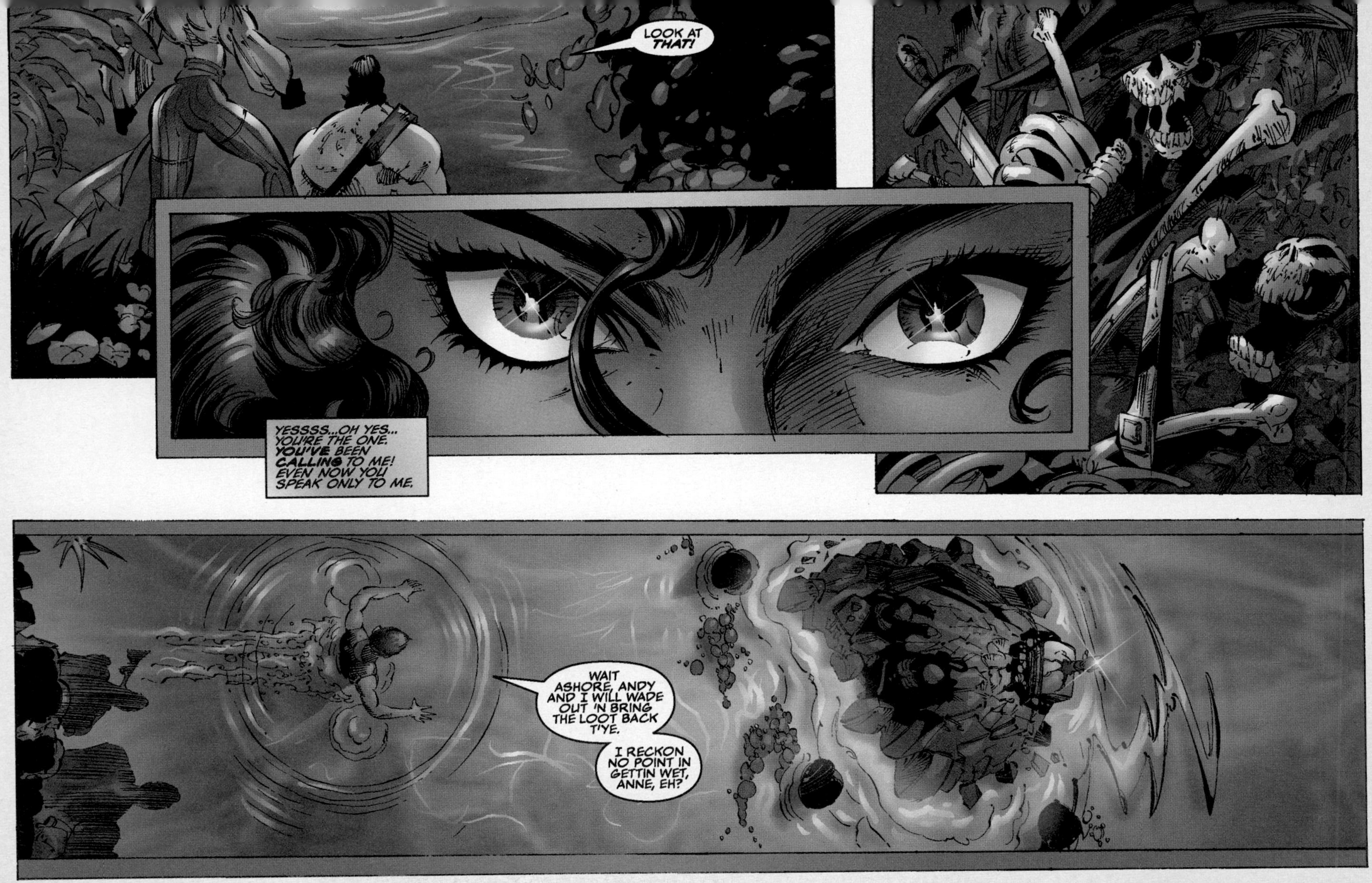
LOOK AT *THAT!*
YESSSS...OH YES... YOU'RE THE ONE. **YOU'VE** BEEN **CALLING** TO ME! EVEN NOW YOU SPEAK ONLY TO ME.
WAIT ASHORE, ANDY AND I WILL WADE OUT 'N BRING THE LOOT BACK T'YE.
I RECKON NO POINT IN GETTIN WET, ANNE, EH?

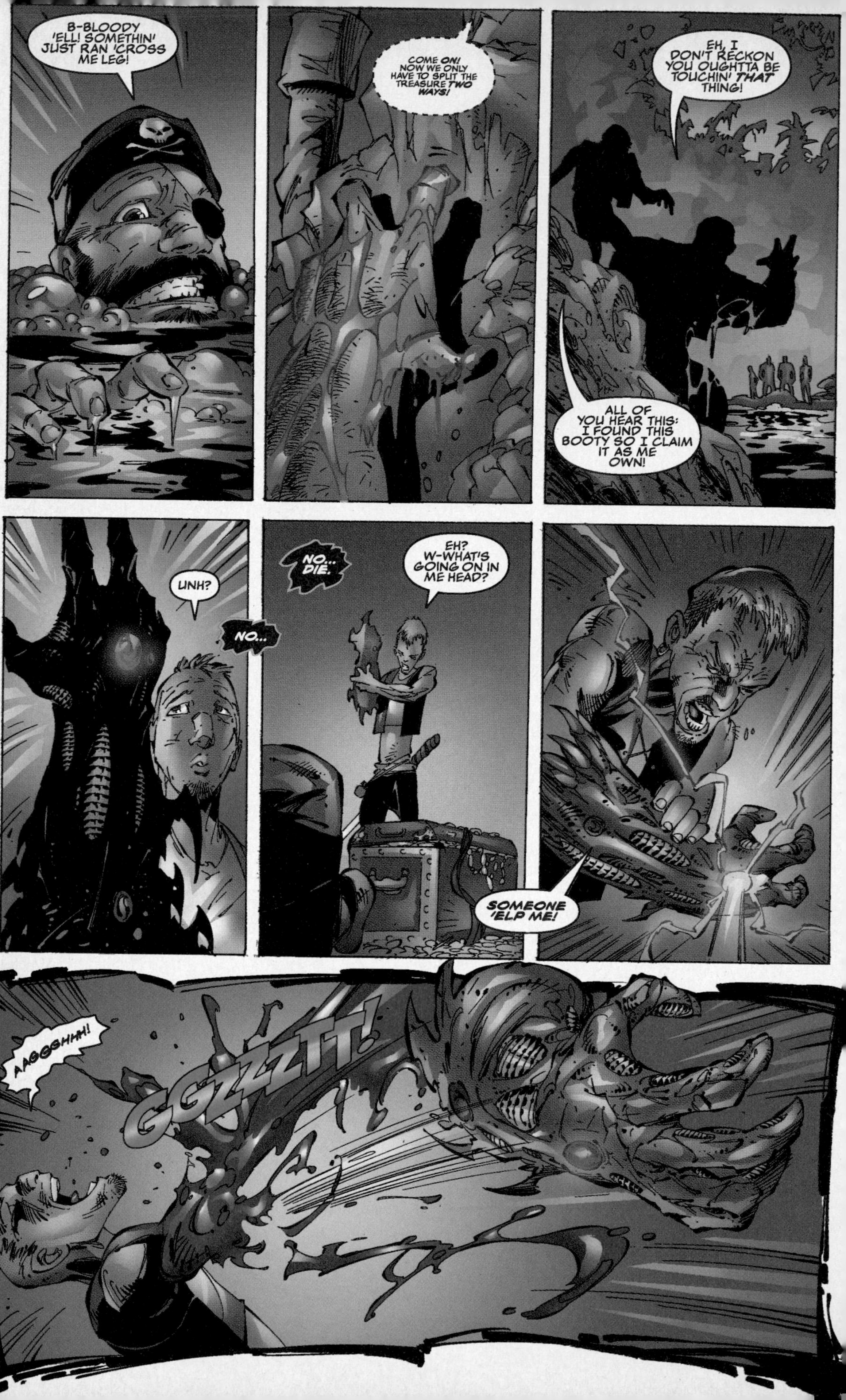
B-BLOODY 'ELL! SOMETHIN' JUST RAN 'CROSS ME LEG!
COME ON! NOW WE ONLY HAVE TO SPLIT THE TREASURE TWO WAYS!
EH, I DON'T RECKON YOU OUGHTTA BE TOUCHIN' THAT THING!
ALL OF YOU HEAR THIS: I FOUND THIS BOOTY SO I CLAIM IT AS ME OWN!
UNH?
NO...
NO... DIE.
EH? W-WHAT'S GOING ON IN ME HEAD?
SOMEONE 'ELP ME!
AAGGGHHH!
GGZZZTT!

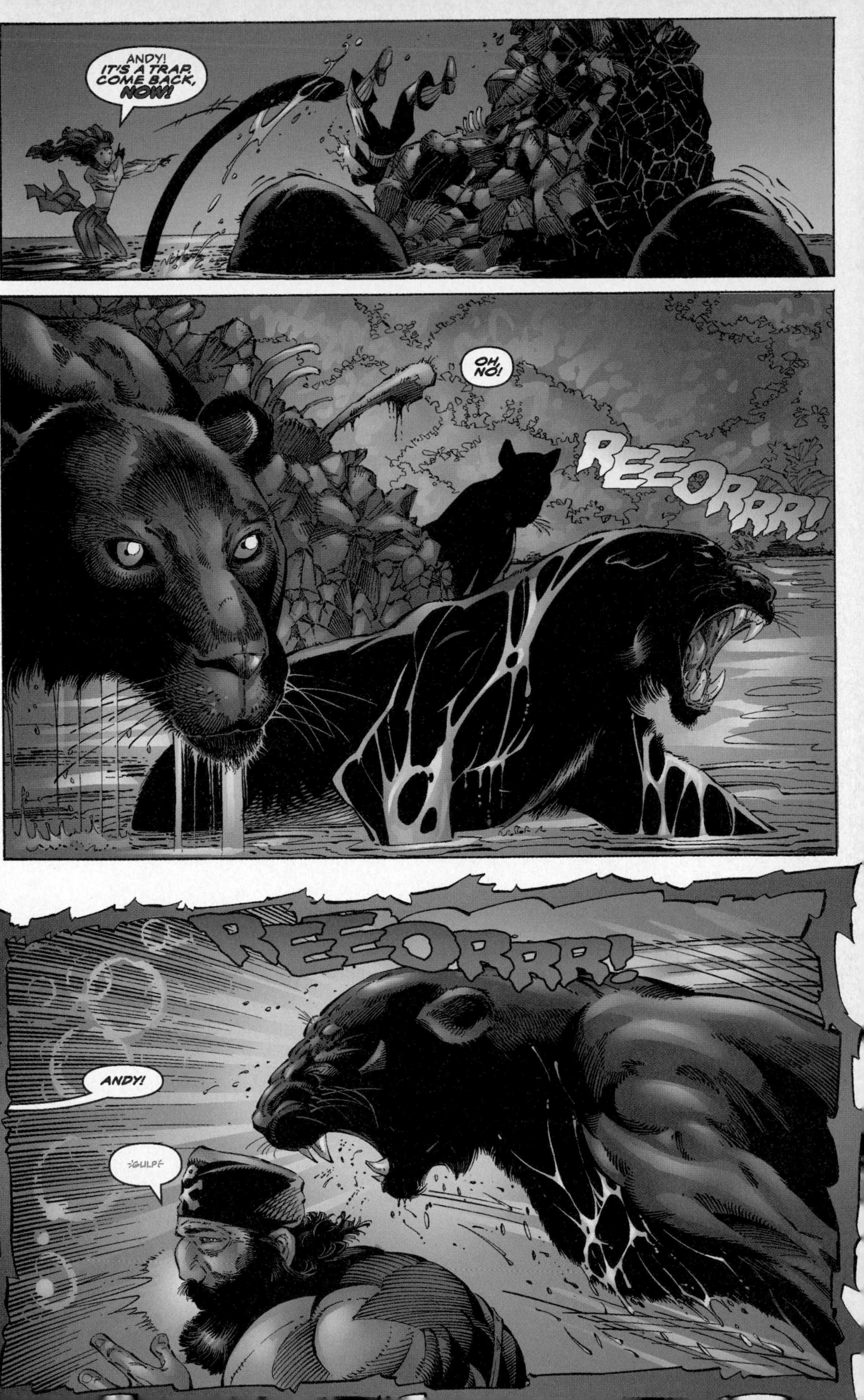
ANDY! IT'S A TRAP. COME BACK, NOW!
OH, NO!
REEEORRR!
REEEORRR!
ANDY!
GULP

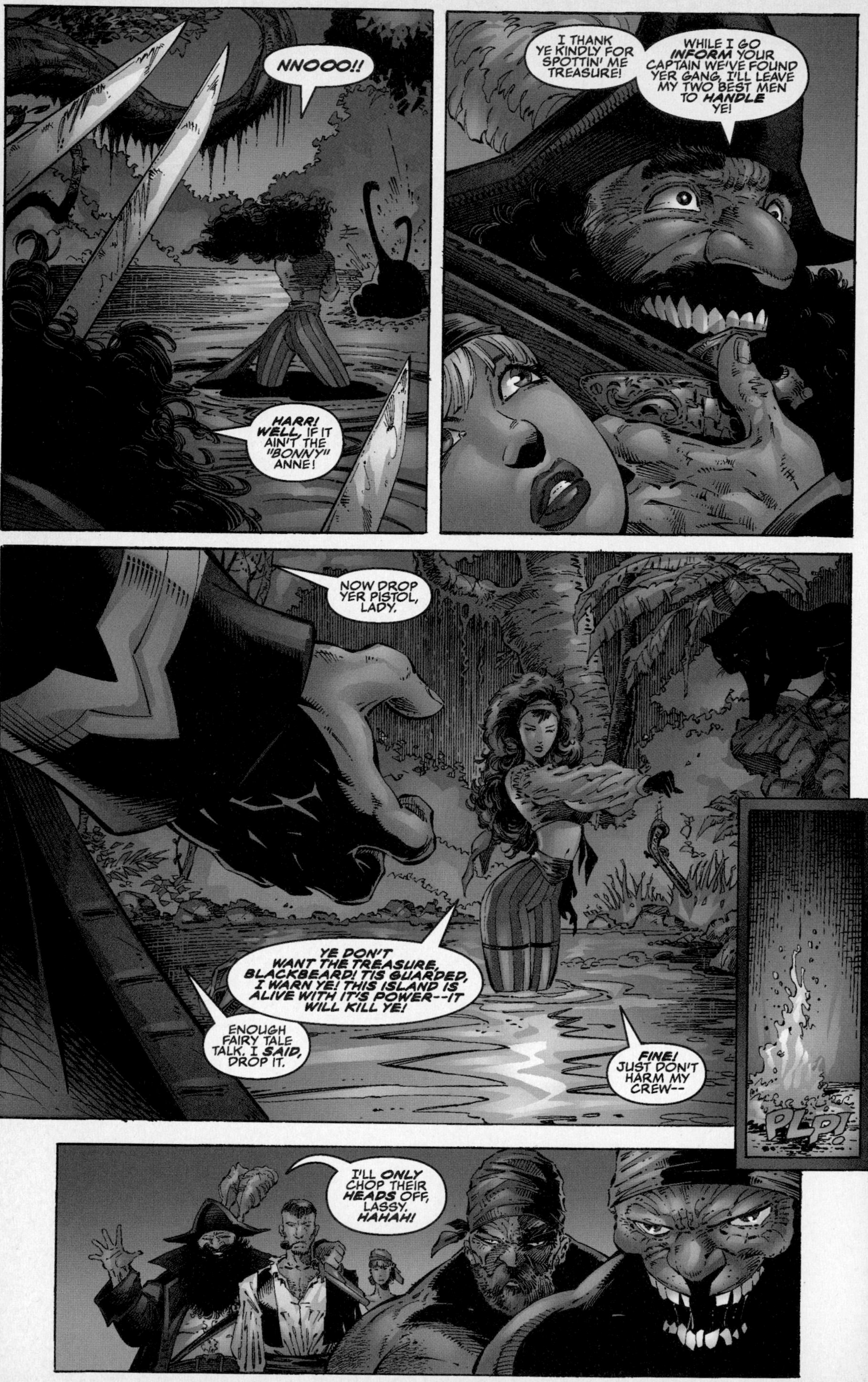
NNOOO!!
HARR! WELL, IF IT AIN'T THE "BONNY" ANNE!
I THANK YE KINDLY FOR SPOTTIN' ME TREASURE!
WHILE I GO INFORM YOUR CAPTAIN WE'VE FOUND YER GANG, I'LL LEAVE MY TWO BEST MEN TO HANDLE YE!
NOW DROP YER PISTOL, LADY.
YE DON'T WANT THE TREASURE, BLACKBEARD! TIS GUARDED, I WARN YE! THIS ISLAND IS ALIVE WITH IT'S POWER--IT WILL KILL YE!
ENOUGH FAIRY TALE TALK. I SAID, DROP IT.
FINE! JUST DON'T HARM MY CREW--
PLP!
I'LL ONLY CHOP THEIR HEADS OFF, LASSY. HAHAH!

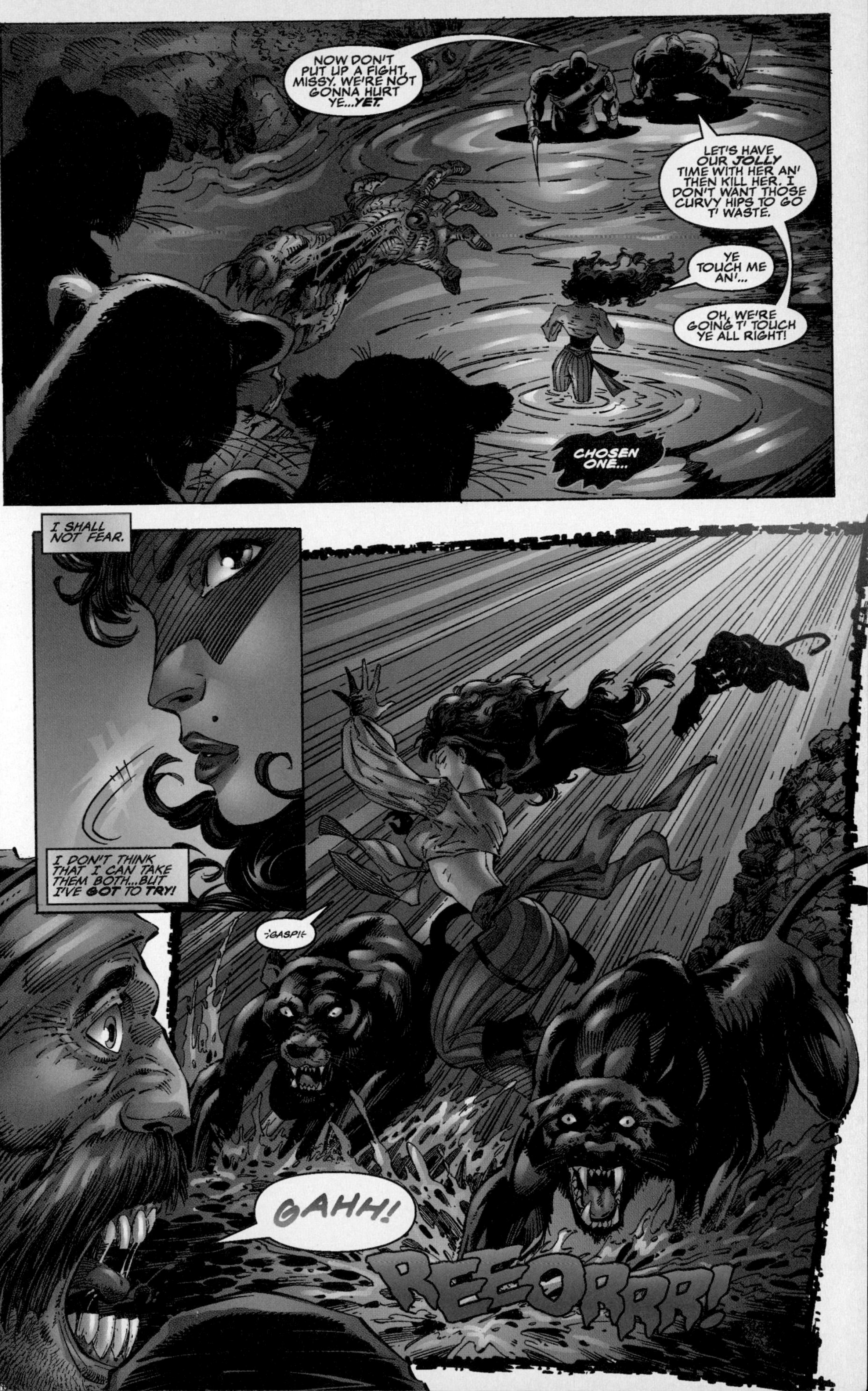

NOW DON'T PUT UP A FIGHT, MISSY. WE'RE NOT GONNA HURT YE...YET.
LET'S HAVE OUR JOLLY TIME WITH HER AN' THEN KILL HER. I DON'T WANT THOSE CURVY HIPS TO GO T' WASTE.
YE TOUCH ME AN'...
OH, WE'RE GOING T' TOUCH YE ALL RIGHT!
CHOSEN ONE...
I SHALL NOT FEAR.
I DON'T THINK THAT I CAN TAKE THEM BOTH...BUT I'VE GOT TO TRY!
GASP!
GAHH!
REEORRR!

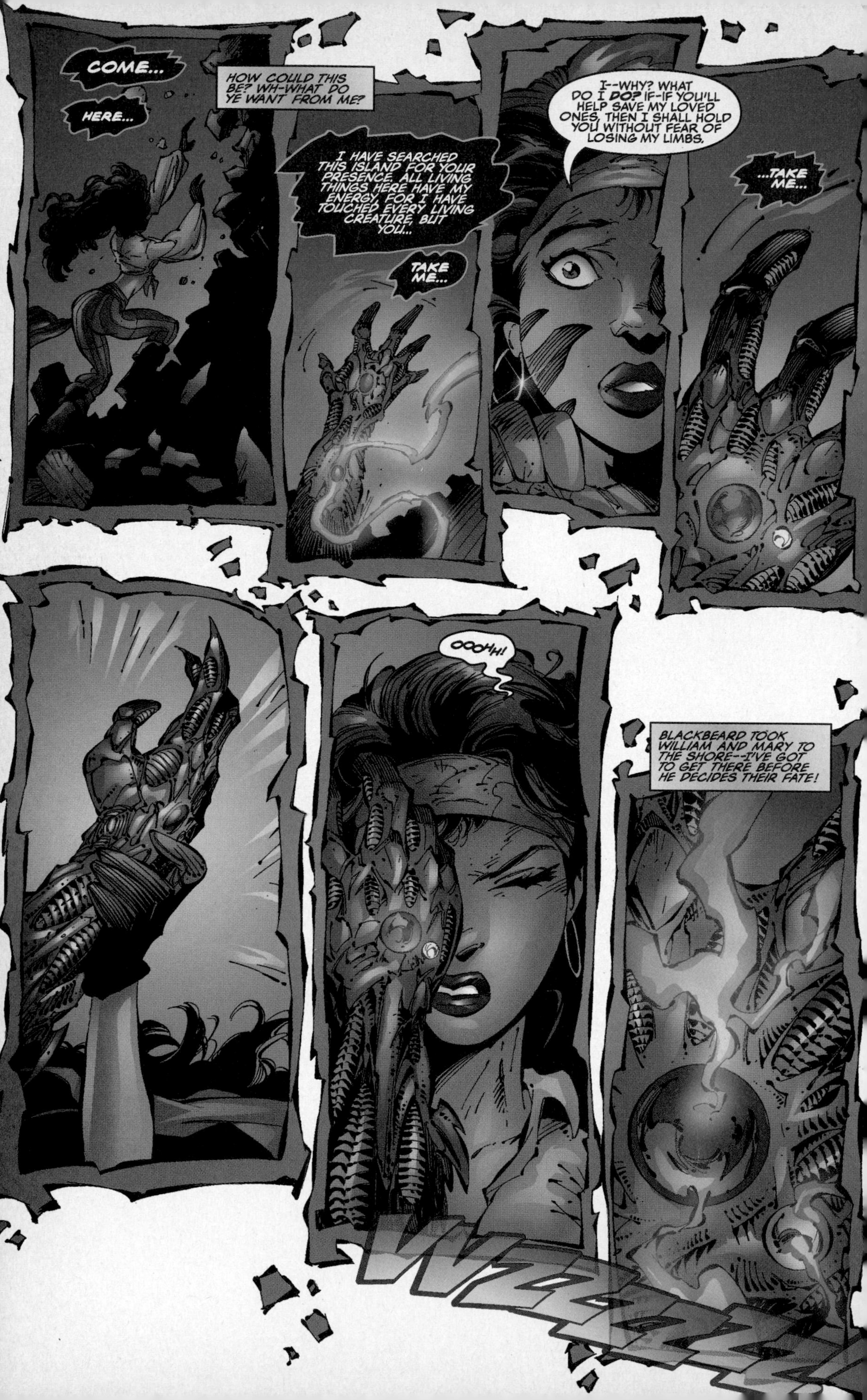
COME...
HERE...
HOW COULD THIS BE? WH-WHAT DO YE WANT FROM ME?
I HAVE SEARCHED THIS ISLAND FOR YOUR PRESENCE. ALL LIVING THINGS HERE HAVE MY ENERGY, FOR I HAVE TOUCHED EVERY LIVING CREATURE, BUT YOU...
TAKE ME...
I--WHY? WHAT DO I DO? IF--IF YOU'LL HELP SAVE MY LOVED ONES, THEN I SHALL HOLD YOU WITHOUT FEAR OF LOSING MY LIMBS.
...TAKE ME...
OOOHH!
BLACKBEARD TOOK WILLIAM AND MARY TO THE SHORE--I'VE GOT TO GET THERE BEFORE HE DECIDES THEIR FATE!

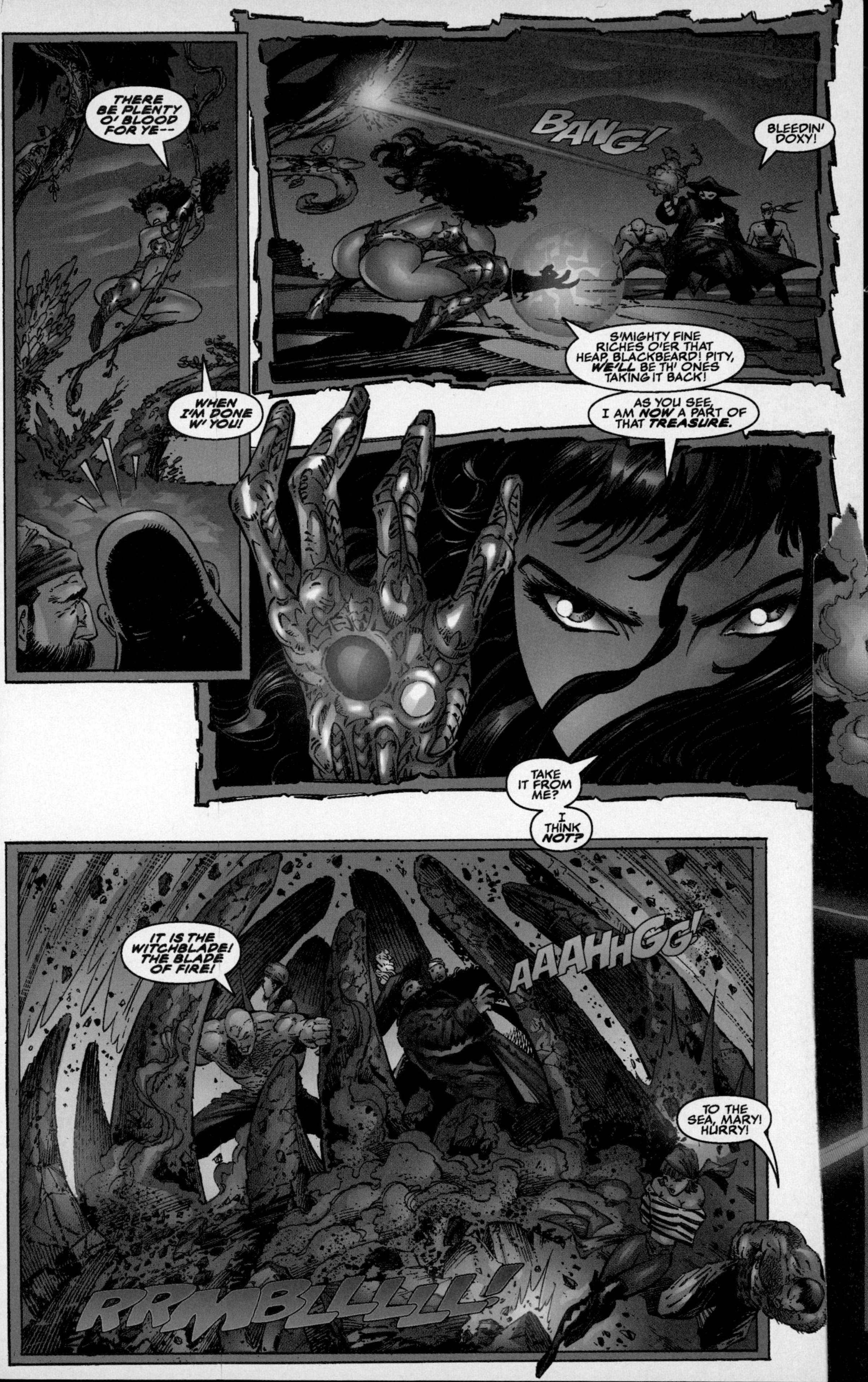
THERE BE PLENTY O' BLOOD FOR YE--
BANG!
BLEEDIN' DOXY!
S'MIGHTY FINE RICHES O'ER THAT HEAP, BLACKBEARD! PITY, WE'LL BE TH' ONES TAKING IT BACK!
WHEN I'M DONE W' YOU!
AS YOU SEE, I AM NOW A PART OF THAT TREASURE.
TAKE IT FROM ME?
I THINK NOT?
IT IS THE WITCHBLADE! THE BLADE OF FIRE!
AAAHHGG!
TO THE SEA, MARY! HURRY!
RRMBLLLLL!

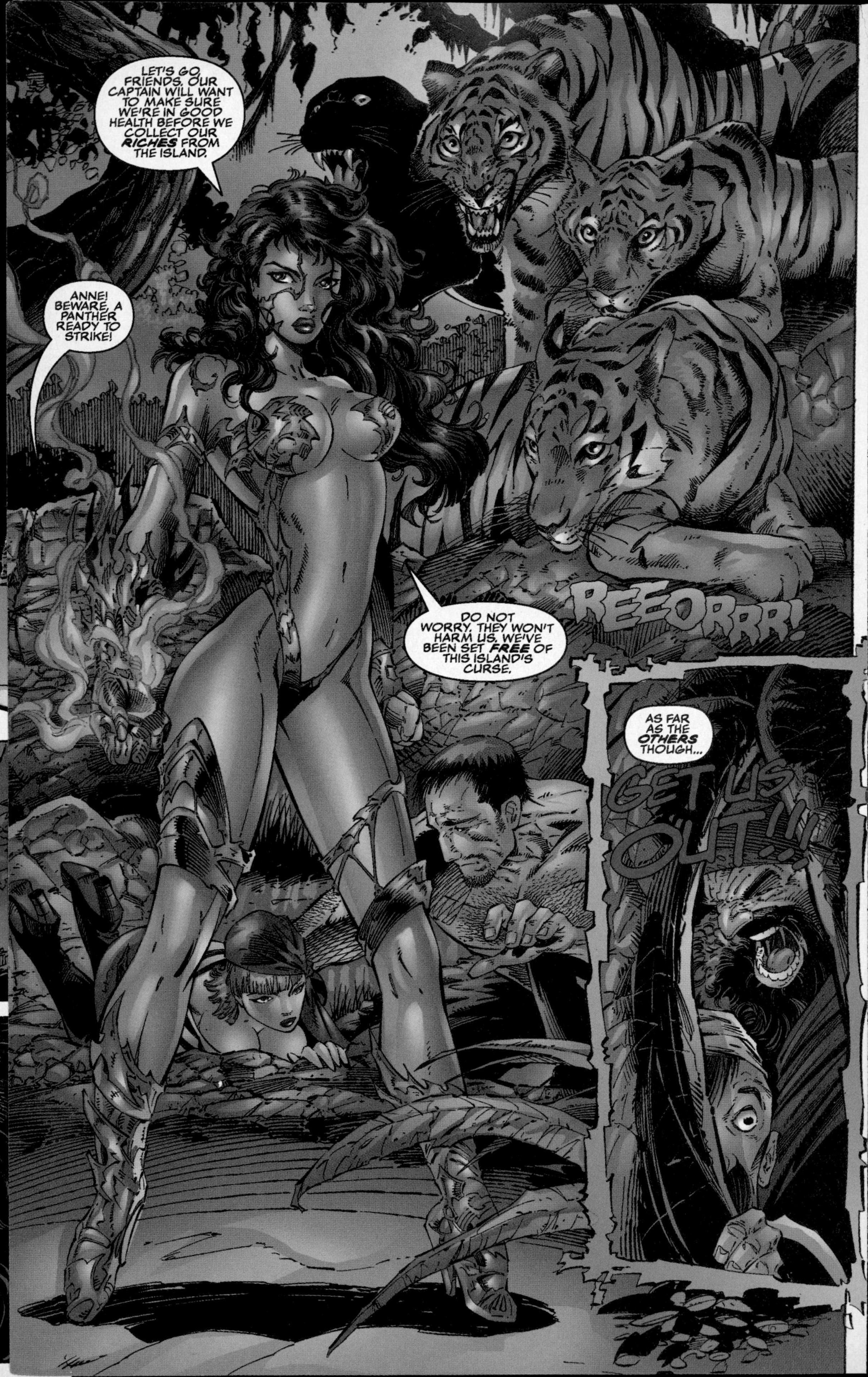
LET'S GO, FRIENDS. OUR CAPTAIN WILL WANT TO MAKE SURE WE'RE IN GOOD HEALTH BEFORE WE COLLECT OUR RICHES FROM THE ISLAND.
ANNE! BEWARE, A PANTHER READY TO STRIKE!
REEORRR!
DO NOT WORRY. THEY WON'T HARM US. WE'VE BEEN SET FREE OF THIS ISLAND'S CURSE.
AS FAR AS THE OTHERS THOUGH...
GET US OUT!!!

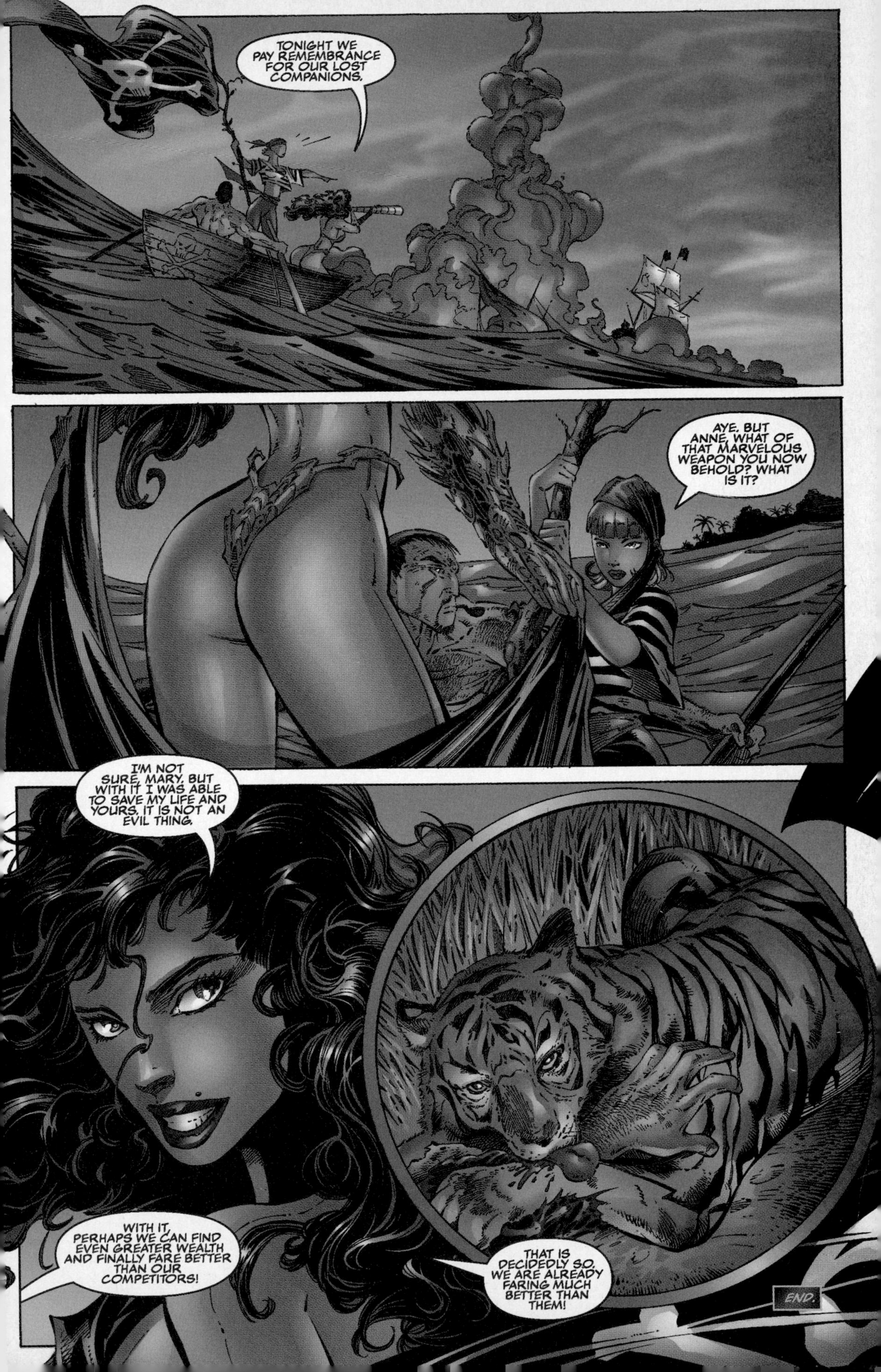
TONIGHT WE PAY REMEMBRANCE FOR OUR LOST COMPANIONS.
AYE. BUT ANNE, WHAT OF THAT MARVELOUS WEAPON YOU NOW BEHOLD? WHAT IS IT?
I'M NOT SURE, MARY. BUT WITH IT I WAS ABLE TO SAVE MY LIFE AND YOURS. IT IS NOT AN EVIL THING.
WITH IT, PERHAPS WE CAN FIND EVEN GREATER WEALTH AND FINALLY FARE BETTER THAN OUR COMPETITORS!
THAT IS DECIDEDLY SO. WE ARE ALREADY FARING MUCH BETTER THAN THEM!
END.

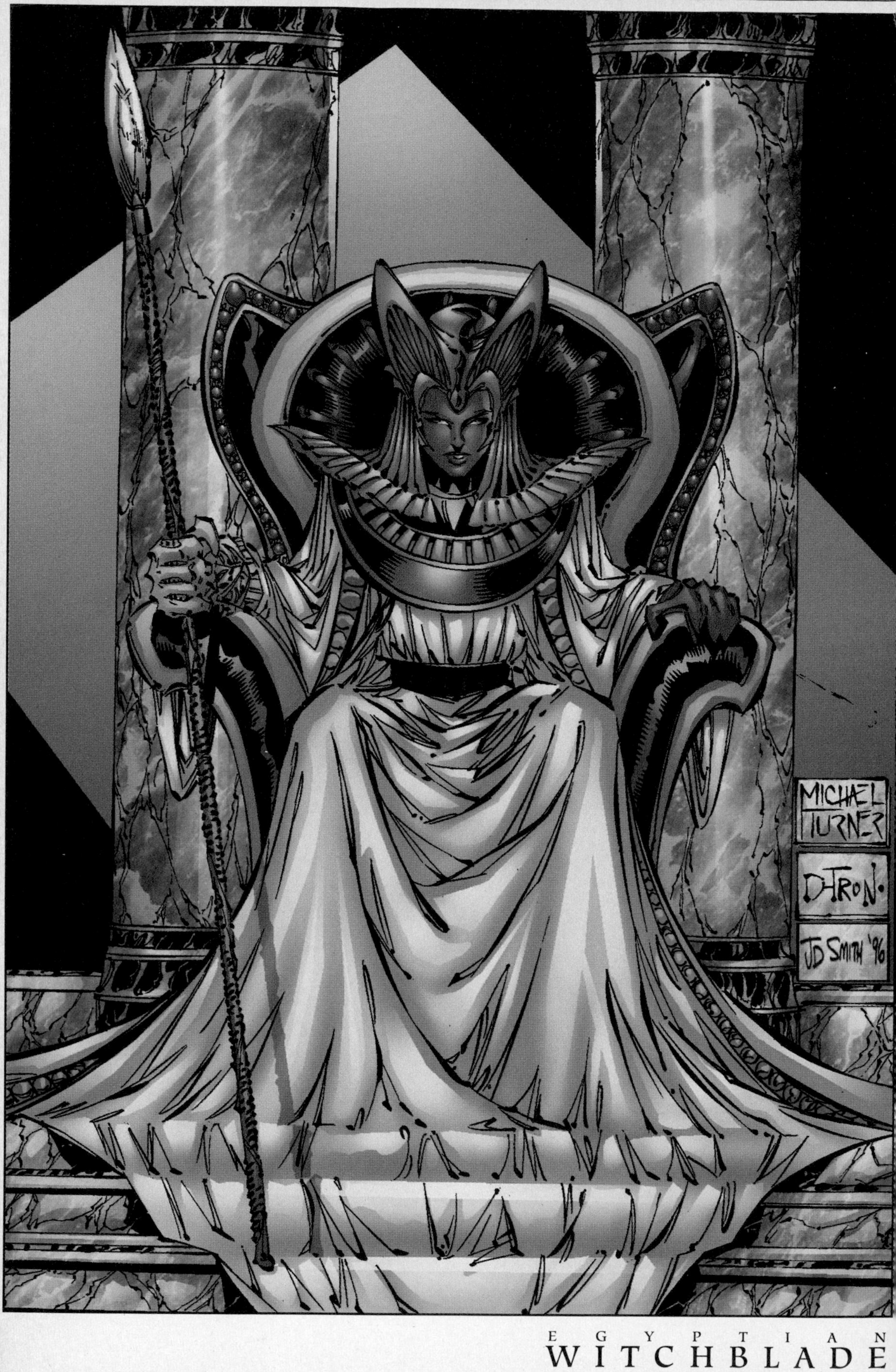
MICHAEL TURNER
D-TRON
JD SMITH '96

EGYPTIAN
WITCHBLADE
MICHAEL TURNER, D-TRON & JONATHAN D. SMITH

TALES *of the* WITCHBLADE

02

PLOTTED by
David Finch

SCRIPTED by
Christina Z.
David Wohl
David Finch

PENCILED by
David Finch
Billy Tan (pgs. 42-45)

INKED by
Batt (10, 15 and 19)
Joe Weems V (pgs. 36-39, 51, 56)
Billy Tan (pgs. 42-44)
D-Tron· (pg. 45)
Livesay (pg. 40)

COLORED by
Jonathan D. Smith
Tyson Wengler

LETTERED by
Dennis Heisler

INK ASSISTS
Victor Llamas
Marco Galli

LETTERING ASSISTS
Robin Spehar

COVER by
David Finch,
Batt
and
Jonathan D. Smith

ANNABELLA ALTAVISTA

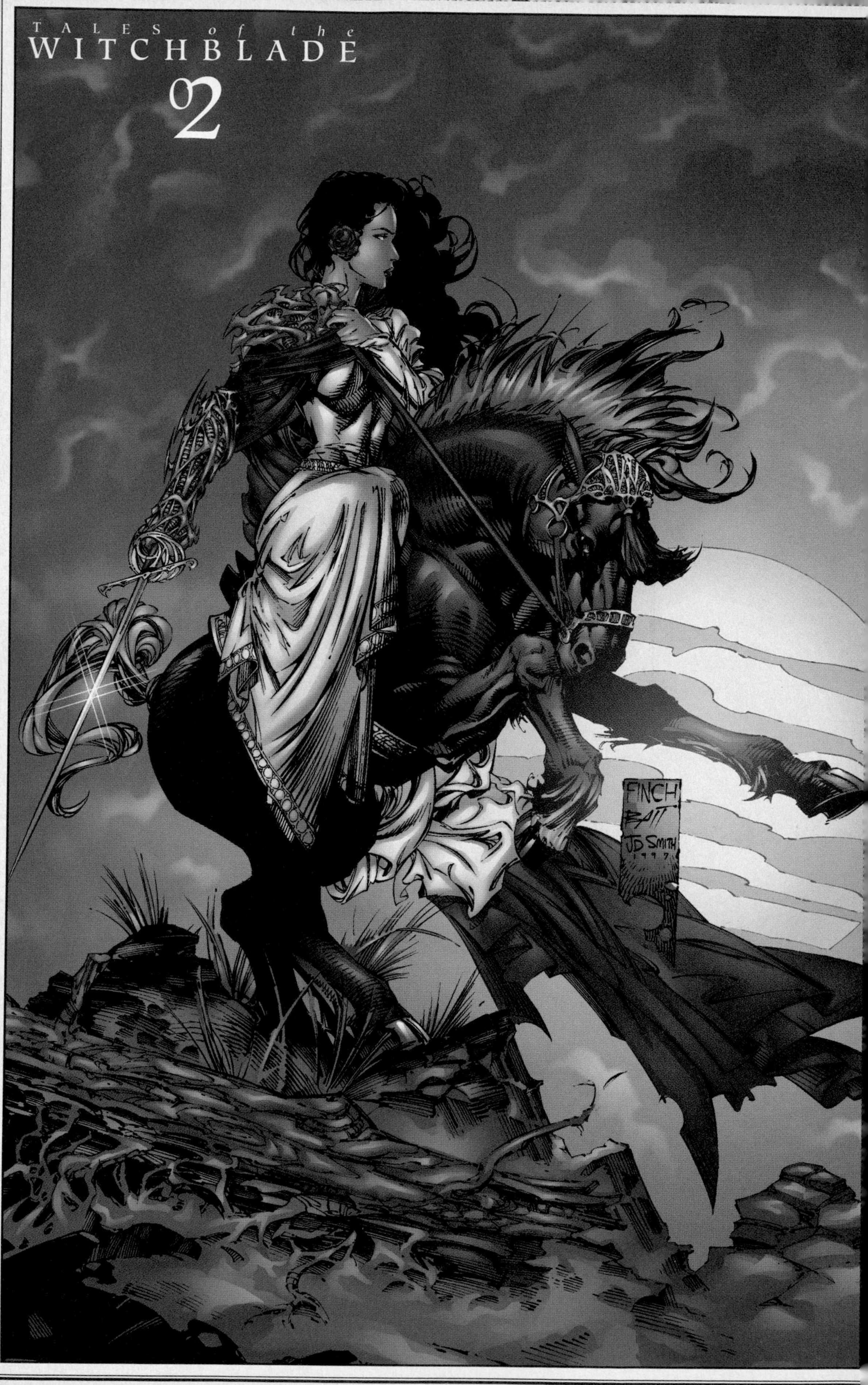
TALES of the
WITCHBLADE
2
FINCH
BATT
J.D. SMITH
1997

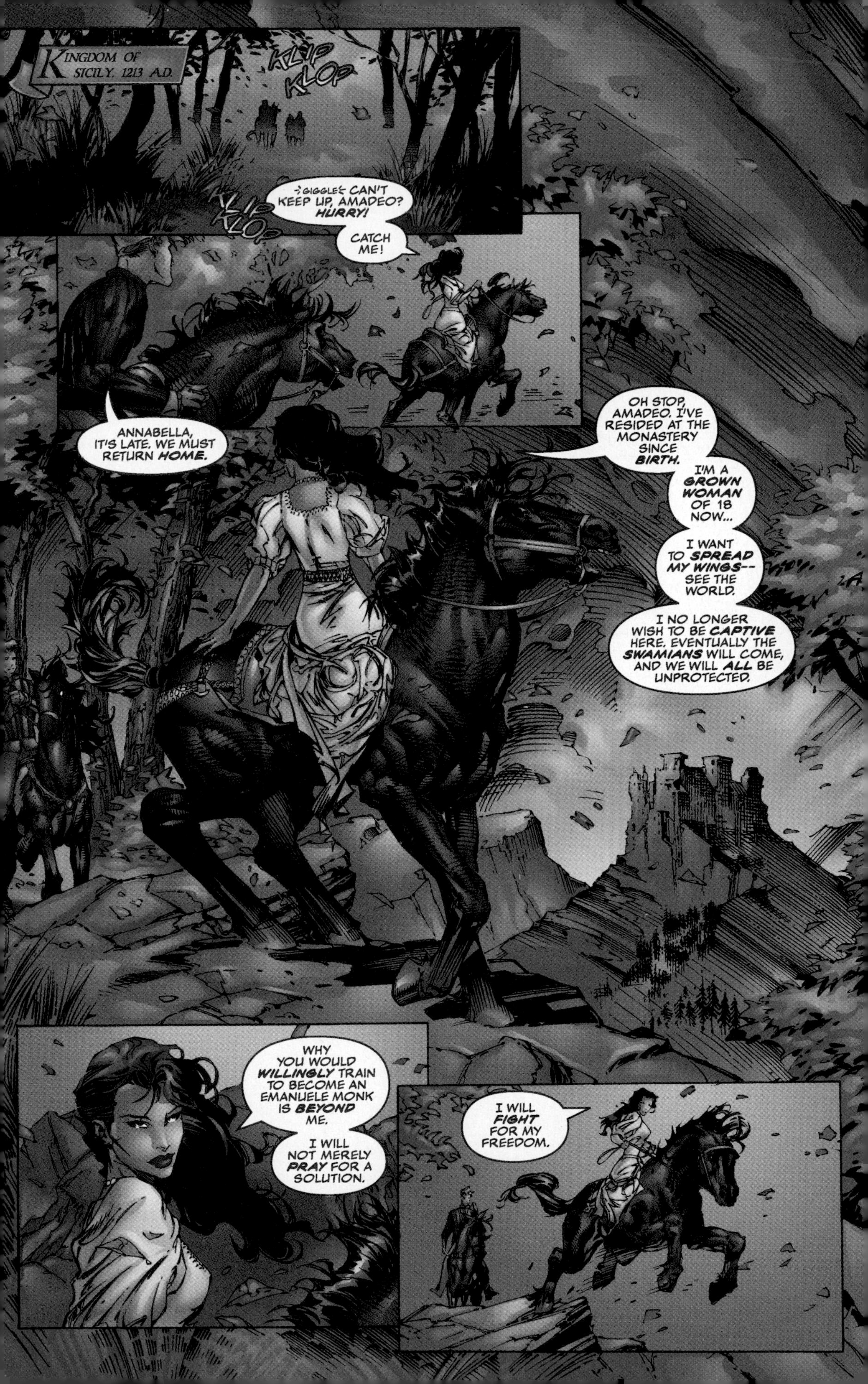
KINGDOM OF SICILY. 1213 A.D.
KLIP KLOP
KLIP KLOP
~GIGGLE~ CAN'T KEEP UP, AMADEO? HURRY!
CATCH ME!
ANNABELLA, IT'S LATE. WE MUST RETURN HOME.
OH STOP, AMADEO. I'VE RESIDED AT THE MONASTERY SINCE BIRTH.
I'M A GROWN WOMAN OF 18 NOW...
I WANT TO SPREAD MY WINGS-- SEE THE WORLD.
I NO LONGER WISH TO BE CAPTIVE HERE. EVENTUALLY THE SWAMIANS WILL COME, AND WE WILL ALL BE UNPROTECTED.
WHY YOU WOULD WILLINGLY TRAIN TO BECOME AN EMANUELE MONK IS BEYOND ME.
I WILL NOT MERELY PRAY FOR A SOLUTION.
I WILL FIGHT FOR MY FREEDOM.

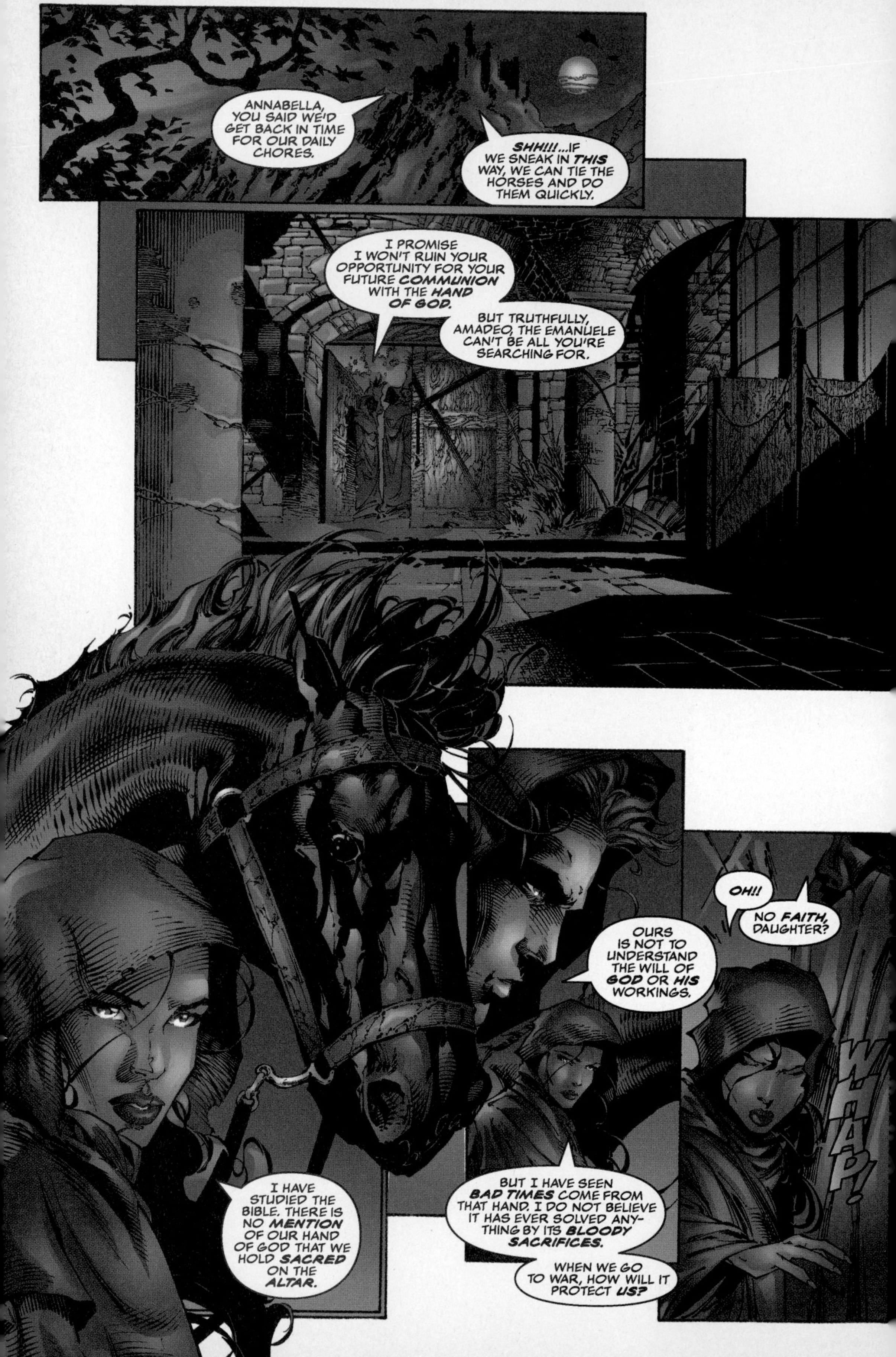

ANNABELLA, YOU SAID WE'D GET BACK IN TIME FOR OUR DAILY CHORES.
SHH!!!...IF WE SNEAK IN THIS WAY, WE CAN TIE THE HORSES AND DO THEM QUICKLY.
I PROMISE I WON'T RUIN YOUR OPPORTUNITY FOR YOUR FUTURE COMMUNION WITH THE HAND OF GOD.
BUT TRUTHFULLY, AMADEO, THE EMANUELE CAN'T BE ALL YOU'RE SEARCHING FOR.
I HAVE STUDIED THE BIBLE. THERE IS NO MENTION OF OUR HAND OF GOD THAT WE HOLD SACRED ON THE ALTAR.
OURS IS NOT TO UNDERSTAND THE WILL OF GOD OR HIS WORKINGS.
BUT I HAVE SEEN BAD TIMES COME FROM THAT HAND. I DO NOT BELIEVE IT HAS EVER SOLVED ANY-THING BY ITS BLOODY SACRIFICES.
WHEN WE GO TO WAR, HOW WILL IT PROTECT US?
WHAP!
OH!!
NO FAITH, DAUGHTER?

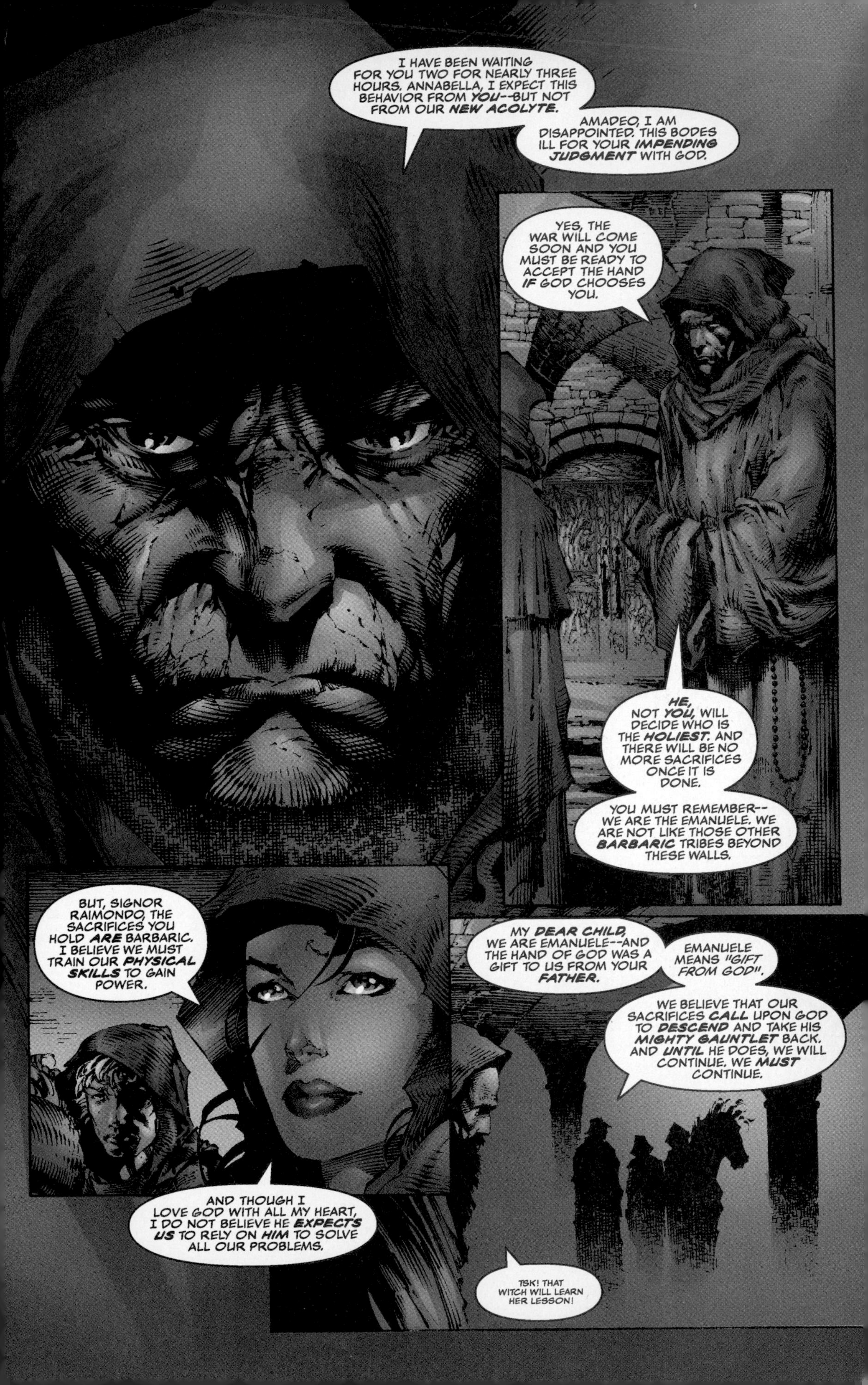

I HAVE BEEN WAITING FOR YOU TWO FOR NEARLY THREE HOURS. ANNABELLA, I EXPECT THIS BEHAVIOR FROM YOU--BUT NOT FROM OUR NEW ACOLYTE.
AMADEO, I AM DISAPPOINTED. THIS BODES ILL FOR YOUR IMPENDING JUDGMENT WITH GOD.
YES, THE WAR WILL COME SOON AND YOU MUST BE READY TO ACCEPT THE HAND IF GOD CHOOSES YOU.
HE, NOT YOU, WILL DECIDE WHO IS THE HOLIEST. AND THERE WILL BE NO MORE SACRIFICES ONCE IT IS DONE.
YOU MUST REMEMBER--WE ARE THE EMANUELE. WE ARE NOT LIKE THOSE OTHER BARBARIC TRIBES BEYOND THESE WALLS.
BUT, SIGNOR RAIMONDO, THE SACRIFICES YOU HOLD ARE BARBARIC. I BELIEVE WE MUST TRAIN OUR PHYSICAL SKILLS TO GAIN POWER.
AND THOUGH I LOVE GOD WITH ALL MY HEART, I DO NOT BELIEVE HE EXPECTS US TO RELY ON HIM TO SOLVE ALL OUR PROBLEMS.
MY DEAR CHILD, WE ARE EMANUELE--AND THE HAND OF GOD WAS A GIFT TO US FROM YOUR FATHER.
EMANUELE MEANS "GIFT FROM GOD".
WE BELIEVE THAT OUR SACRIFICES CALL UPON GOD TO DESCEND AND TAKE HIS MIGHTY GAUNTLET BACK. AND UNTIL HE DOES, WE WILL CONTINUE. WE MUST CONTINUE.
TSK! THAT WITCH WILL LEARN HER LESSON!

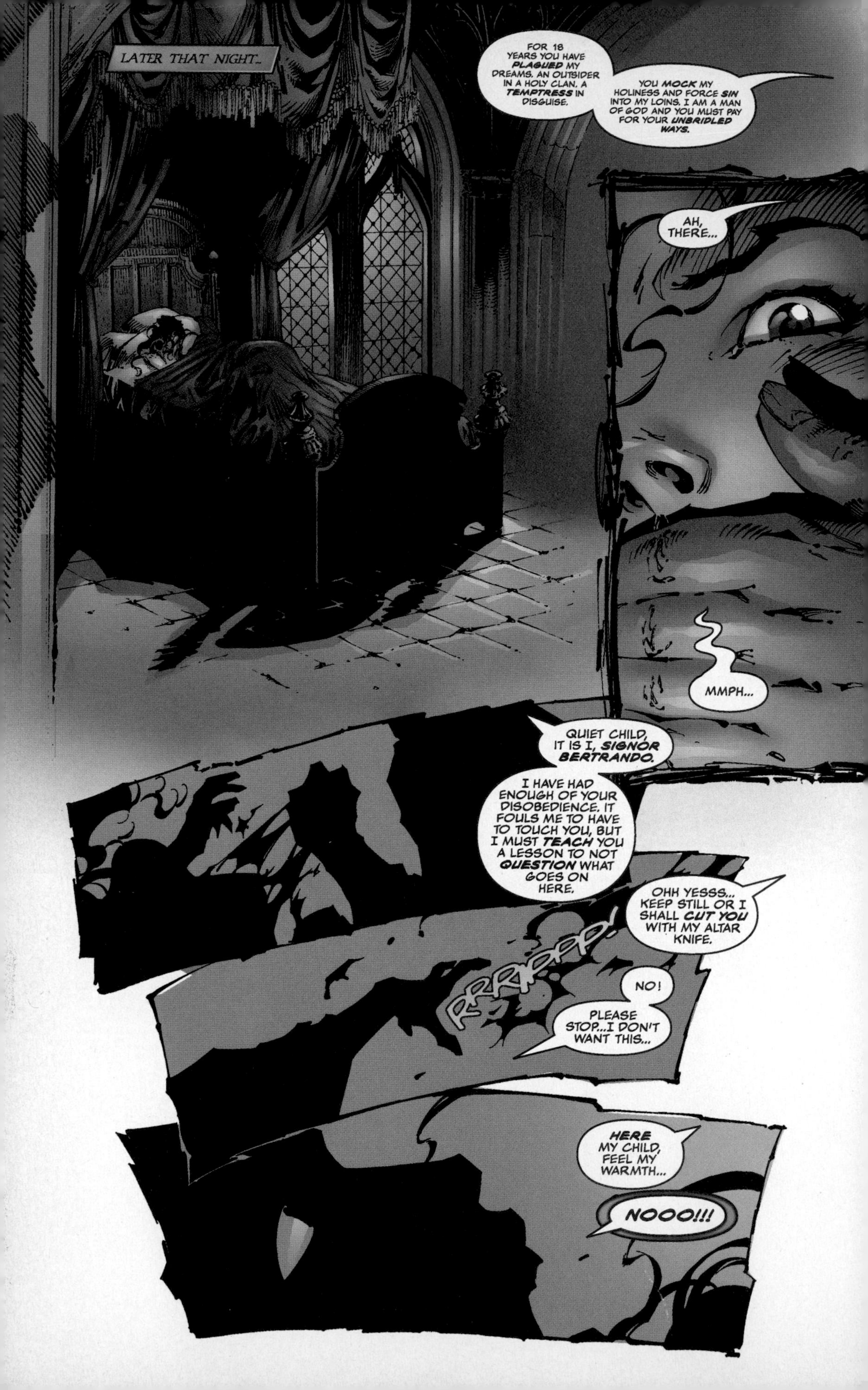
LATER THAT NIGHT...
FOR 18 YEARS YOU HAVE PLAGUED MY DREAMS. AN OUTSIDER IN A HOLY CLAN. A TEMPTRESS IN DISGUISE.
YOU MOCK MY HOLINESS AND FORCE SIN INTO MY LOINS. I AM A MAN OF GOD AND YOU MUST PAY FOR YOUR UNBRIDLED WAYS.
AH, THERE...
MMPH...
QUIET CHILD, IT IS I, SIGNOR BERTRANDO.
I HAVE HAD ENOUGH OF YOUR DISOBEDIENCE. IT FOULS ME TO HAVE TO TOUCH YOU, BUT I MUST TEACH YOU A LESSON TO NOT QUESTION WHAT GOES ON HERE.
OHH YESSS... KEEP STILL OR I SHALL CUT YOU WITH MY ALTAR KNIFE.
NO!
PLEASE STOP...I DON'T WANT THIS...
HERE MY CHILD, FEEL MY WARMTH...
NOOO!!!

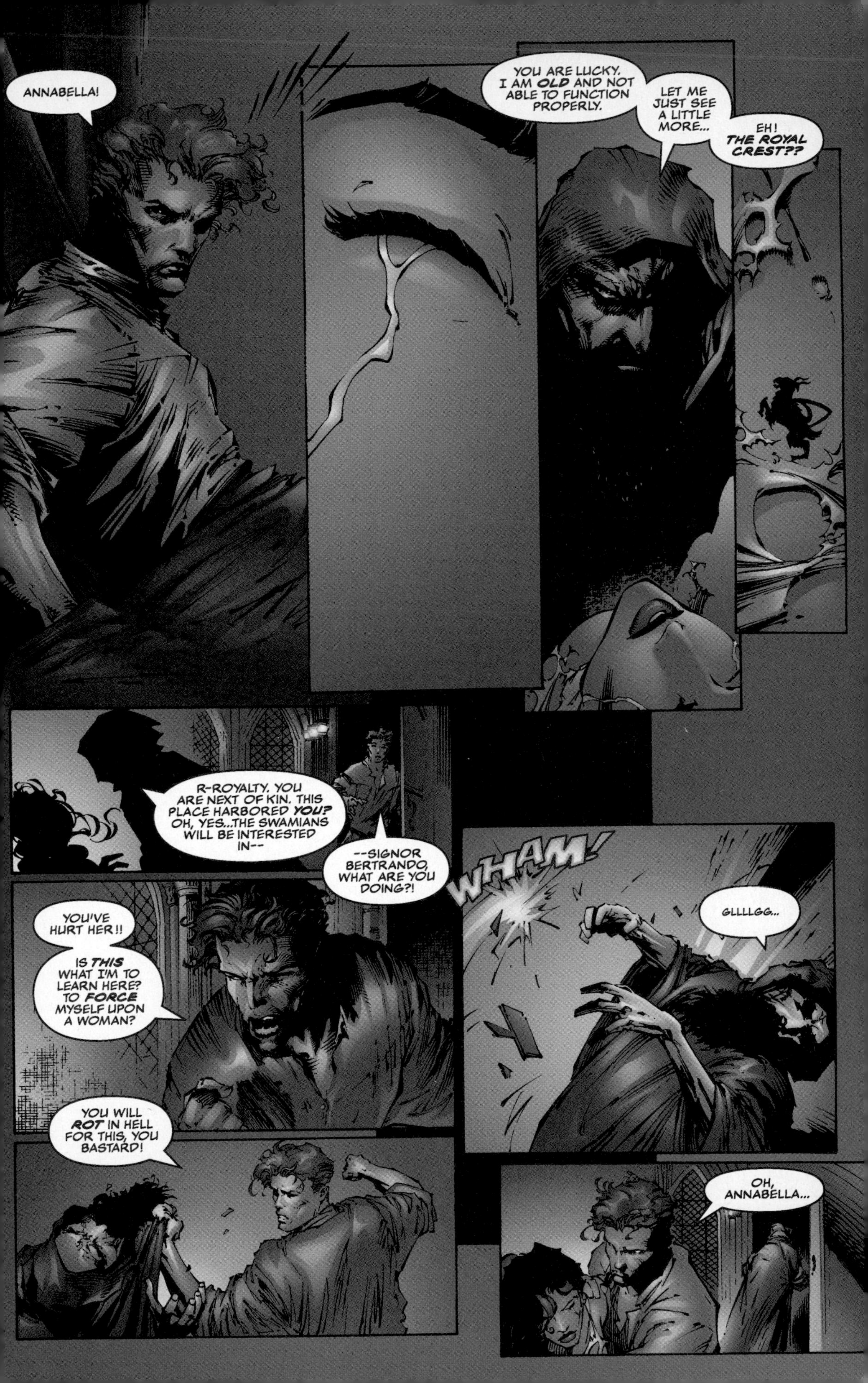
ANNABELLA!
YOU ARE LUCKY. I AM OLD AND NOT ABLE TO FUNCTION PROPERLY.
LET ME JUST SEE A LITTLE MORE...
EH! THE ROYAL CREST??
R-ROYALTY. YOU ARE NEXT OF KIN. THIS PLACE HARBORED YOU? OH, YES...THE SWAMIANS WILL BE INTERESTED IN--
--SIGNOR BERTRANDO, WHAT ARE YOU DOING?!
YOU'VE HURT HER!!
IS THIS WHAT I'M TO LEARN HERE? TO FORCE MYSELF UPON A WOMAN?
WHAM!
GLLLLGG...
YOU WILL ROT IN HELL FOR THIS, YOU BASTARD!
OH, ANNABELLA...

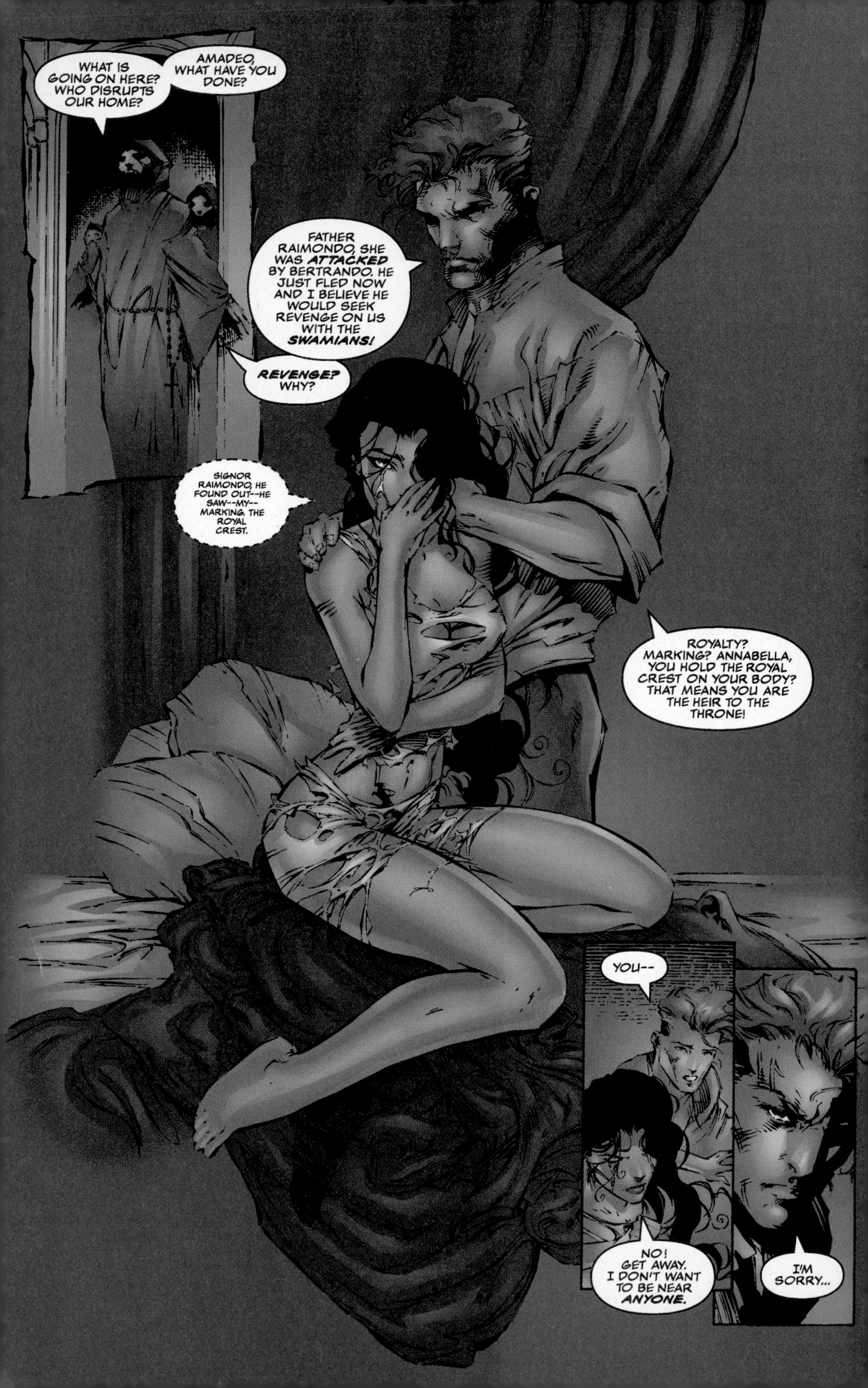
WHAT IS GOING ON HERE? WHO DISRUPTS OUR HOME?
AMADEO, WHAT HAVE YOU DONE?
FATHER RAIMONDO, SHE WAS *ATTACKED* BY BERTRANDO. HE JUST FLED NOW AND I BELIEVE HE WOULD SEEK REVENGE ON US WITH THE *SWAMIANS!*
REVENGE? WHY?
SIGNOR RAIMONDO, HE FOUND OUT--HE SAW--MY--MARKING, THE ROYAL CREST.
ROYALTY? MARKING? ANNABELLA, YOU HOLD THE ROYAL CREST ON YOUR BODY? THAT MEANS YOU ARE THE HEIR TO THE THRONE!
YOU--
NO! GET AWAY. I DON'T WANT TO BE NEAR *ANYONE.*
I'M SORRY...

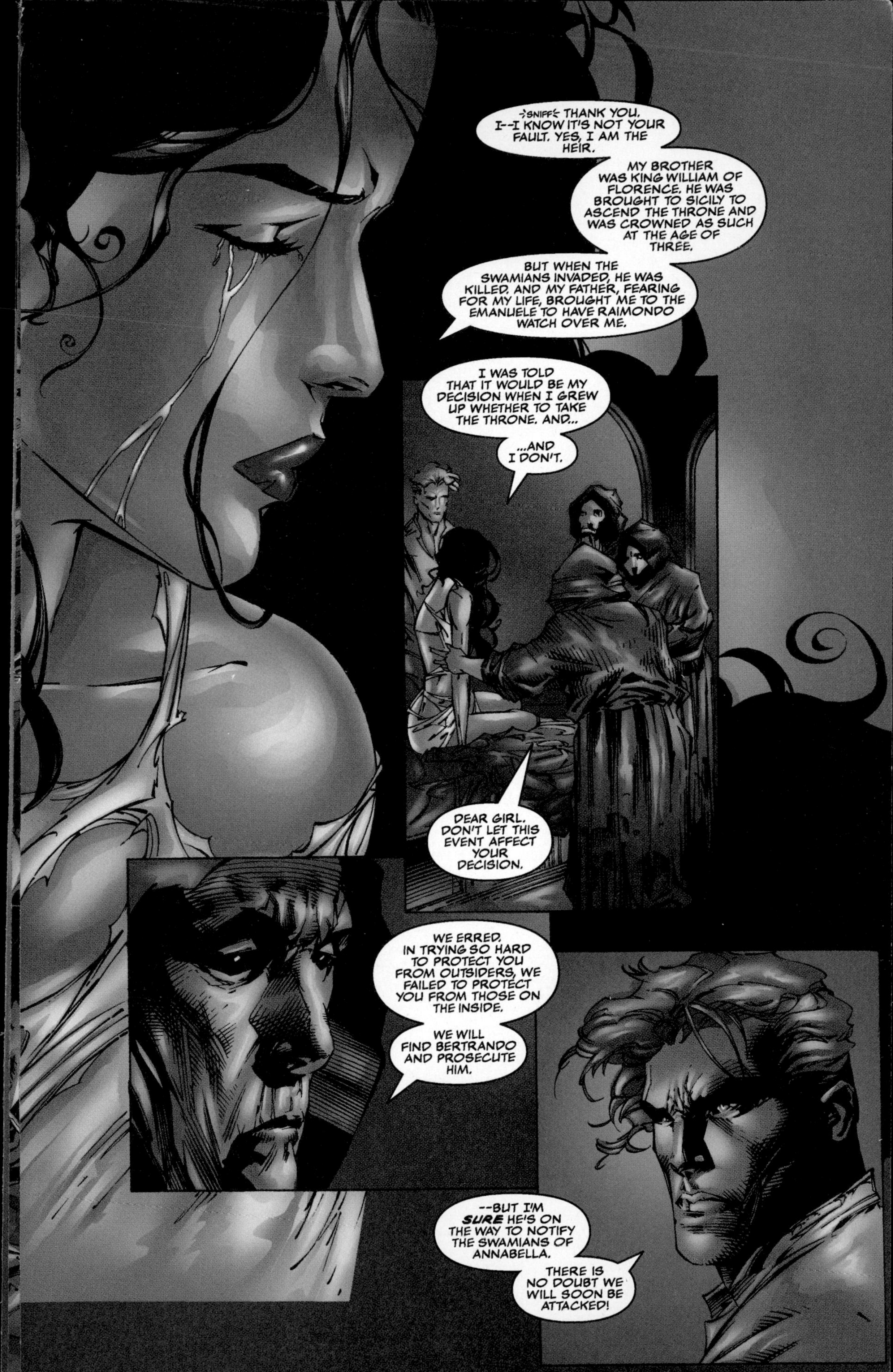
-SNIFF- THANK YOU. I--I KNOW IT'S NOT YOUR FAULT. YES, I AM THE HEIR.
MY BROTHER WAS KING WILLIAM OF FLORENCE. HE WAS BROUGHT TO SICILY TO ASCEND THE THRONE AND WAS CROWNED AS SUCH AT THE AGE OF THREE.
BUT WHEN THE SWAMIANS INVADED, HE WAS KILLED, AND MY FATHER, FEARING FOR MY LIFE, BROUGHT ME TO THE EMANUELE TO HAVE RAIMONDO WATCH OVER ME.
I WAS TOLD THAT IT WOULD BE MY DECISION WHEN I GREW UP WHETHER TO TAKE THE THRONE. AND...
...AND I DON'T.
DEAR GIRL. DON'T LET THIS EVENT AFFECT YOUR DECISION.
WE ERRED. IN TRYING SO HARD TO PROTECT YOU FROM OUTSIDERS, WE FAILED TO PROTECT YOU FROM THOSE ON THE INSIDE.
WE WILL FIND BERTRANDO AND PROSECUTE HIM.
--BUT I'M SURE HE'S ON THE WAY TO NOTIFY THE SWAMIANS OF ANNABELLA.
THERE IS NO DOUBT WE WILL SOON BE ATTACKED!

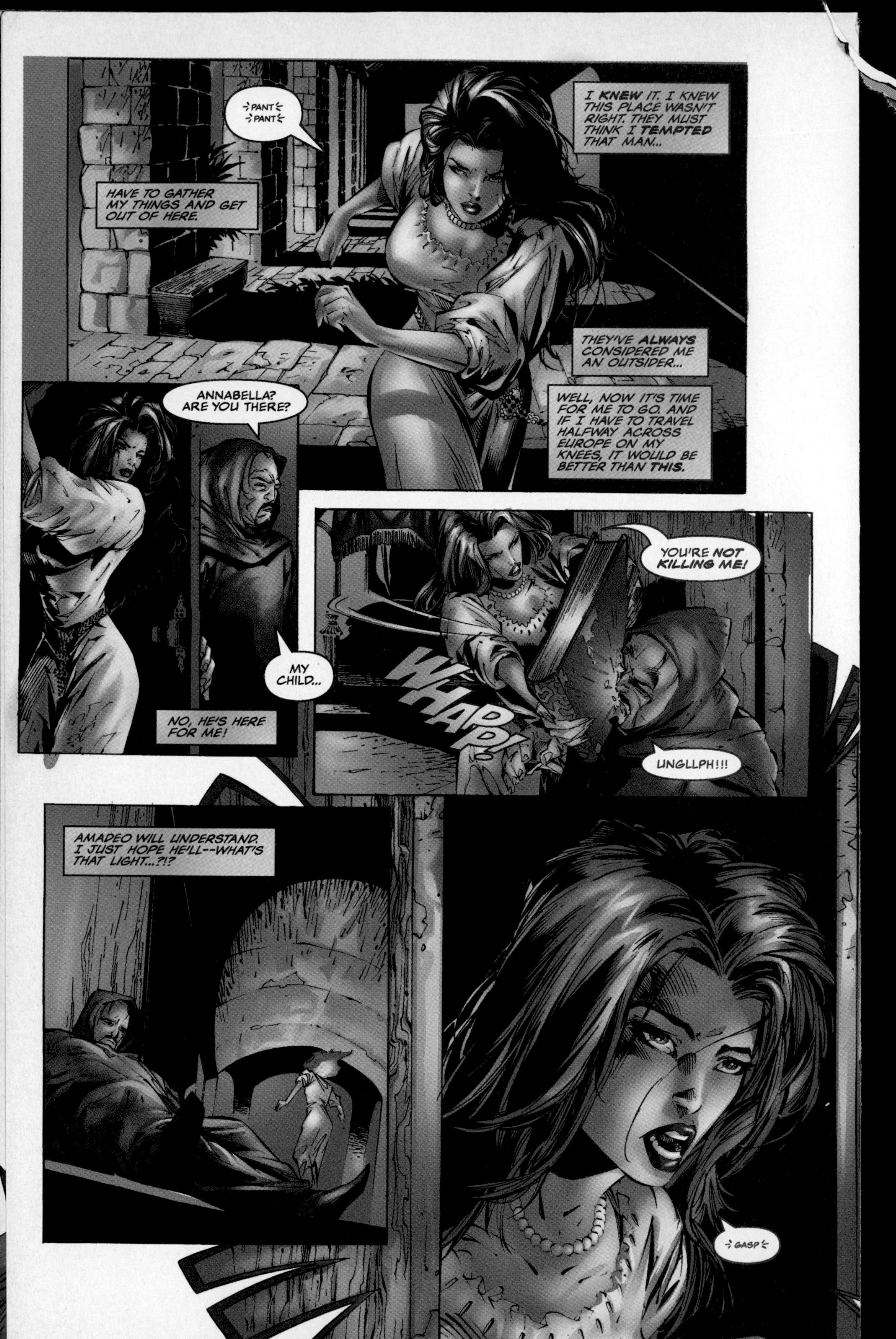
PANT
PANT
I KNEW IT. I KNEW THIS PLACE WASN'T RIGHT. THEY MUST THINK I TEMPTED THAT MAN...
HAVE TO GATHER MY THINGS AND GET OUT OF HERE.
THEY'VE ALWAYS CONSIDERED ME AN OUTSIDER...
WELL, NOW IT'S TIME FOR ME TO GO. AND IF I HAVE TO TRAVEL HALFWAY ACROSS EUROPE ON MY KNEES, IT WOULD BE BETTER THAN THIS.
ANNABELLA? ARE YOU THERE?
MY CHILD...
NO, HE'S HERE FOR ME!
YOU'RE NOT KILLING ME!
WHAP!
UNGLLPH!!!
AMADEO WILL UNDERSTAND. I JUST HOPE HE'LL--WHAT'S THAT LIGHT...?!?
GASP

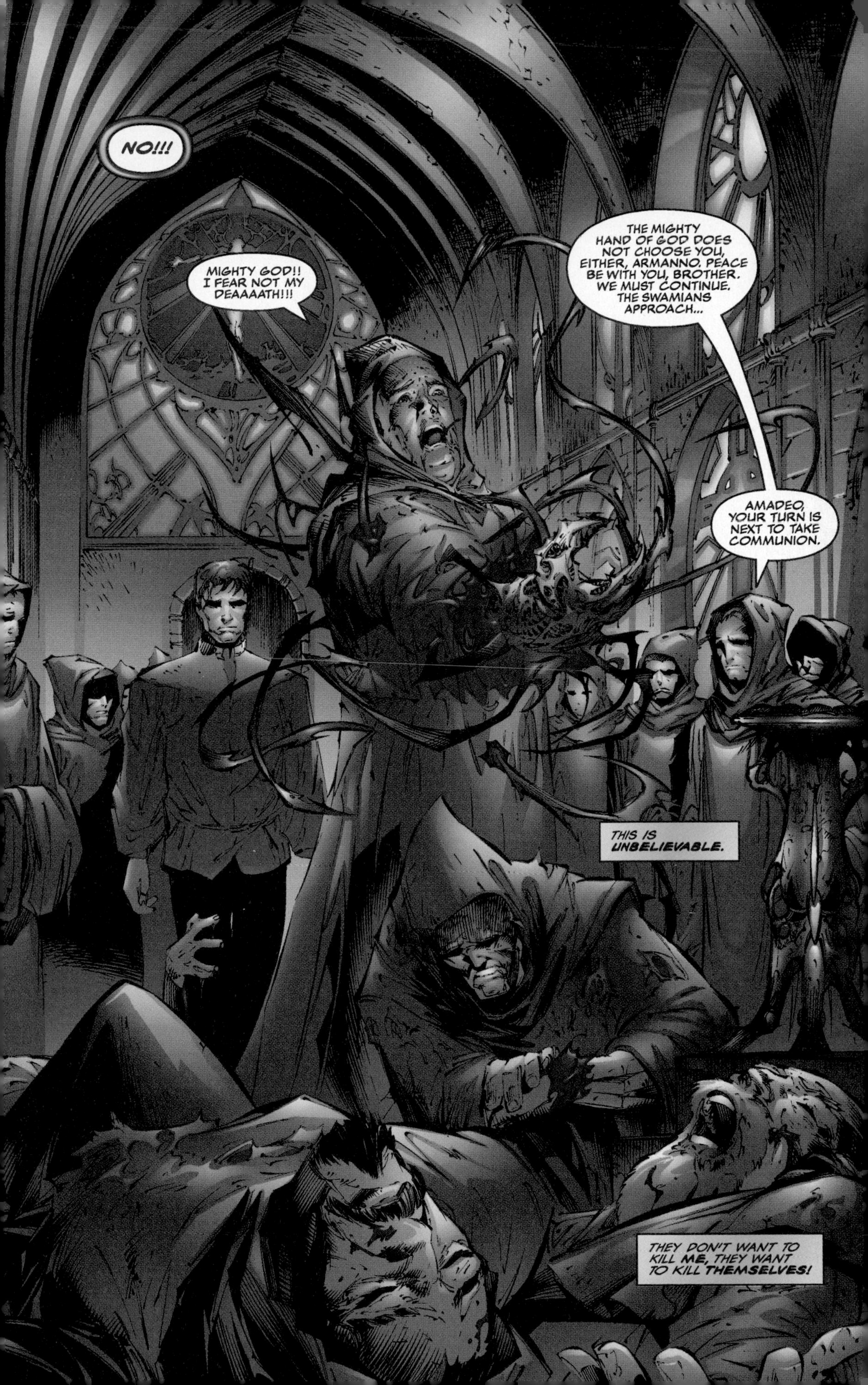
NO!!!
MIGHTY GOD!! I FEAR NOT MY DEAAAATH!!!
THE MIGHTY HAND OF GOD DOES NOT CHOOSE YOU, EITHER, ARMANNO. PEACE BE WITH YOU, BROTHER. WE MUST CONTINUE. THE SWAMIANS APPROACH...
AMADEO, YOUR TURN IS NEXT TO TAKE COMMUNION.
THIS IS UNBELIEVABLE.
THEY DON'T WANT TO KILL ME, THEY WANT TO KILL THEMSELVES!

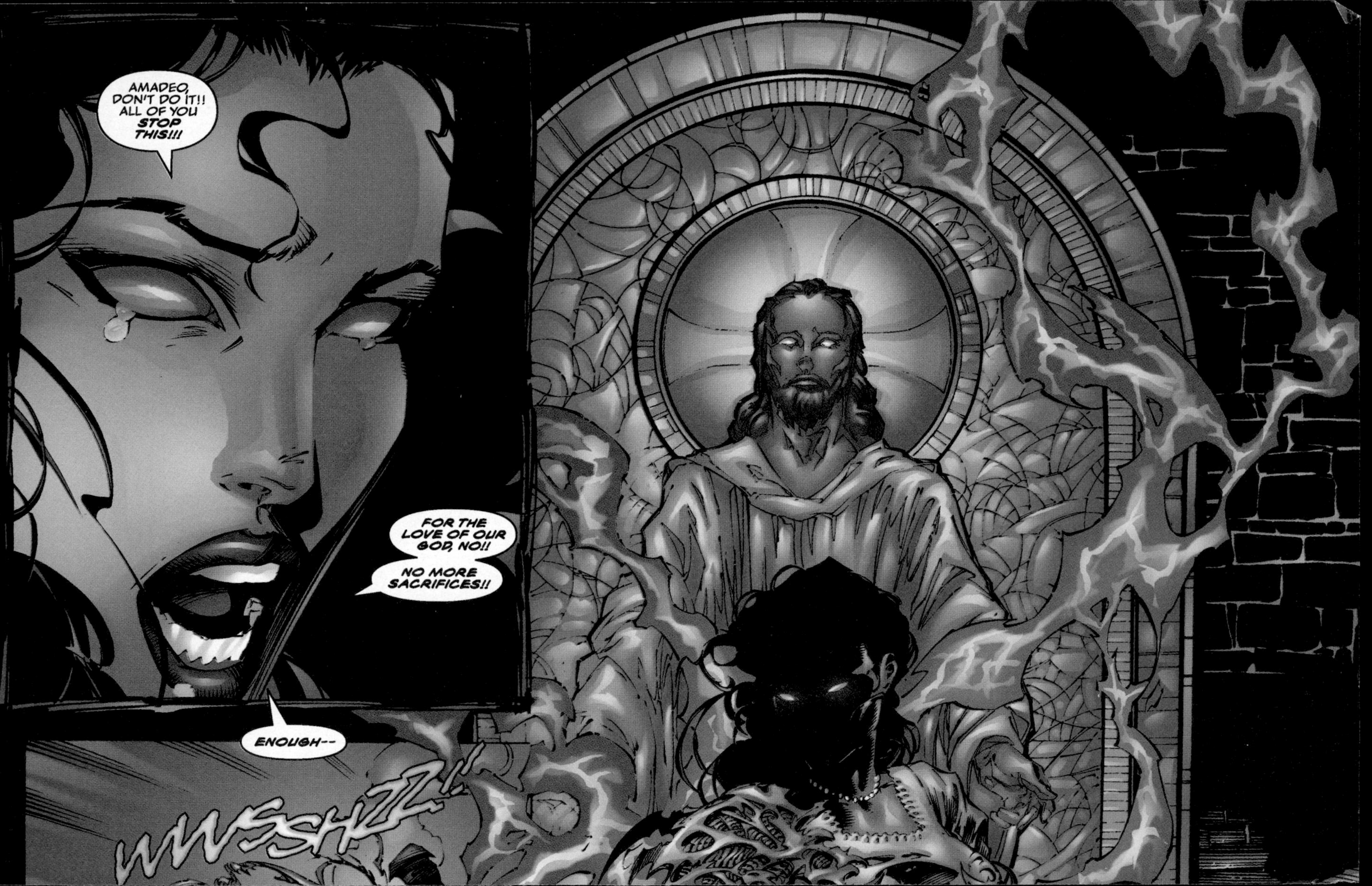
AMADEO, DON'T DO IT!! ALL OF YOU STOP THIS!!!
FOR THE LOVE OF OUR GOD, NO!!
NO MORE SACRIFICES!!
ENOUGH--
WWSHZZ!!

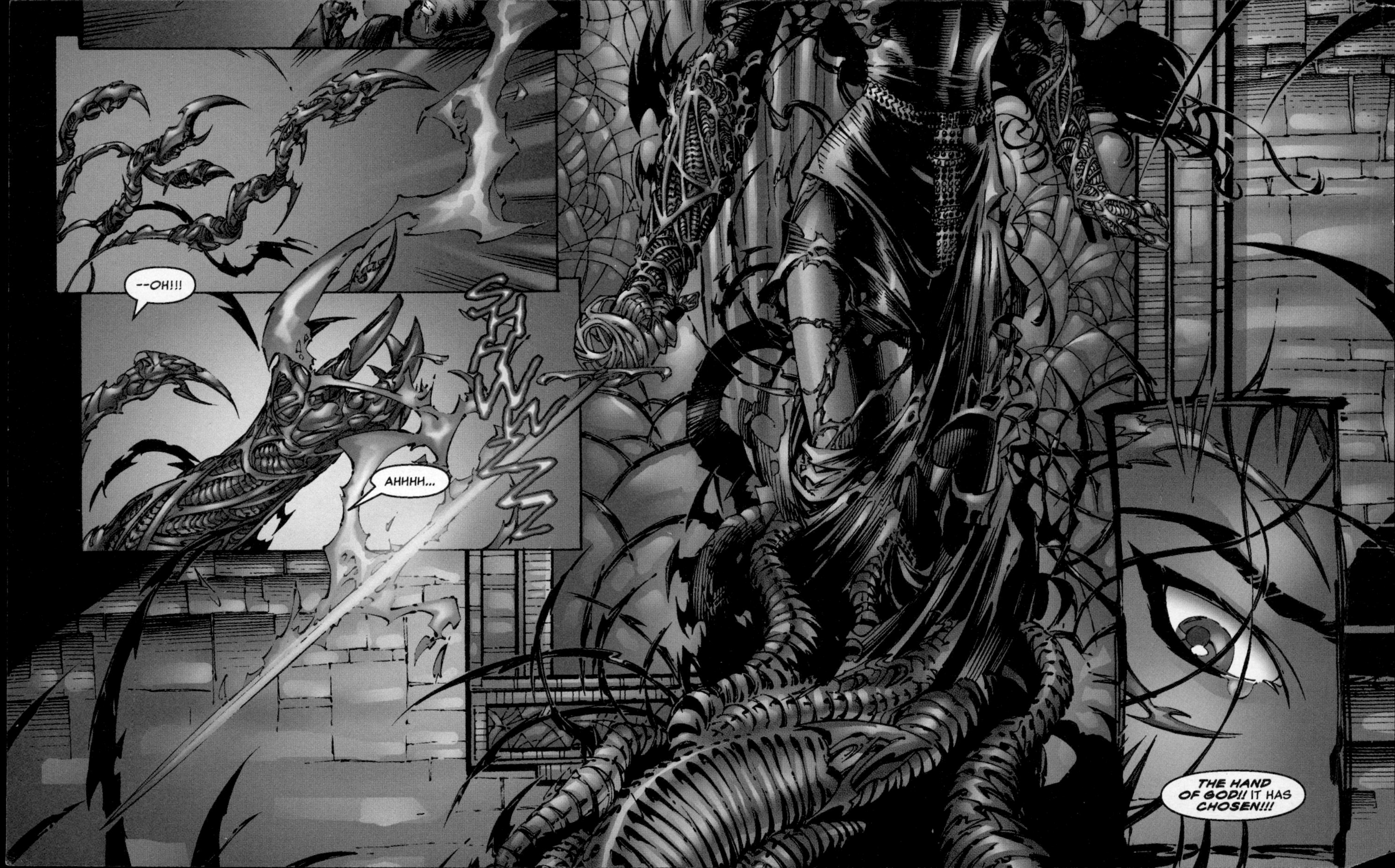
--OH!!!
SHWZZ
AHHHH...
THE HAND OF GOD!! IT HAS CHOSEN!!!

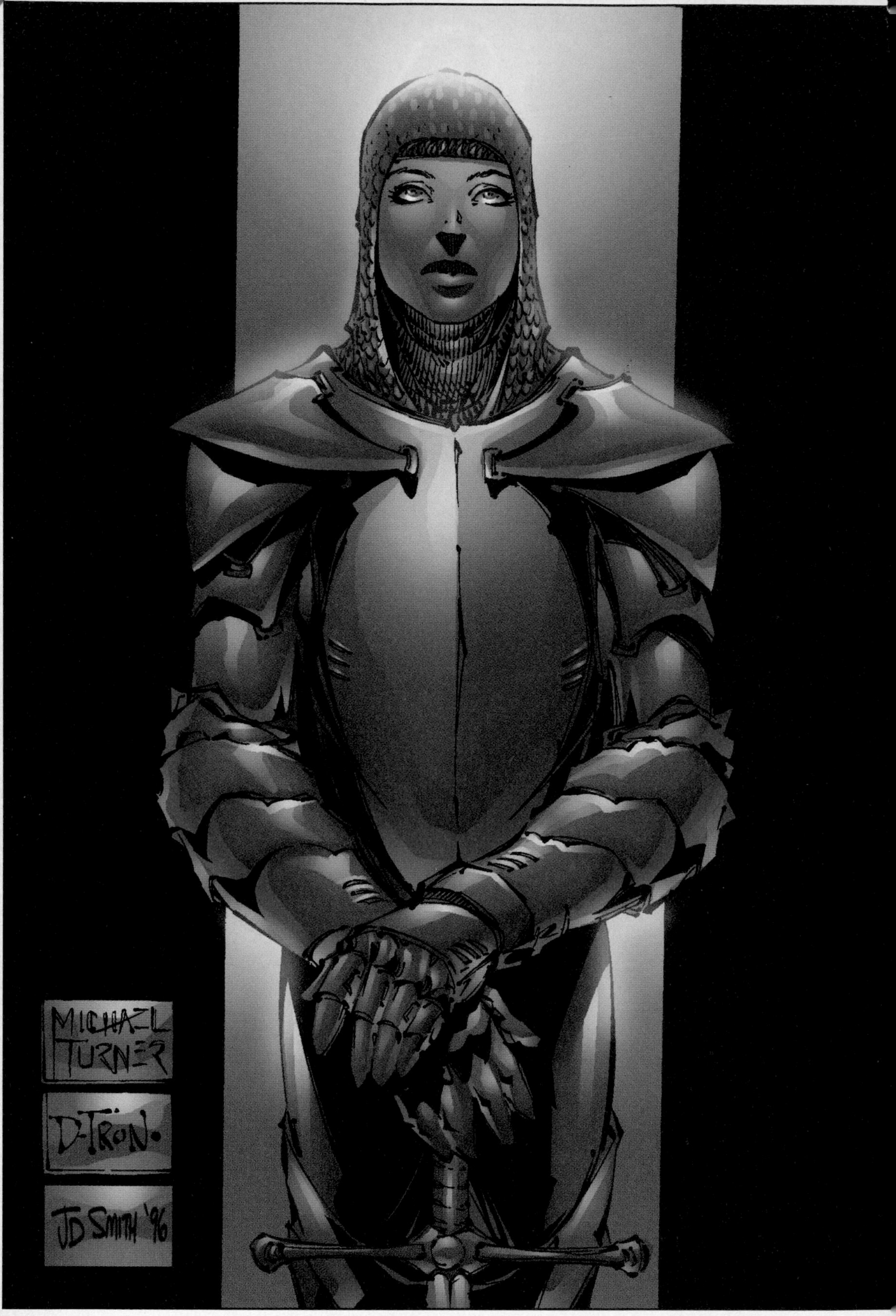
MICHAEL TURNER
D-TRON
JD SMITH '96

F R E N C H
WITCHBLADE
Michael Turner, D-Tron & Jonathan D. Smith

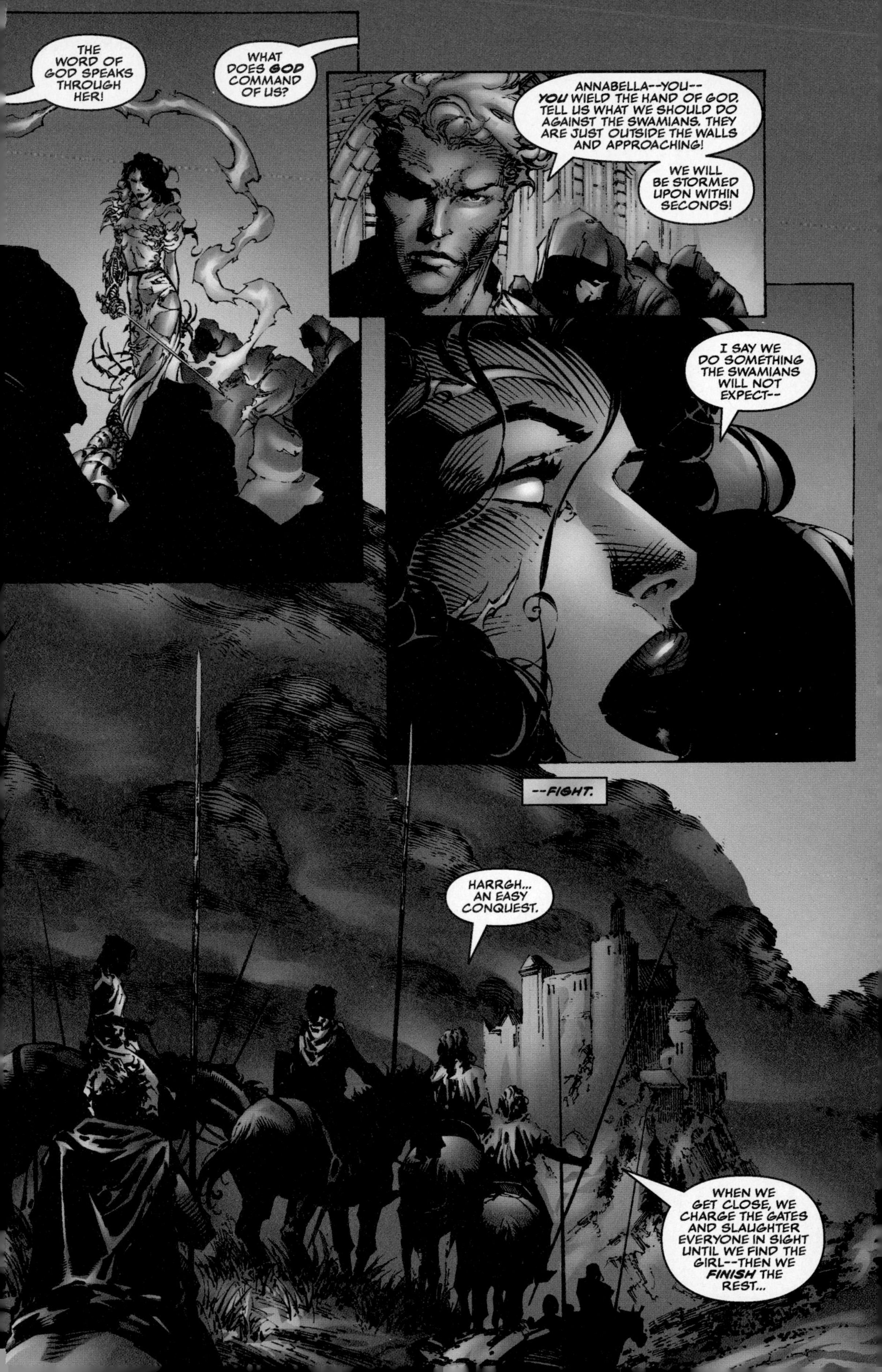
THE WORD OF GOD SPEAKS THROUGH HER!
WHAT DOES GOD COMMAND OF US?
ANNABELLA--YOU-- YOU WIELD THE HAND OF GOD. TELL US WHAT WE SHOULD DO AGAINST THE SWAMIANS. THEY ARE JUST OUTSIDE THE WALLS AND APPROACHING!
WE WILL BE STORMED UPON WITHIN SECONDS!
I SAY WE DO SOMETHING THE SWAMIANS WILL NOT EXPECT--
--FIGHT.
HARRGH... AN EASY CONQUEST.
WHEN WE GET CLOSE, WE CHARGE THE GATES AND SLAUGHTER EVERYONE IN SIGHT UNTIL WE FIND THE GIRL--THEN WE FINISH THE REST...

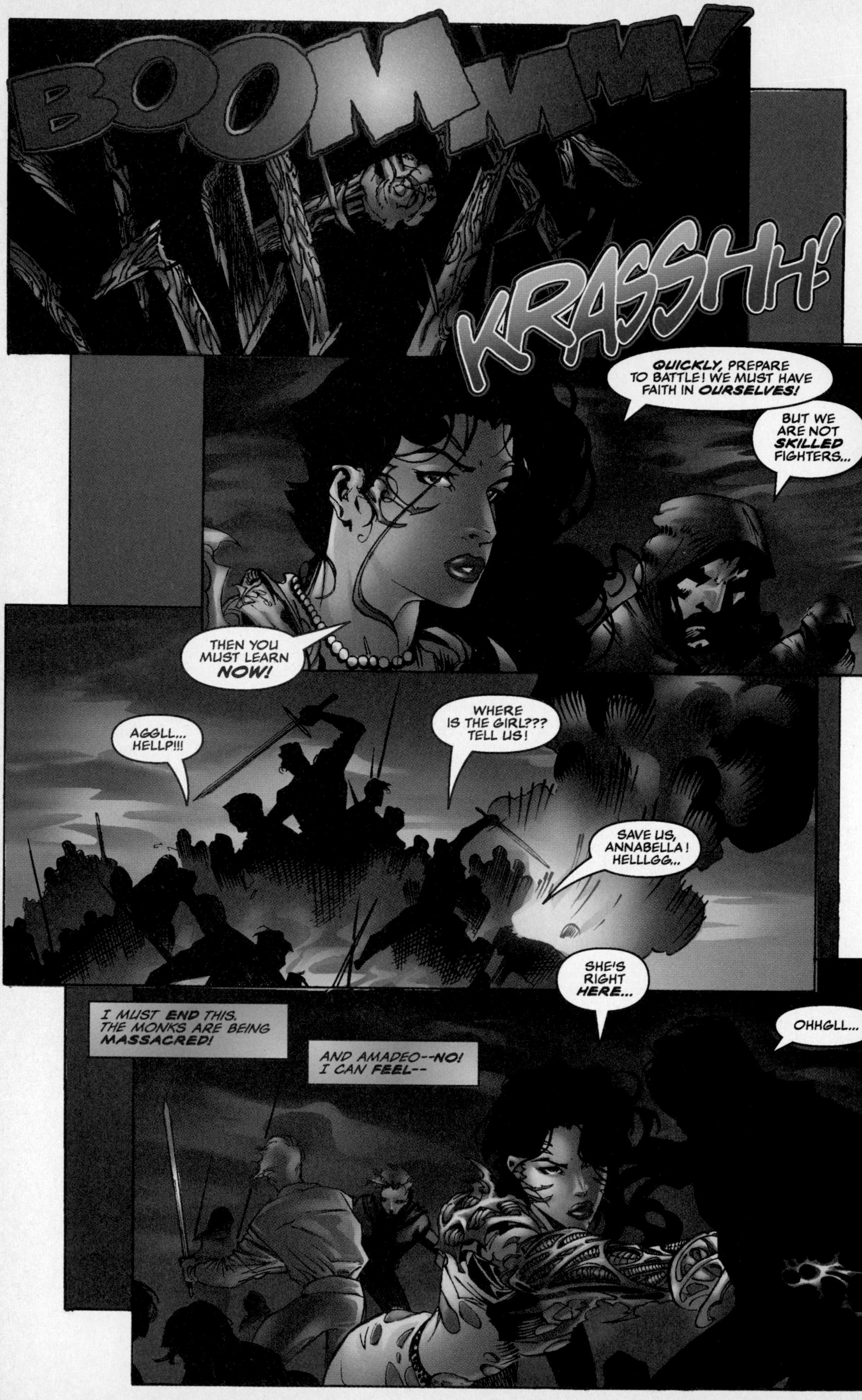
BOOMMM!
KRASSHH!
QUICKLY, PREPARE TO BATTLE! WE MUST HAVE FAITH IN OURSELVES!
BUT WE ARE NOT SKILLED FIGHTERS...
THEN YOU MUST LEARN NOW!
AGGLL... HELLP!!!
WHERE IS THE GIRL??? TELL US!
SAVE US, ANNABELLA! HELLLGG...
SHE'S RIGHT HERE...
OHHGLL...
I MUST END THIS. THE MONKS ARE BEING MASSACRED!
AND AMADEO--NO! I CAN FEEL--

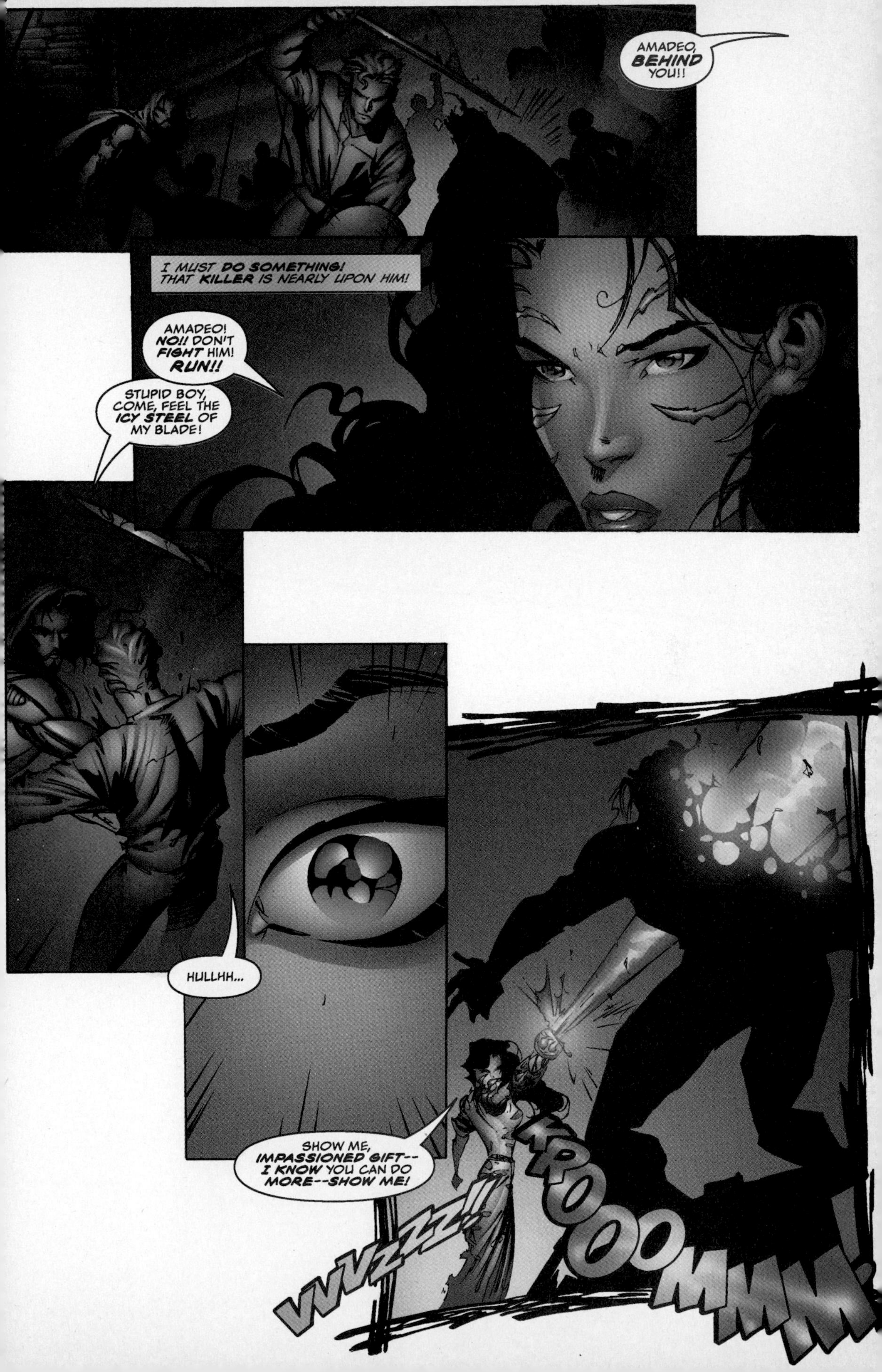
AMADEO, BEHIND YOU!!
I MUST DO SOMETHING! THAT KILLER IS NEARLY UPON HIM!
AMADEO! NO!! DON'T FIGHT HIM! RUN!!
STUPID BOY, COME, FEEL THE ICY STEEL OF MY BLADE!
HULLHH...
SHOW ME, IMPASSIONED GIFT-- I KNOW YOU CAN DO MORE--SHOW ME!
VVVZZZ!!
KROOOOMMMM!

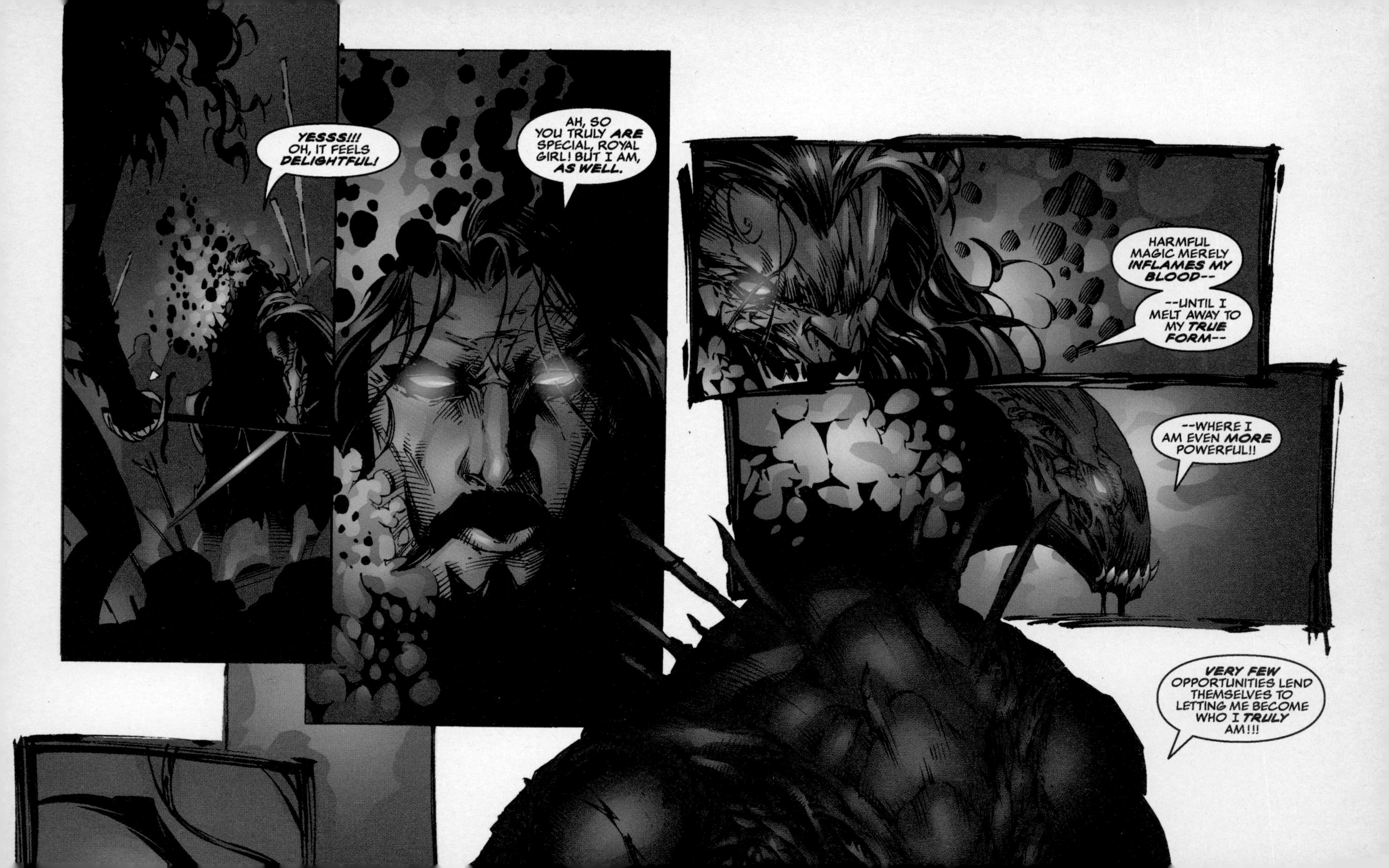
YESSS!!! OH, IT FEELS DELIGHTFUL!
AH, SO YOU TRULY ARE SPECIAL, ROYAL GIRL! BUT I AM, AS WELL.
HARMFUL MAGIC MERELY INFLAMES MY BLOOD--
--UNTIL I MELT AWAY TO MY TRUE FORM--
--WHERE I AM EVEN MORE POWERFUL!!
VERY FEW OPPORTUNITIES LEND THEMSELVES TO LETTING ME BECOME WHO I TRULY AM!!!

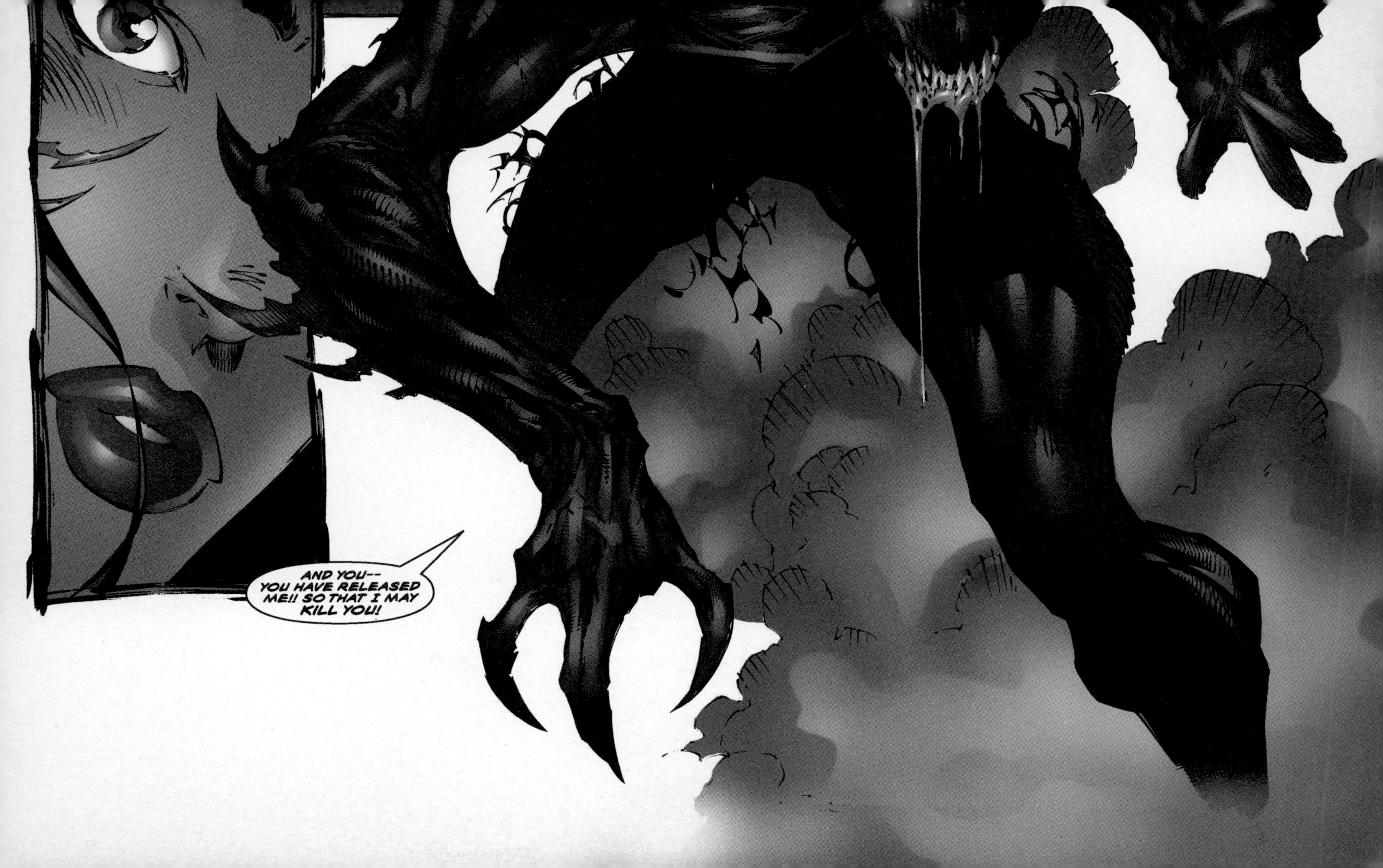
AND YOU-- YOU HAVE RELEASED ME!! SO THAT I MAY KILL YOU!

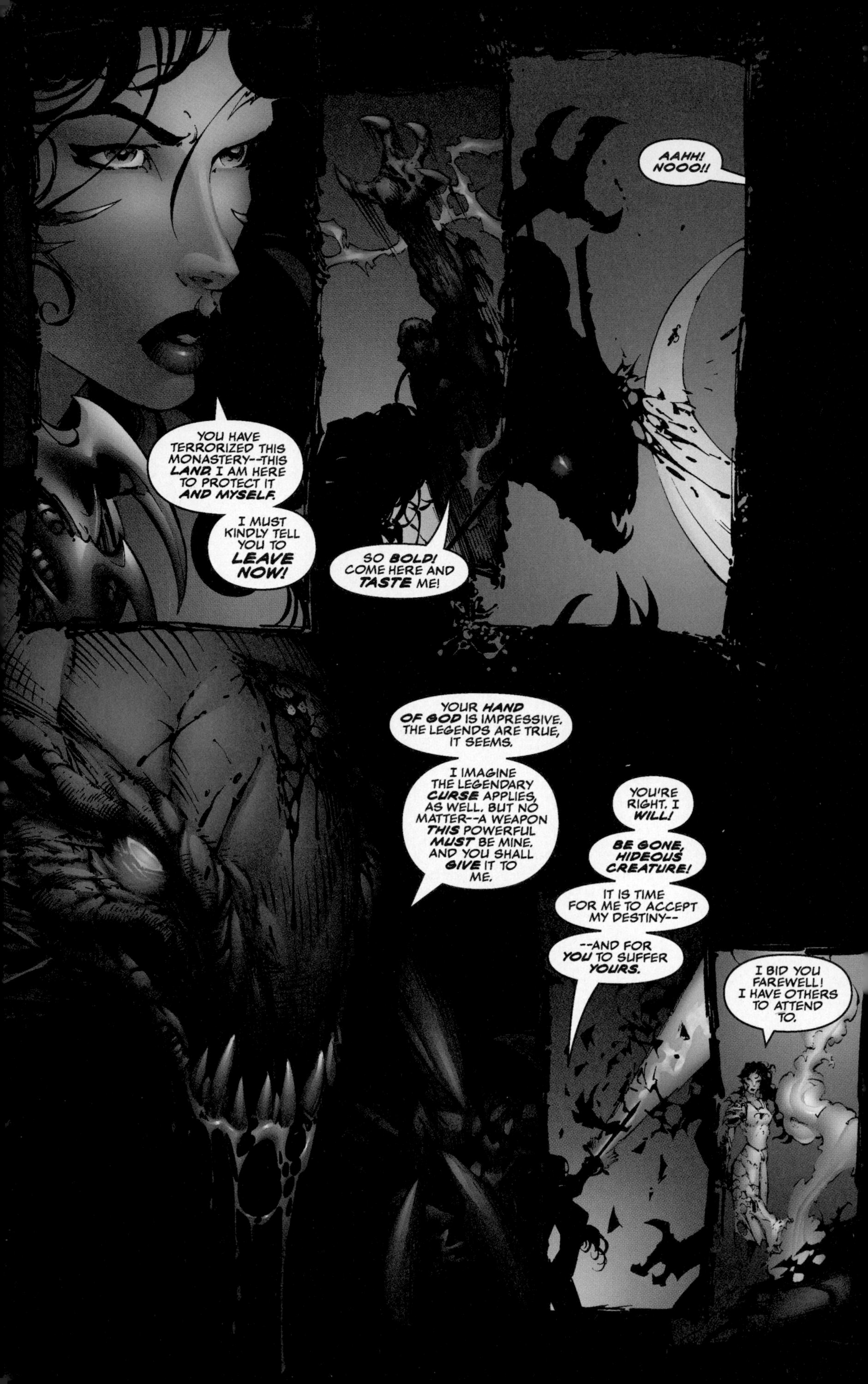

YOU HAVE TERRORIZED THIS MONASTERY--THIS LAND. I AM HERE TO PROTECT IT AND MYSELF.
I MUST KINDLY TELL YOU TO LEAVE NOW!
SO BOLD! COME HERE AND TASTE ME!
AAHH! NOOO!!
YOUR HAND OF GOD IS IMPRESSIVE. THE LEGENDS ARE TRUE, IT SEEMS.
I IMAGINE THE LEGENDARY CURSE APPLIES, AS WELL. BUT NO MATTER--A WEAPON THIS POWERFUL MUST BE MINE. AND YOU SHALL GIVE IT TO ME.
YOU'RE RIGHT. I WILL!
BE GONE, HIDEOUS CREATURE!
IT IS TIME FOR ME TO ACCEPT MY DESTINY--
--AND FOR YOU TO SUFFER YOURS.
I BID YOU FAREWELL! I HAVE OTHERS TO ATTEND TO.

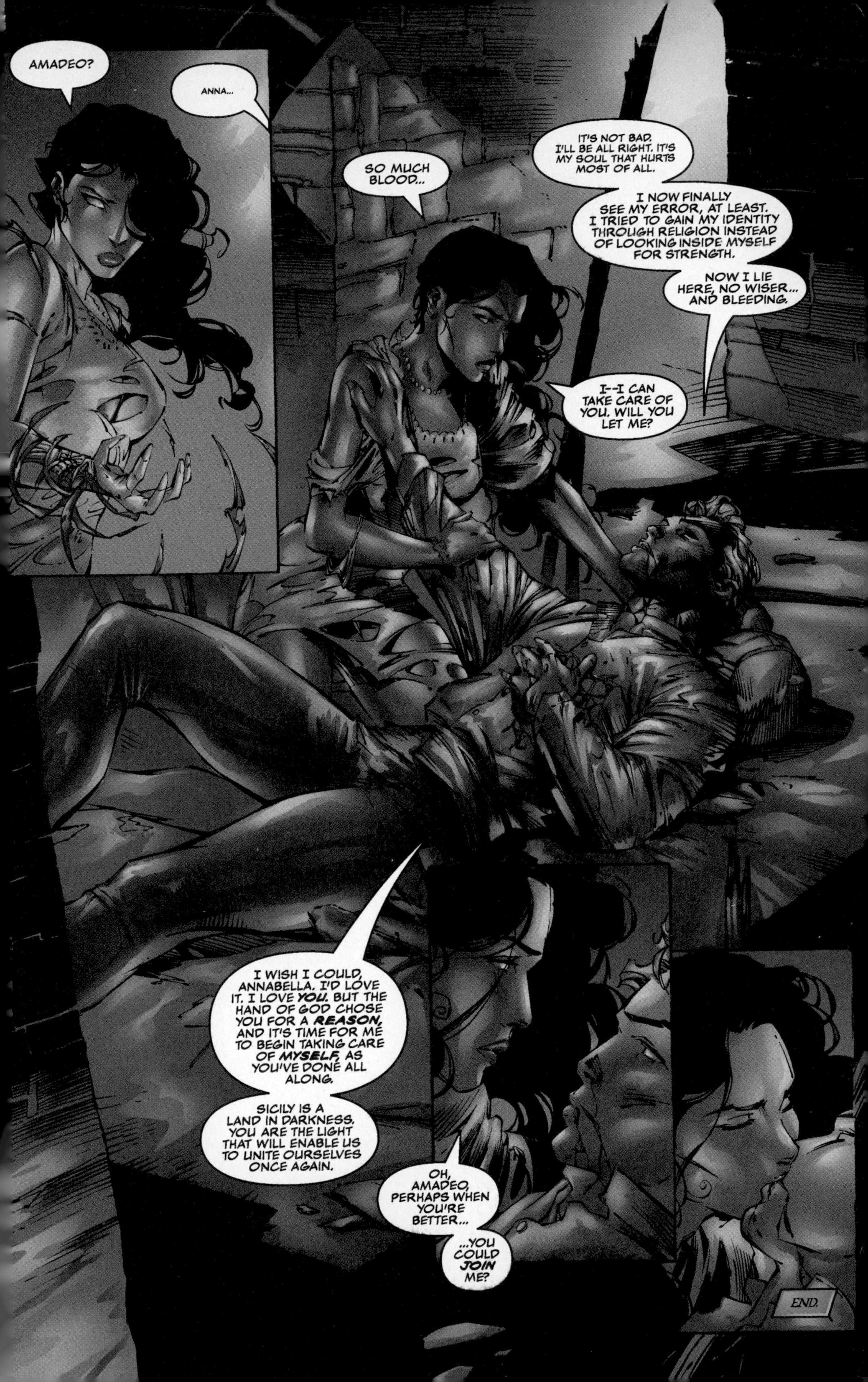
AMADEO?
ANNA...
SO MUCH BLOOD...
IT'S NOT BAD. I'LL BE ALL RIGHT. IT'S MY SOUL THAT HURTS MOST OF ALL.
I NOW FINALLY SEE MY ERROR, AT LEAST. I TRIED TO GAIN MY IDENTITY THROUGH RELIGION INSTEAD OF LOOKING INSIDE MYSELF FOR STRENGTH.
NOW I LIE HERE, NO WISER... AND BLEEDING.
I--I CAN TAKE CARE OF YOU. WILL YOU LET ME?
I WISH I COULD, ANNABELLA. I'D LOVE IT. I LOVE YOU. BUT THE HAND OF GOD CHOSE YOU FOR A REASON, AND IT'S TIME FOR ME TO BEGIN TAKING CARE OF MYSELF, AS YOU'VE DONE ALL ALONG.
SICILY IS A LAND IN DARKNESS. YOU ARE THE LIGHT THAT WILL ENABLE US TO UNITE OURSELVES ONCE AGAIN.
OH, AMADEO, PERHAPS WHEN YOU'RE BETTER...
...YOU COULD JOIN ME?
END.

TALES *of the* WITCHBLADE

03

STORY by
Warren Ellis

PENCILED by
Billy Tan
Brian Ching (pgs. 67-70; CHAPTER 3)

INKED by
D-Tron· w/ Team Tron
Jeff de los Santos
Marcia Chen
Jose "Jag" Guillen
Andy Kim
Viet Truong

COLORED by
Jonathan D. Smith
Steve Firchow (CHAPTER 4)
Peter Steigerwald (CHAPTER 4)

LETTERED by
Dennis Heisler

COVERS 3 & 4 by
Billy Tan,
D-Tron·
and
Jonathan D. Smith

SELENA

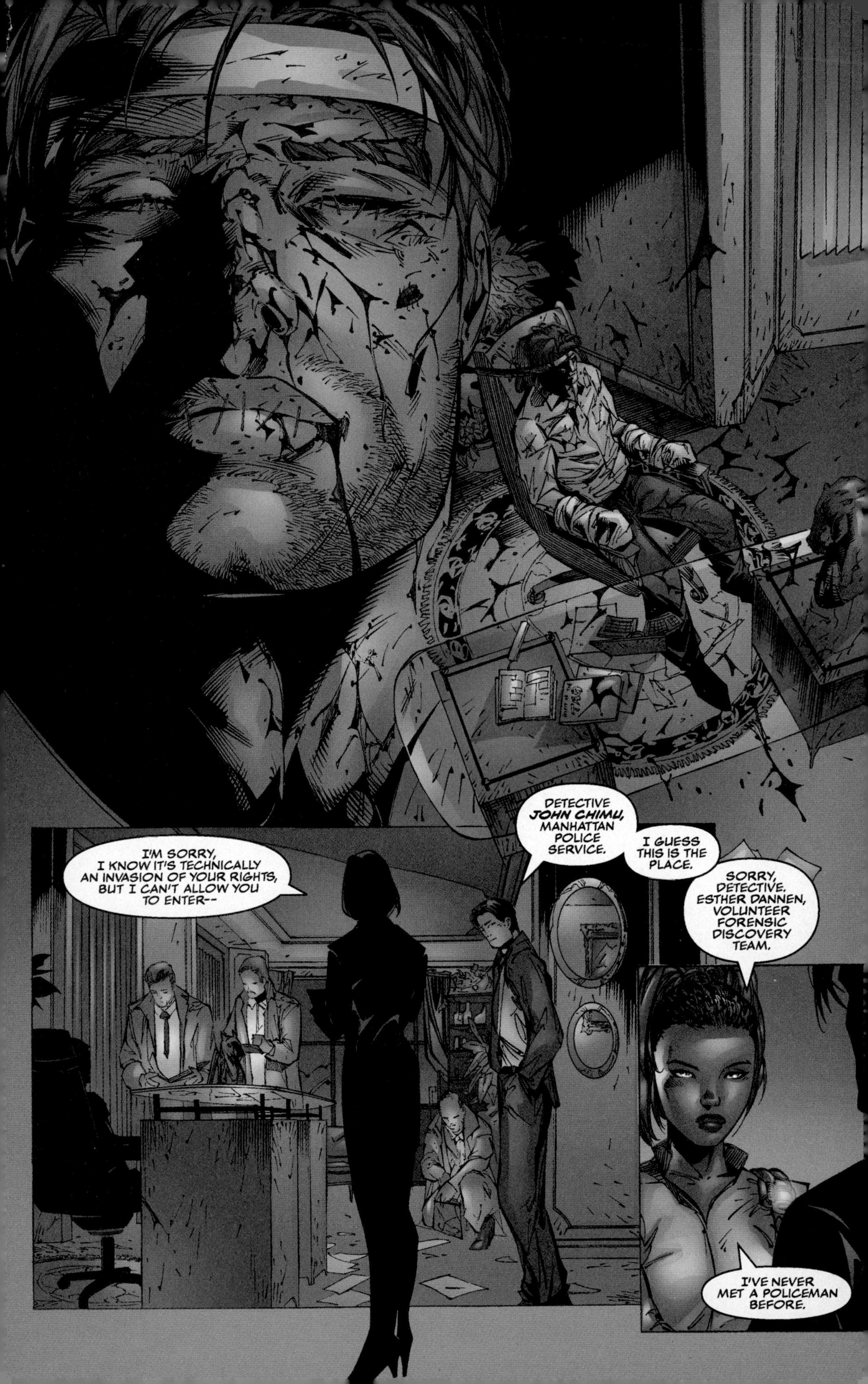

I'M SORRY, I KNOW IT'S TECHNICALLY AN INVASION OF YOUR RIGHTS, BUT I CAN'T ALLOW YOU TO ENTER--
DETECTIVE JOHN CHIMU, MANHATTAN POLICE SERVICE.
I GUESS THIS IS THE PLACE.
SORRY, DETECTIVE. ESTHER DANNEN, VOLUNTEER FORENSIC DISCOVERY TEAM.
I'VE NEVER MET A POLICEMAN BEFORE.

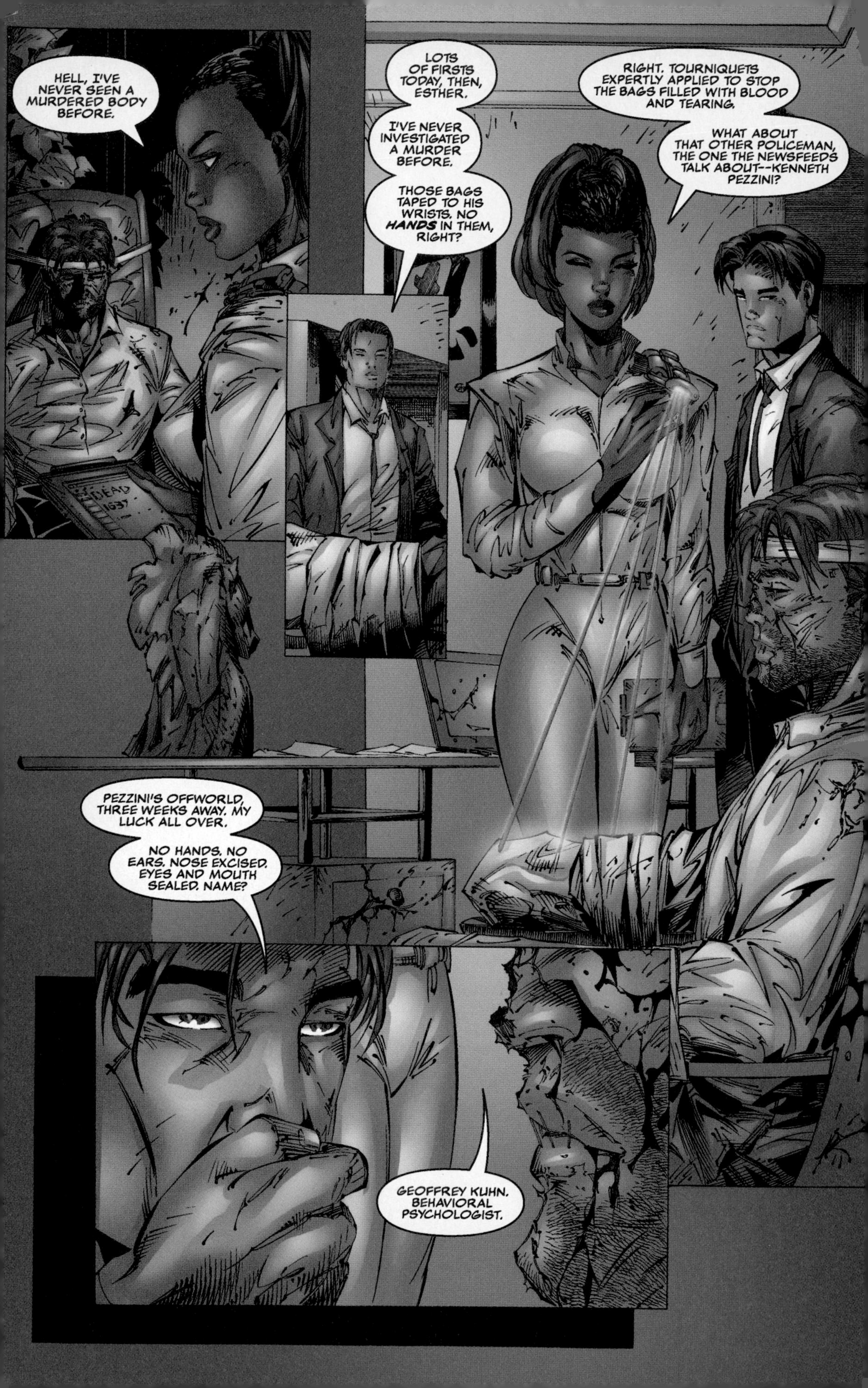
HELL, I'VE NEVER SEEN A MURDERED BODY BEFORE.
LOTS OF FIRSTS TODAY, THEN, ESTHER.
I'VE NEVER INVESTIGATED A MURDER BEFORE.
THOSE BAGS TAPED TO HIS WRISTS. NO HANDS IN THEM, RIGHT?
RIGHT. TOURNIQUETS EXPERTLY APPLIED TO STOP THE BAGS FILLED WITH BLOOD AND TEARING.
WHAT ABOUT THAT OTHER POLICEMAN, THE ONE THE NEWSFEEDS TALK ABOUT--KENNETH PEZZINI?
PEZZINI'S OFFWORLD, THREE WEEKS AWAY. MY LUCK ALL OVER.
NO HANDS. NO EARS. NOSE EXCISED. EYES AND MOUTH SEALED. NAME?
GEOFFREY KUHN. BEHAVIORAL PSYCHOLOGIST.

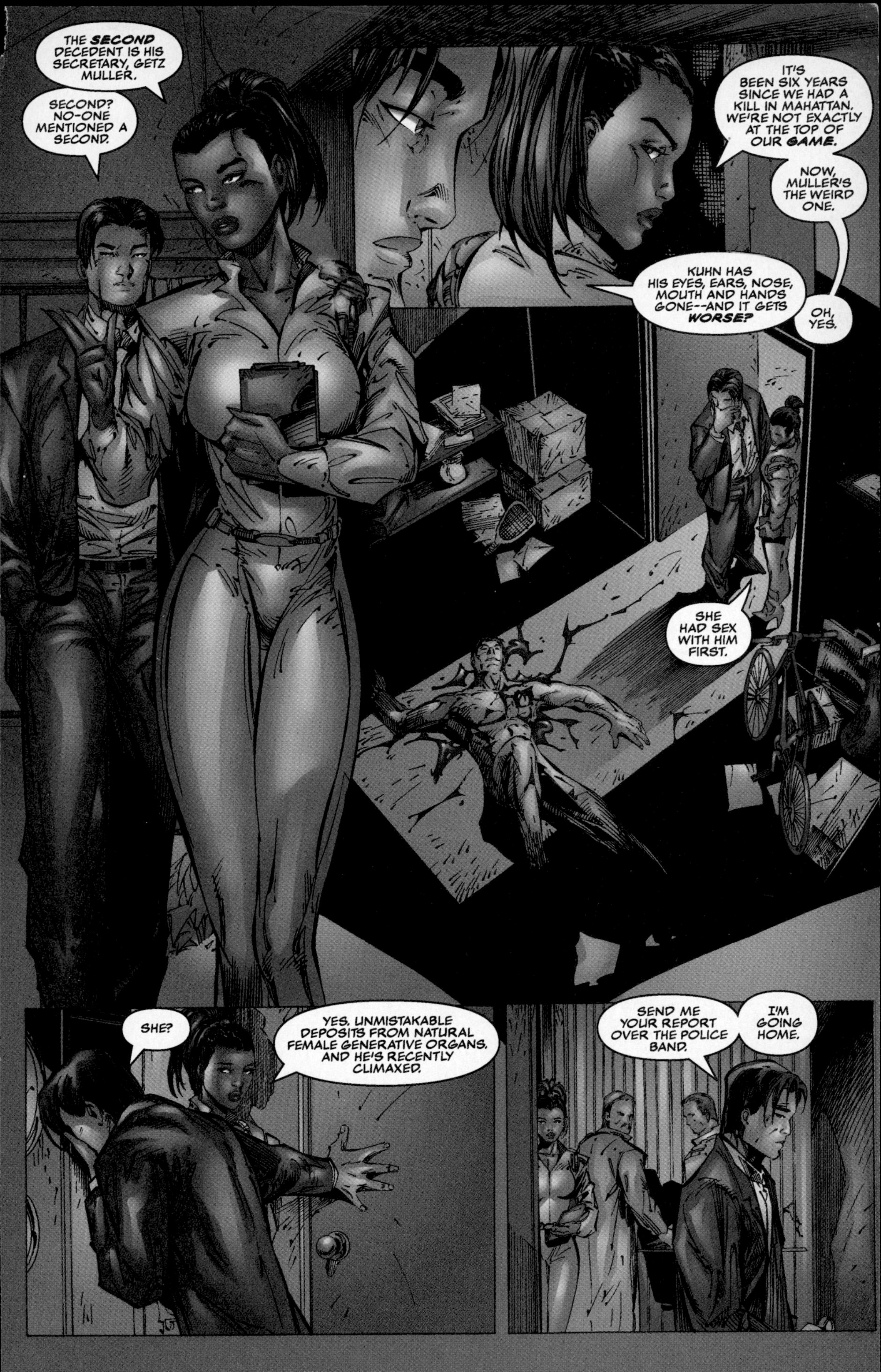
THE SECOND DECEDENT IS HIS SECRETARY, GETZ MULLER.
SECOND? NO-ONE MENTIONED A SECOND.
IT'S BEEN SIX YEARS SINCE WE HAD A KILL IN MAHATTAN. WE'RE NOT EXACTLY AT THE TOP OF OUR GAME.
NOW, MULLER'S THE WEIRD ONE.
KUHN HAS HIS EYES, EARS, NOSE, MOUTH AND HANDS GONE--AND IT GETS WORSE?
OH, YES.
SHE HAD SEX WITH HIM FIRST.
SHE?
YES. UNMISTAKABLE DEPOSITS FROM NATURAL FEMALE GENERATIVE ORGANS. AND HE'S RECENTLY CLIMAXED.
SEND ME YOUR REPORT OVER THE POLICE BAND.
I'M GOING HOME.

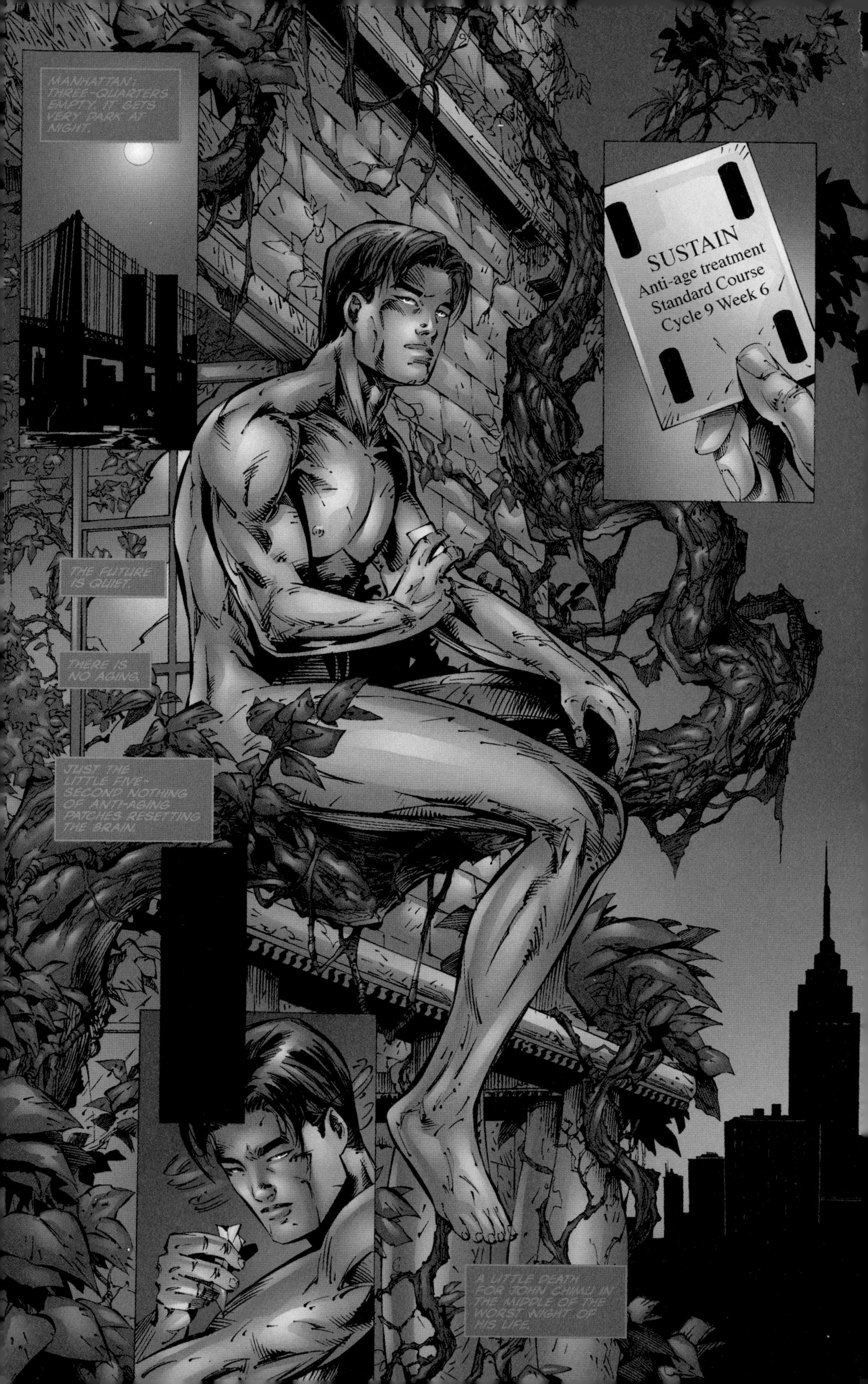
MANHATTAN: THREE-QUARTERS EMPTY. IT GETS VERY DARK AT NIGHT.
SUSTAIN
Anti-age treatment
Standard Course
Cycle 9 Week 6
THE FUTURE IS QUIET.
THERE IS NO AGING.
JUST THE LITTLE FIVE-SECOND NOTHING OF ANTI-AGING PATCHES RESETTING THE BRAIN.
A LITTLE DEATH FOR JOHN CHIAU IN THE MIDDLE OF THE WORST NIGHT OF HIS LIFE.

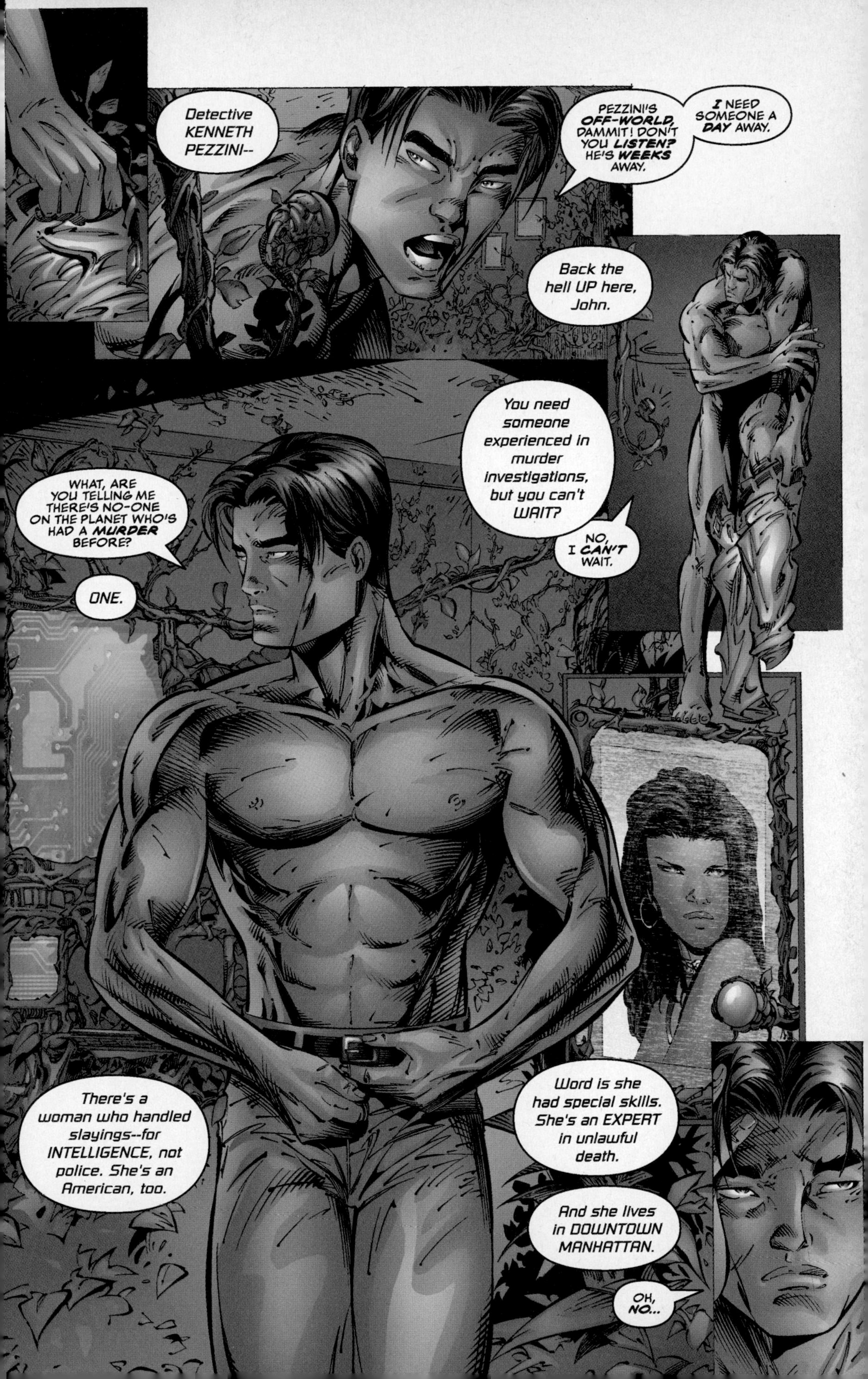
Detective KENNETH PEZZINI--
PEZZINI'S OFF-WORLD, DAMMIT! DON'T YOU LISTEN? HE'S WEEKS AWAY.
I NEED SOMEONE A DAY AWAY.
Back the hell UP here, John.
You need someone experienced in murder investigations, but you can't WAIT?
NO, I CAN'T WAIT.
WHAT, ARE YOU TELLING ME THERE'S NO-ONE ON THE PLANET WHO'S HAD A MURDER BEFORE?
ONE.
There's a woman who handled slayings--for INTELLIGENCE, not police. She's an American, too.
Word is she had special skills. She's an EXPERT in unlawful death.
And she lives in DOWNTOWN MANHATTAN.
OH, NO...

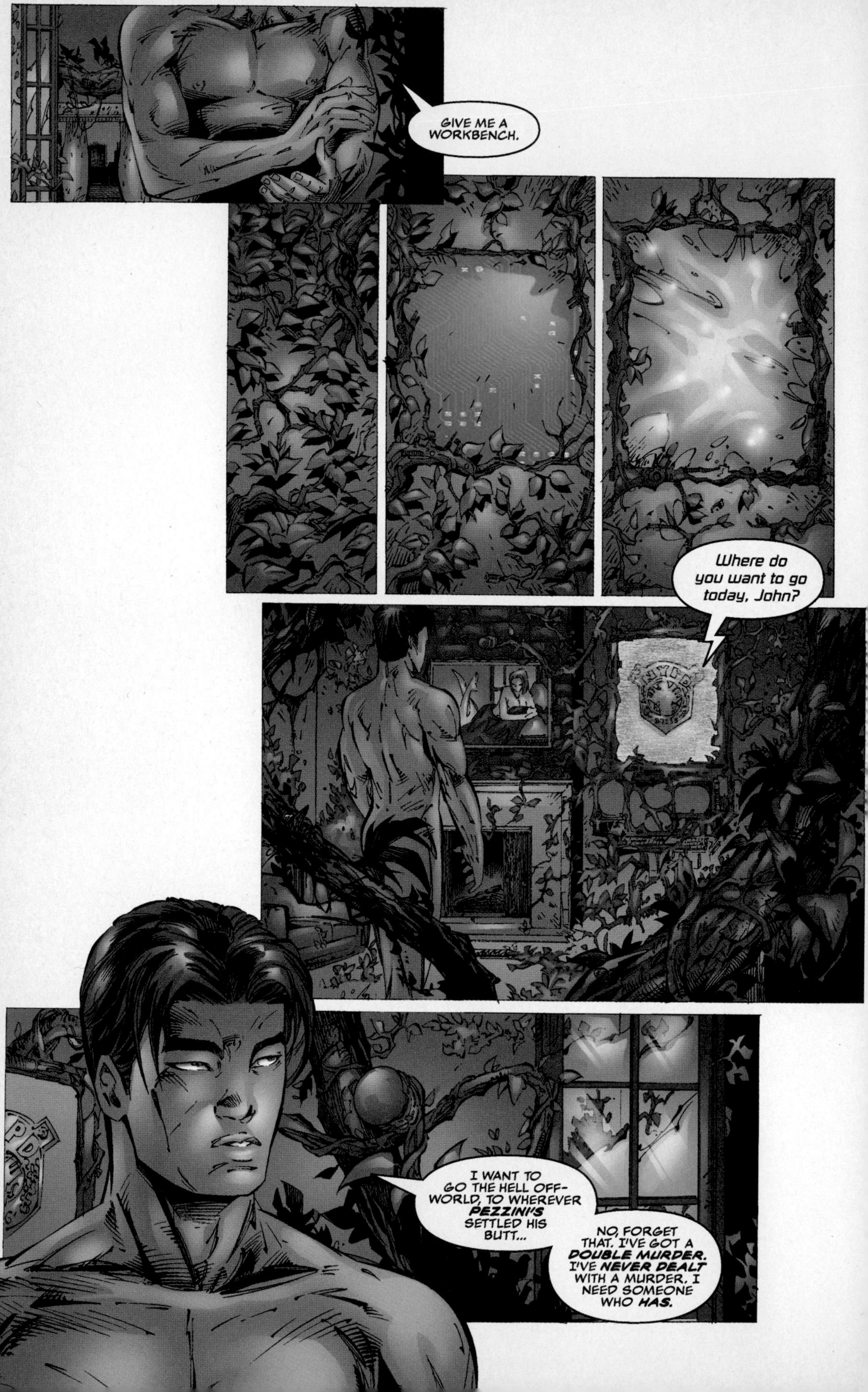
GIVE ME A WORKBENCH.
Where do you want to go today, John?
I WANT TO GO THE HELL OFF-WORLD, TO WHEREVER PEZZINI'S SETTLED HIS BUTT...
NO, FORGET THAT. I'VE GOT A DOUBLE MURDER. I'VE NEVER DEALT WITH A MURDER. I NEED SOMEONE WHO HAS.

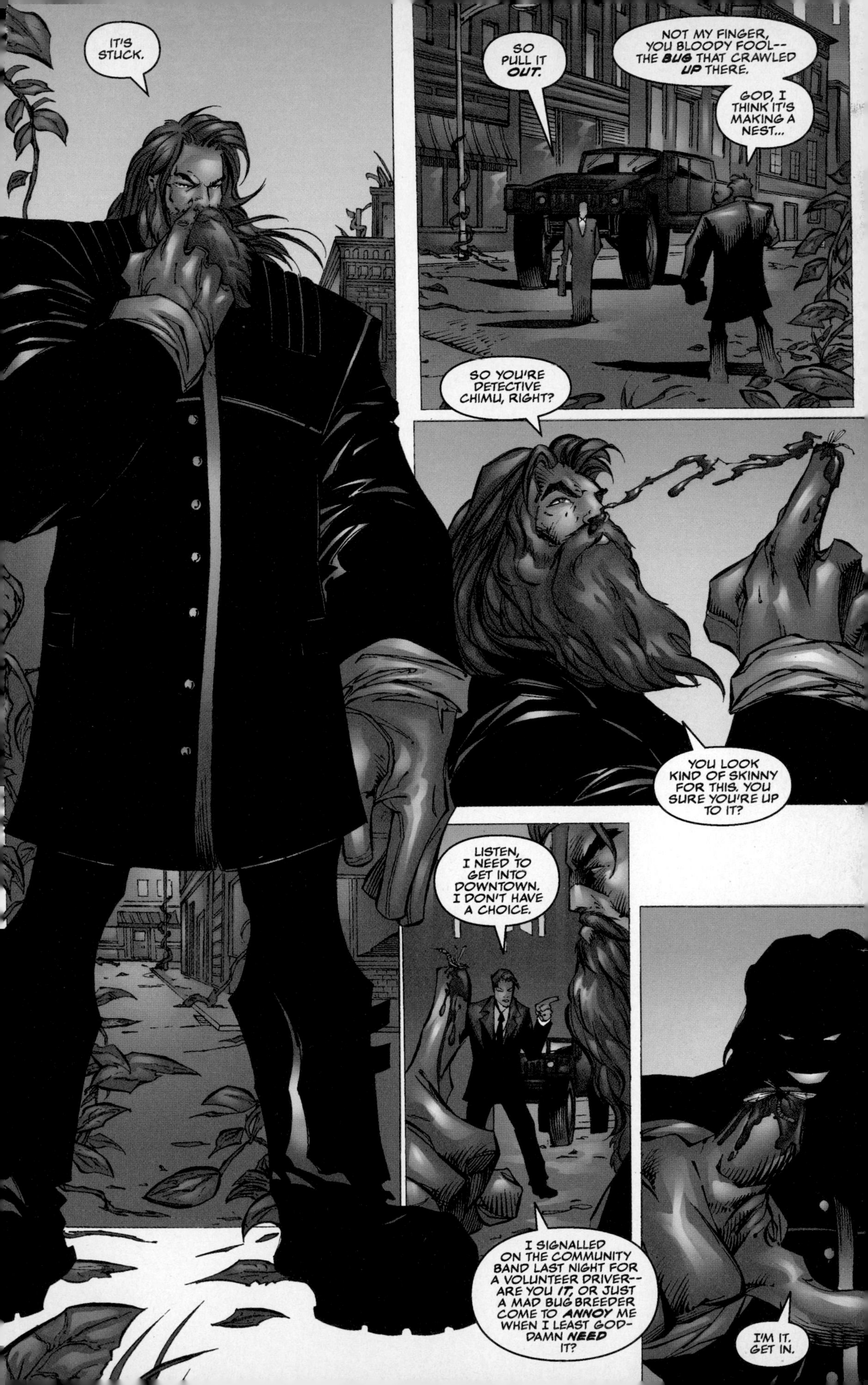
IT'S STUCK.
SO PULL IT OUT.
NOT MY FINGER, YOU BLOODY FOOL-- THE BUG THAT CRAWLED UP THERE.
GOD, I THINK IT'S MAKING A NEST...
SO YOU'RE DETECTIVE CHIMU, RIGHT?
YOU LOOK KIND OF SKINNY FOR THIS. YOU SURE YOU'RE UP TO IT?
LISTEN, I NEED TO GET INTO DOWNTOWN. I DON'T HAVE A CHOICE.
I SIGNALLED ON THE COMMUNITY BAND LAST NIGHT FOR A VOLUNTEER DRIVER-- ARE YOU IT, OR JUST A MAD BUG BREEDER COME TO ANNOY ME WHEN I LEAST GOD-DAMN NEED IT?
I'M IT. GET IN.

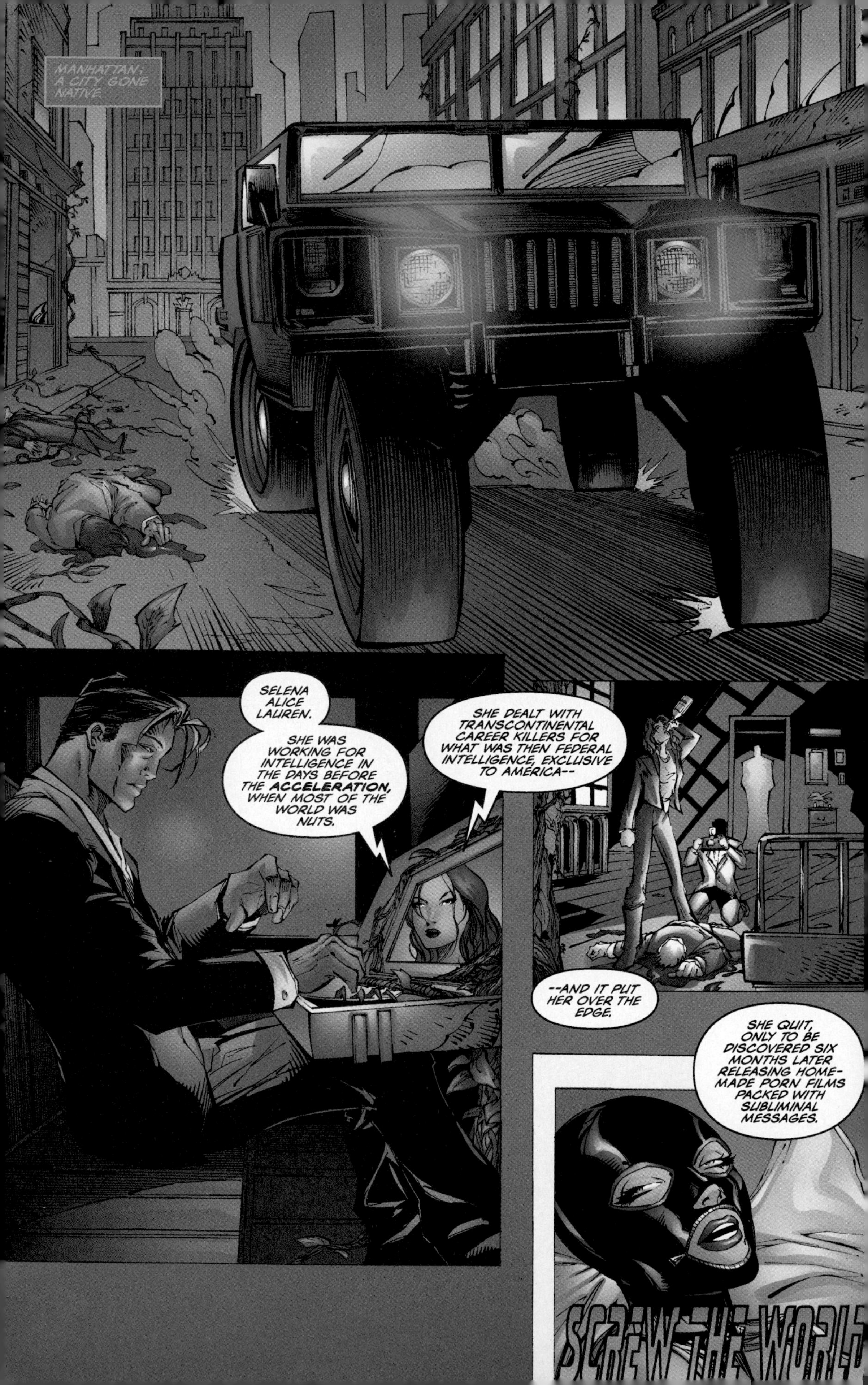
MANHATTAN: A CITY GONE NATIVE.
SELENA ALICE LAUREN.
SHE WAS WORKING FOR INTELLIGENCE IN THE DAYS BEFORE THE ACCELERATION, WHEN MOST OF THE WORLD WAS NUTS.
SHE DEALT WITH TRANSCONTINENTAL CAREER KILLERS FOR WHAT WAS THEN FEDERAL INTELLIGENCE, EXCLUSIVE TO AMERICA--
--AND IT PUT HER OVER THE EDGE.
SHE QUIT, ONLY TO BE DISCOVERED SIX MONTHS LATER RELEASING HOME-MADE PORN FILMS PACKED WITH SUBLIMINAL MESSAGES.
SCREW THE WORLD

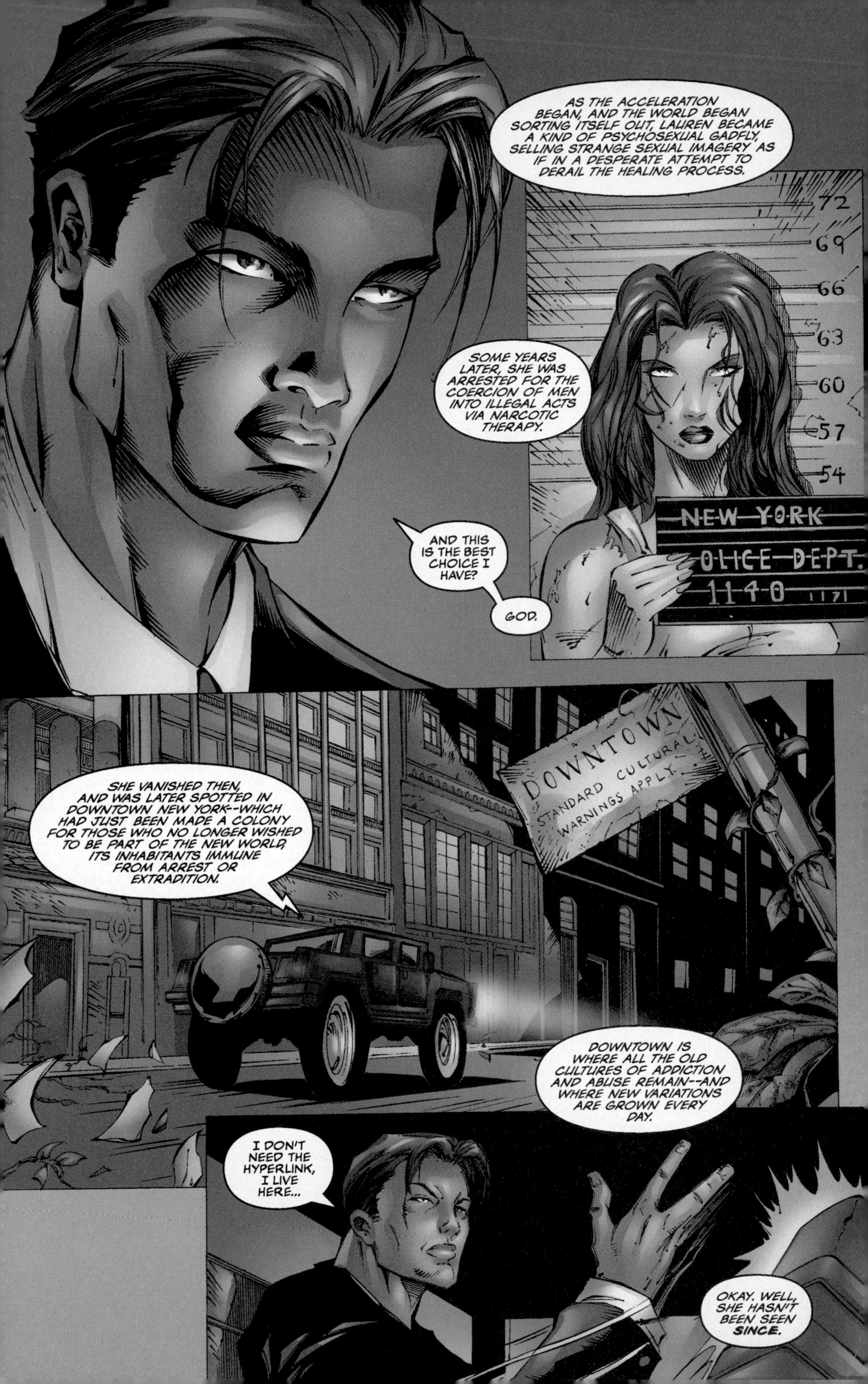
AS THE ACCELERATION BEGAN, AND THE WORLD BEGAN SORTING ITSELF OUT, LAUREN BECAME A KIND OF PSYCHOSEXUAL GADFLY, SELLING STRANGE SEXUAL IMAGERY AS IF IN A DESPERATE ATTEMPT TO DERAIL THE HEALING PROCESS.
72
69
66
63
60
57
54
SOME YEARS LATER, SHE WAS ARRESTED FOR THE COERCION OF MEN INTO ILLEGAL ACTS VIA NARCOTIC THERAPY.
NEW YORK
OLICE DEPT.
1140
AND THIS IS THE BEST CHOICE I HAVE?
GOD.
DOWNTOWN
STANDARD CULTURAL WARNINGS APPLY.
SHE VANISHED THEN, AND WAS LATER SPOTTED IN DOWNTOWN NEW YORK--WHICH HAD JUST BEEN MADE A COLONY FOR THOSE WHO NO LONGER WISHED TO BE PART OF THE NEW WORLD, ITS INHABITANTS IMMUNE FROM ARREST OR EXTRADITION.
DOWNTOWN IS WHERE ALL THE OLD CULTURES OF ADDICTION AND ABUSE REMAIN--AND WHERE NEW VARIATIONS ARE GROWN EVERY DAY.
I DON'T NEED THE HYPERLINK, I LIVE HERE...
OKAY. WELL, SHE HASN'T BEEN SEEN **SINCE.**

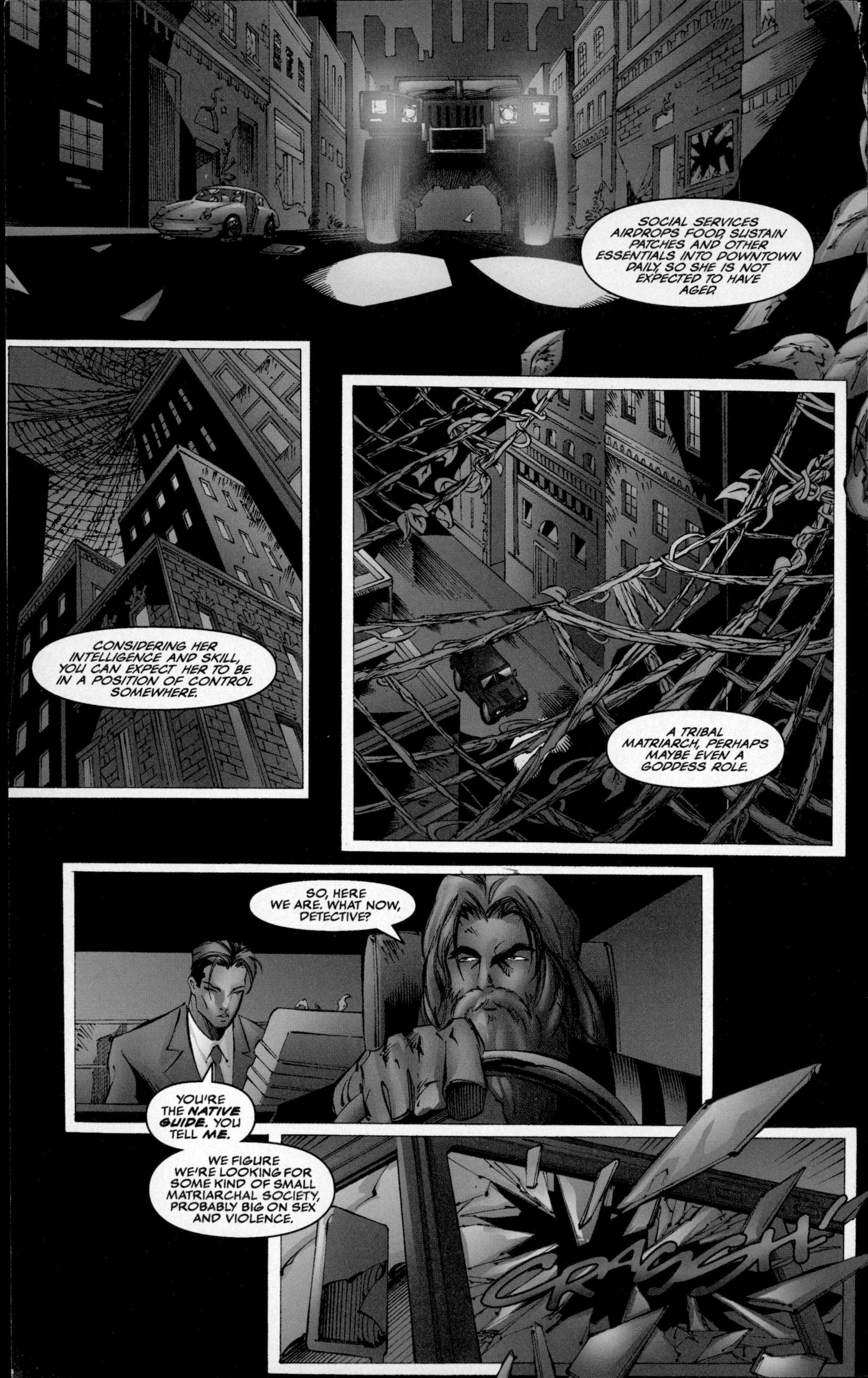

SOCIAL SERVICES AIRDROPS FOOD, SUSTAIN PATCHES AND OTHER ESSENTIALS INTO DOWNTOWN DAILY, SO SHE IS NOT EXPECTED TO HAVE AGED.
CONSIDERING HER INTELLIGENCE AND SKILL, YOU CAN EXPECT HER TO BE IN A POSITION OF CONTROL SOMEWHERE.
A TRIBAL MATRIARCH, PERHAPS MAYBE EVEN A GODDESS ROLE.
SO, HERE WE ARE. WHAT NOW, DETECTIVE?
YOU'RE THE **NATIVE GUIDE**. YOU TELL **ME**.
WE FIGURE WE'RE LOOKING FOR SOME KIND OF SMALL MATRIARCHAL SOCIETY, PROBABLY BIG ON SEX AND VIOLENCE.
CRAAACK!

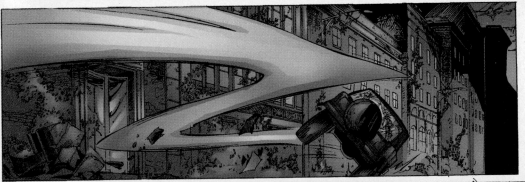

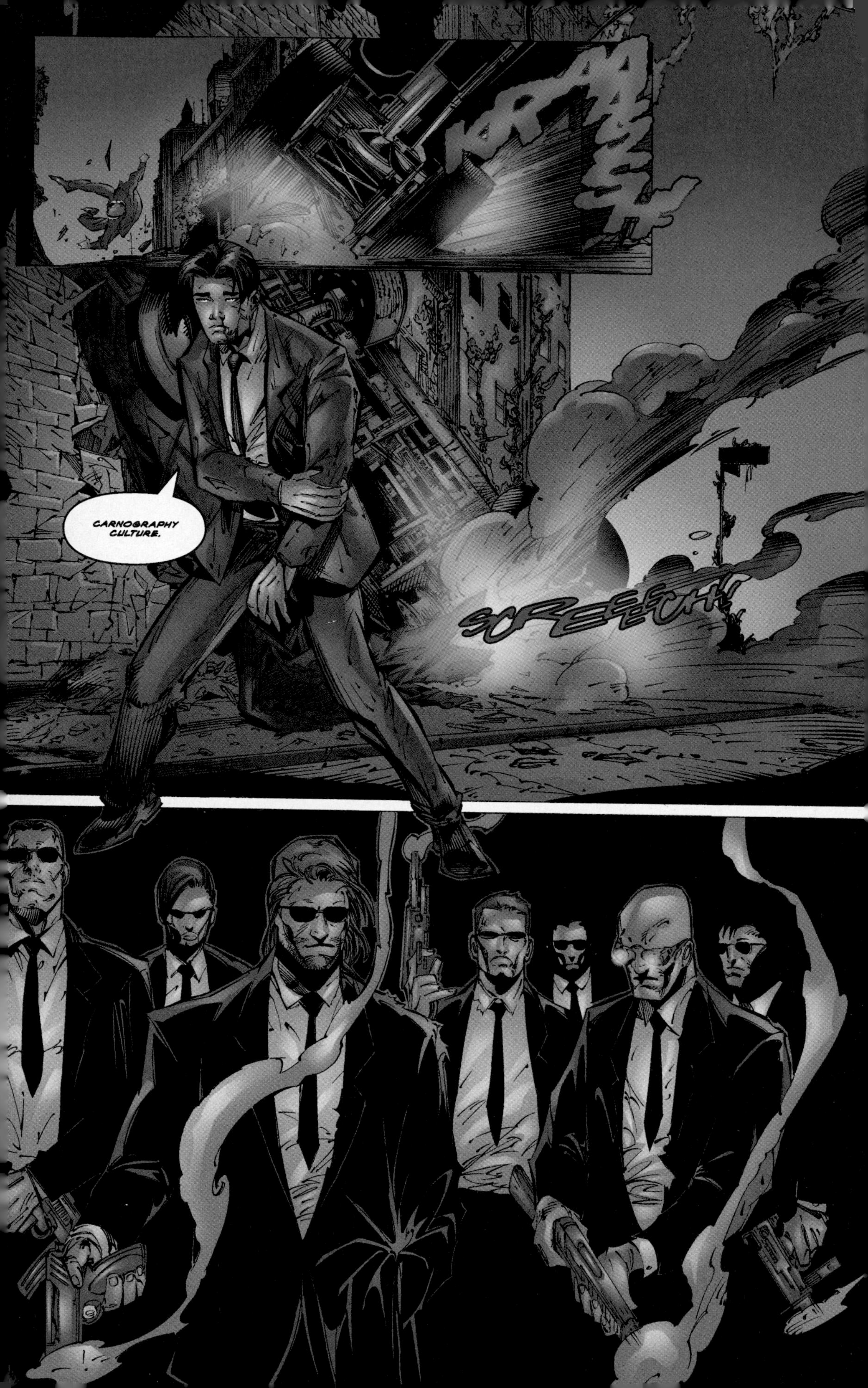
KRAASH
CARNOGRAPHY CULTURE.
SCREEECH!!

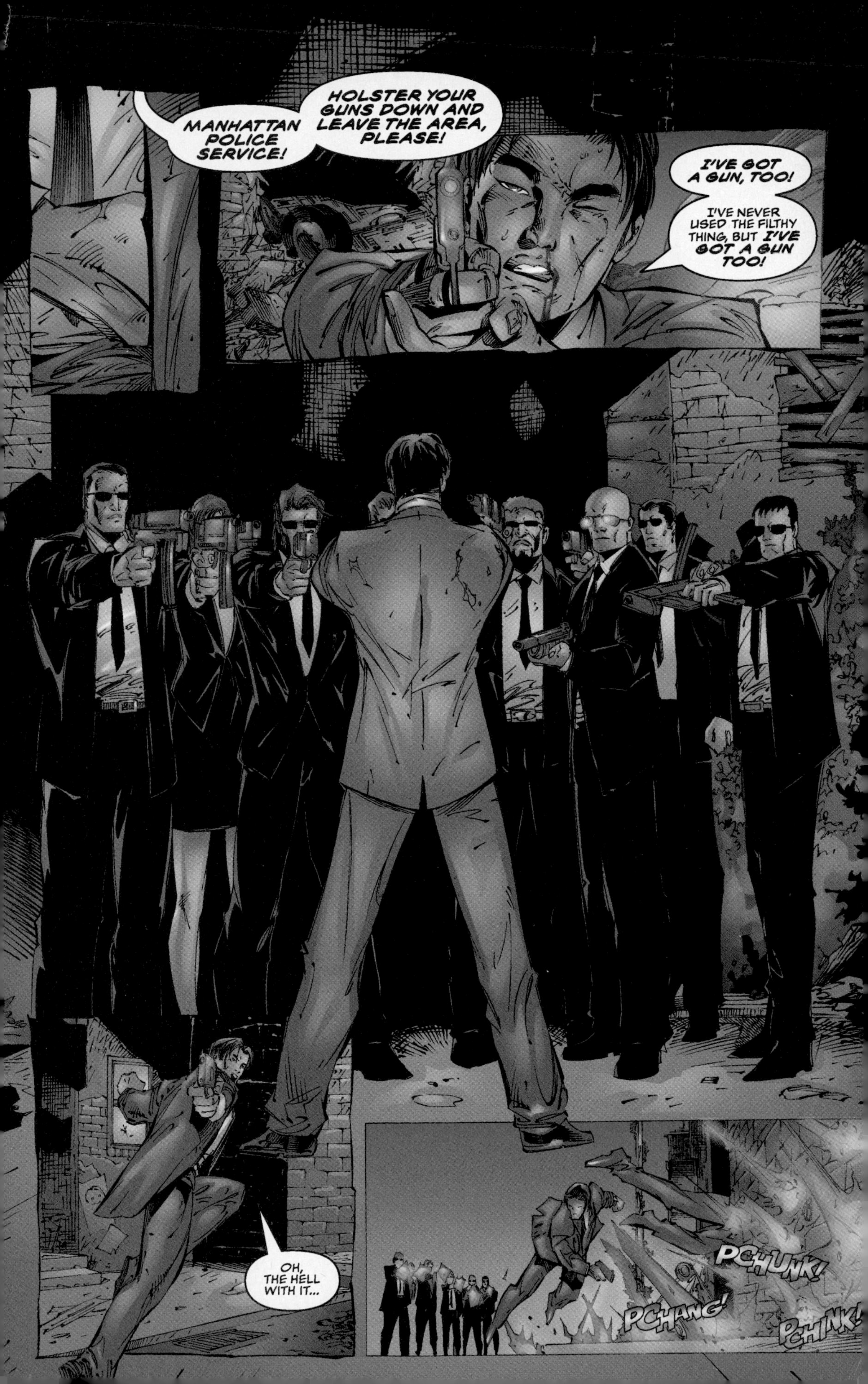
MANHATTAN POLICE SERVICE!
HOLSTER YOUR GUNS DOWN AND LEAVE THE AREA, PLEASE!
I'VE GOT A GUN, TOO!
I'VE NEVER USED THE FILTHY THING, BUT I'VE GOT A GUN TOO!
OH, THE HELL WITH IT...
PCHUNK!
PCHANG!
PCHINK!

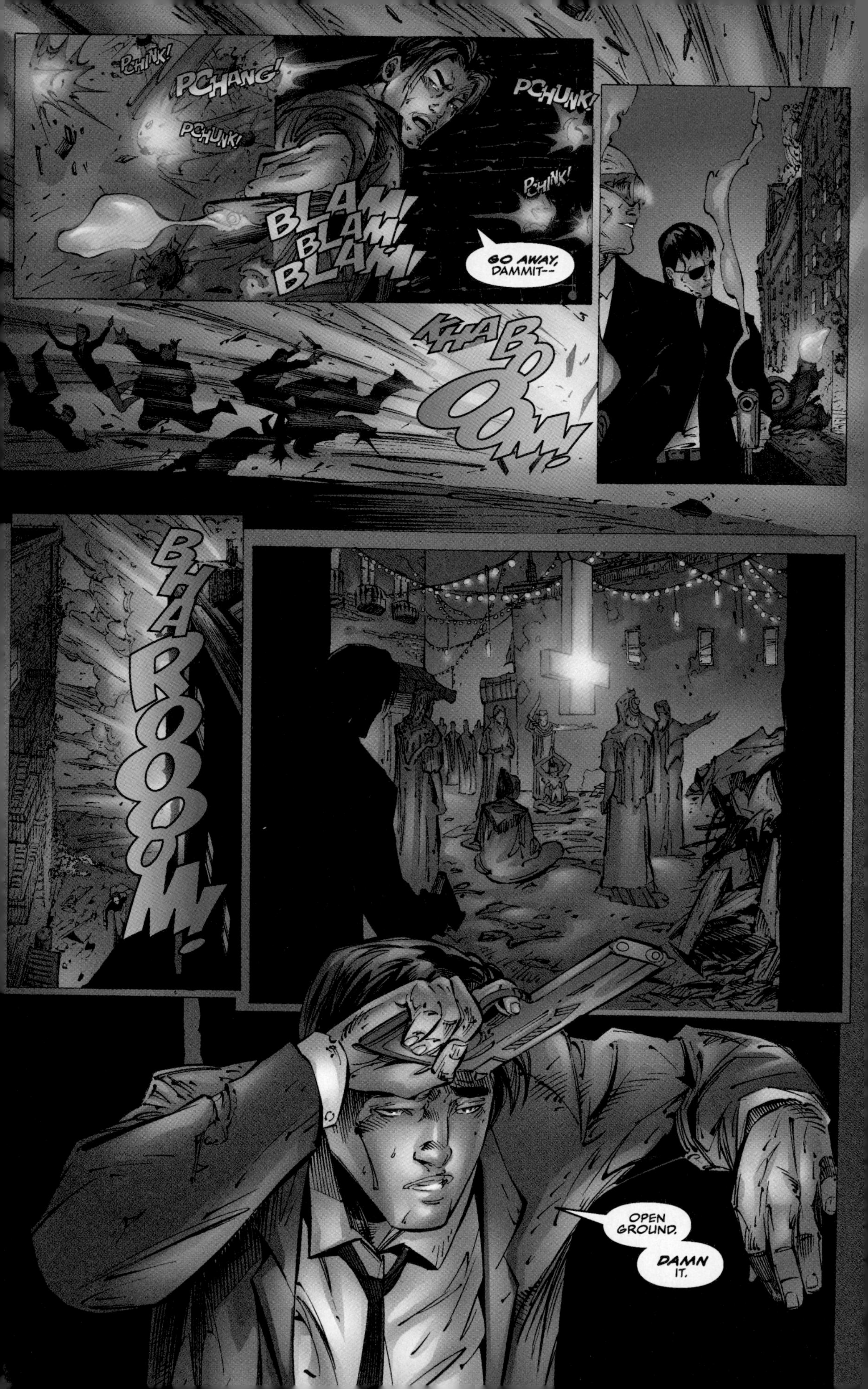
PCHINK!
PCHANG!
PCHUNK!
PCHUNK!
PCHINK!
BLAM! BLAM! BLAM!
GO AWAY, DAMMIT--
KHABOOOM!
BHAROOOOM!
OPEN GROUND.
DAMN IT.

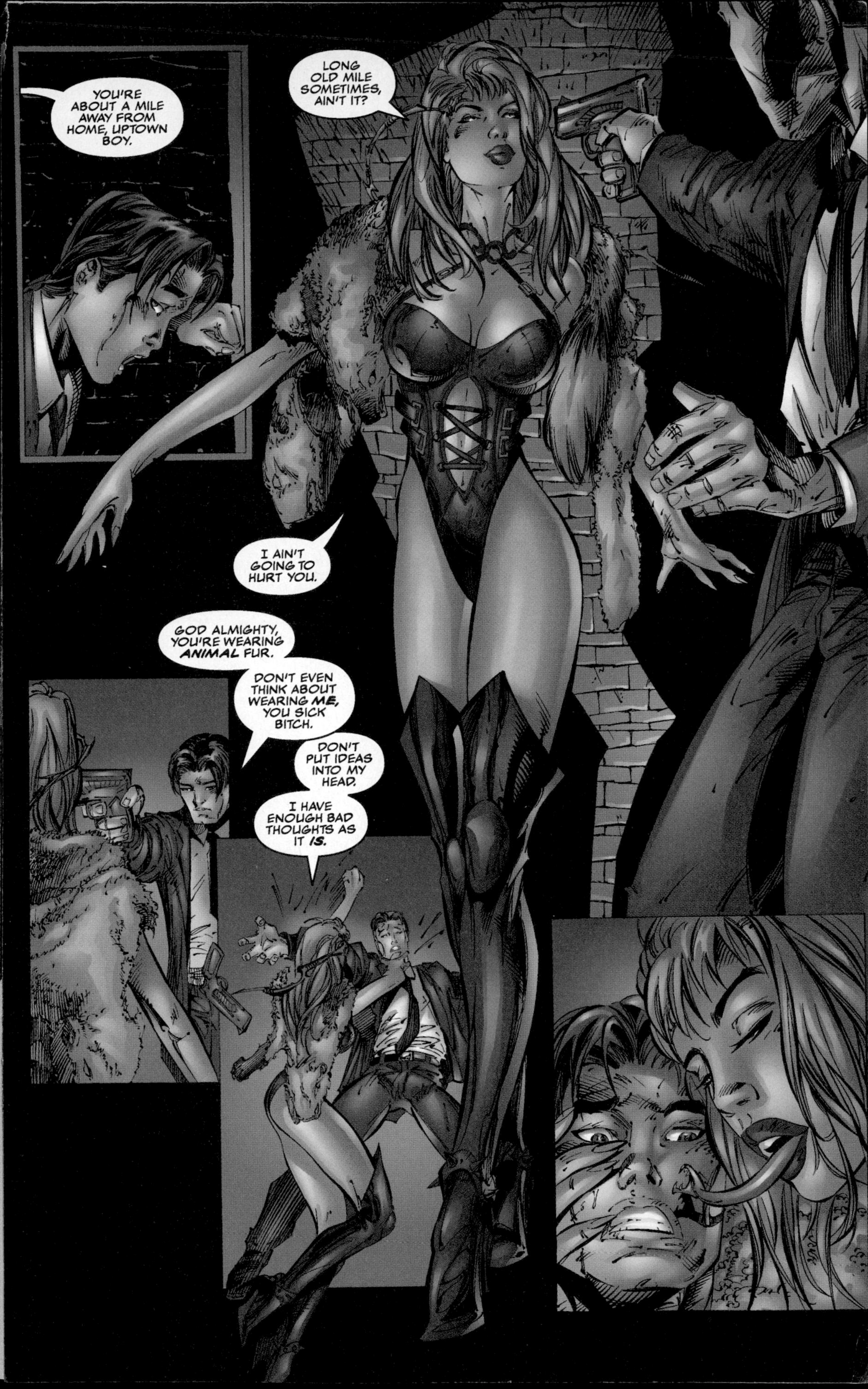
YOU'RE ABOUT A MILE AWAY FROM HOME, UPTOWN BOY.
LONG OLD MILE SOMETIMES, AIN'T IT?
I AIN'T GOING TO HURT YOU.
GOD ALMIGHTY, YOU'RE WEARING *ANIMAL* FUR.
DON'T EVEN THINK ABOUT WEARING *ME,* YOU SICK BITCH.
DON'T PUT IDEAS INTO MY HEAD.
I HAVE ENOUGH BAD THOUGHTS AS IT *IS.*

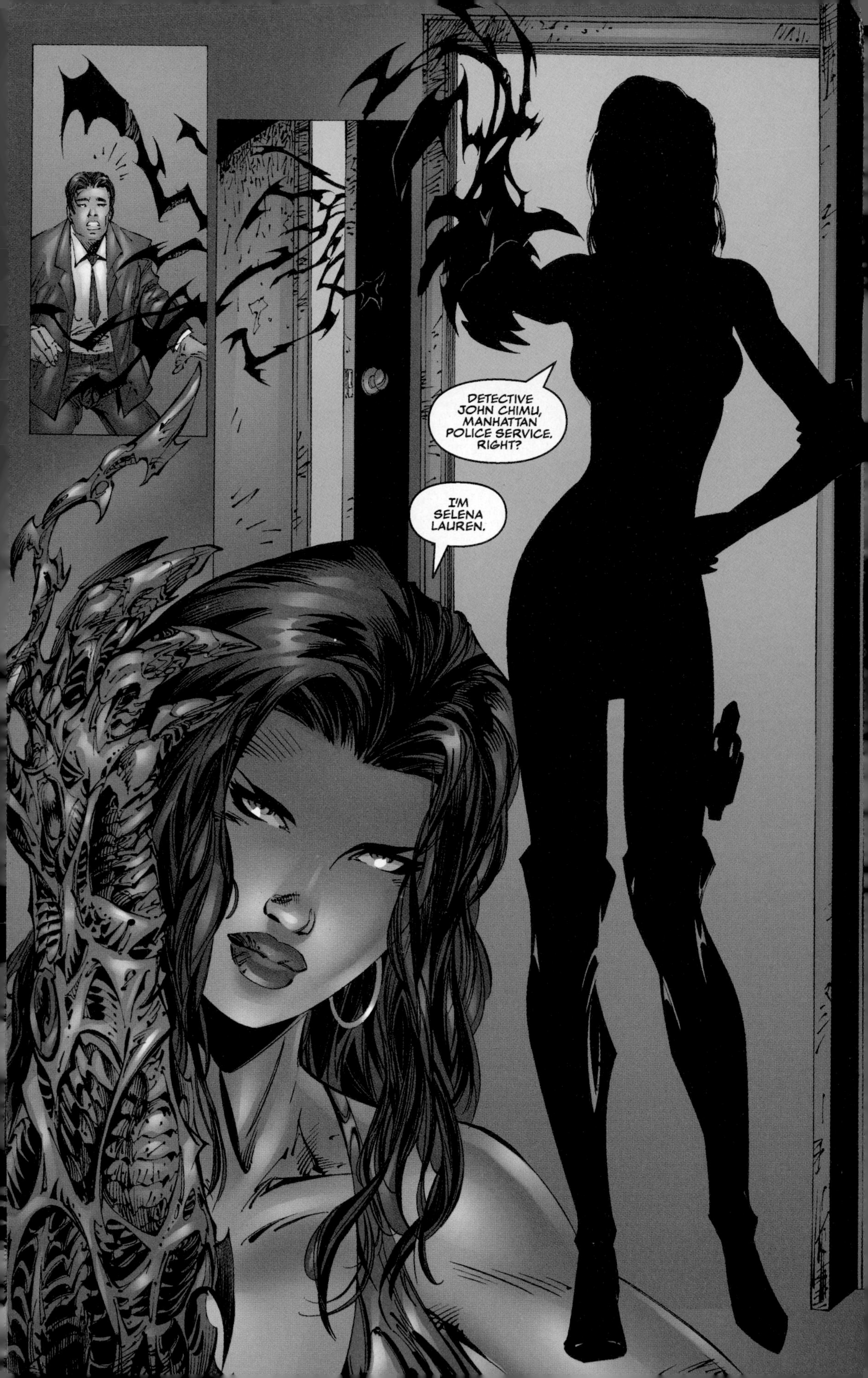
DETECTIVE JOHN CHIMU, MANHATTAN POLICE SERVICE. RIGHT?
I'M SELENA LAUREN.

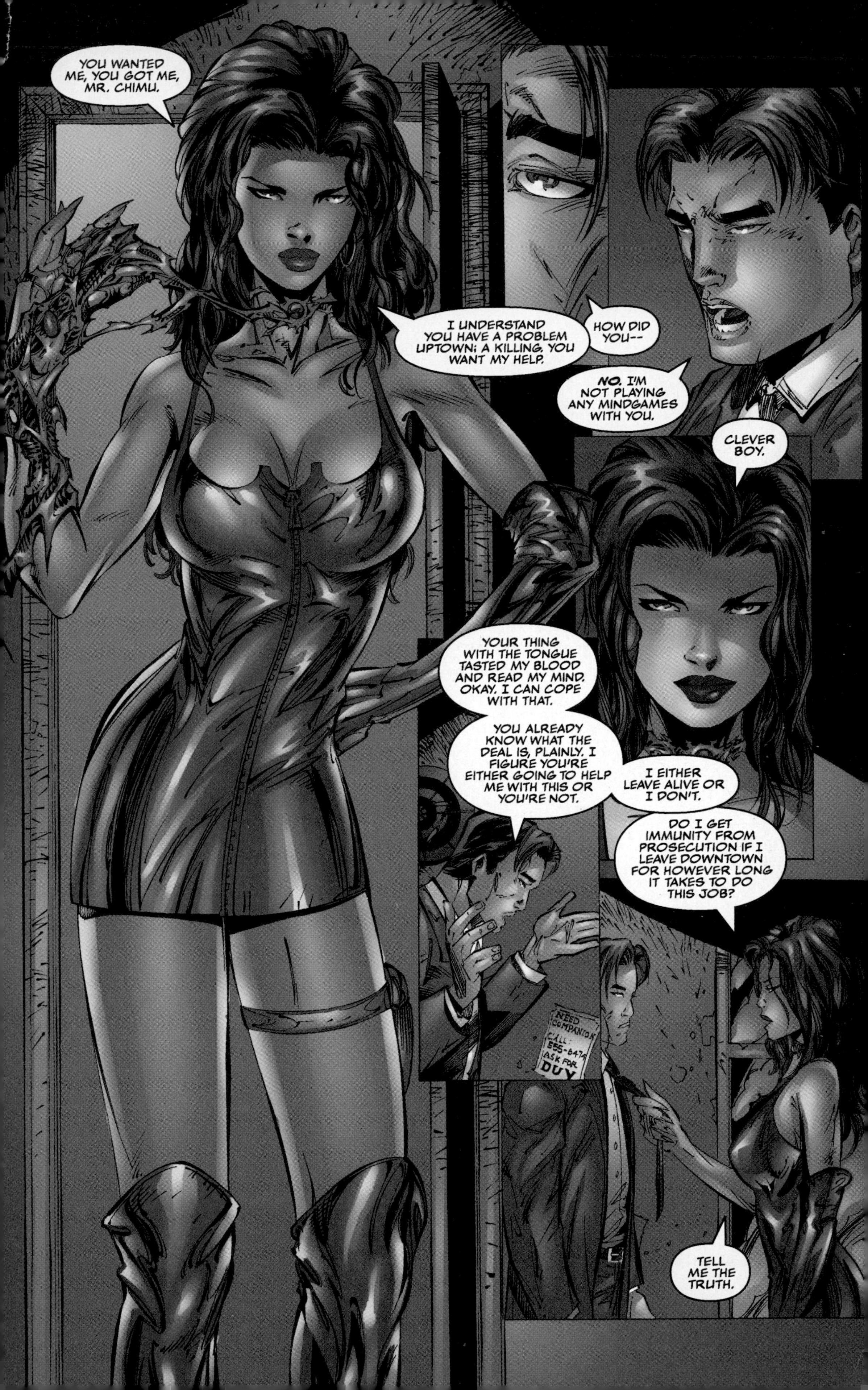

YOU WANTED ME, YOU GOT ME, MR. CHIMU.
I UNDERSTAND YOU HAVE A PROBLEM UPTOWN; A KILLING. YOU WANT MY HELP.
HOW DID YOU--
NO. I'M NOT PLAYING ANY MINDGAMES WITH YOU.
CLEVER BOY.
YOUR THING WITH THE TONGUE TASTED MY BLOOD AND READ MY MIND. OKAY. I CAN COPE WITH THAT.
YOU ALREADY KNOW WHAT THE DEAL IS, PLAINLY. I FIGURE YOU'RE EITHER GOING TO HELP ME WITH THIS OR YOU'RE NOT.
I EITHER LEAVE ALIVE OR I DON'T.
DO I GET IMMUNITY FROM PROSECUTION IF I LEAVE DOWNTOWN FOR HOWEVER LONG IT TAKES TO DO THIS JOB?
NEED COMPANION CALL 555-6474 ASK FOR DUY
TELL ME THE TRUTH.

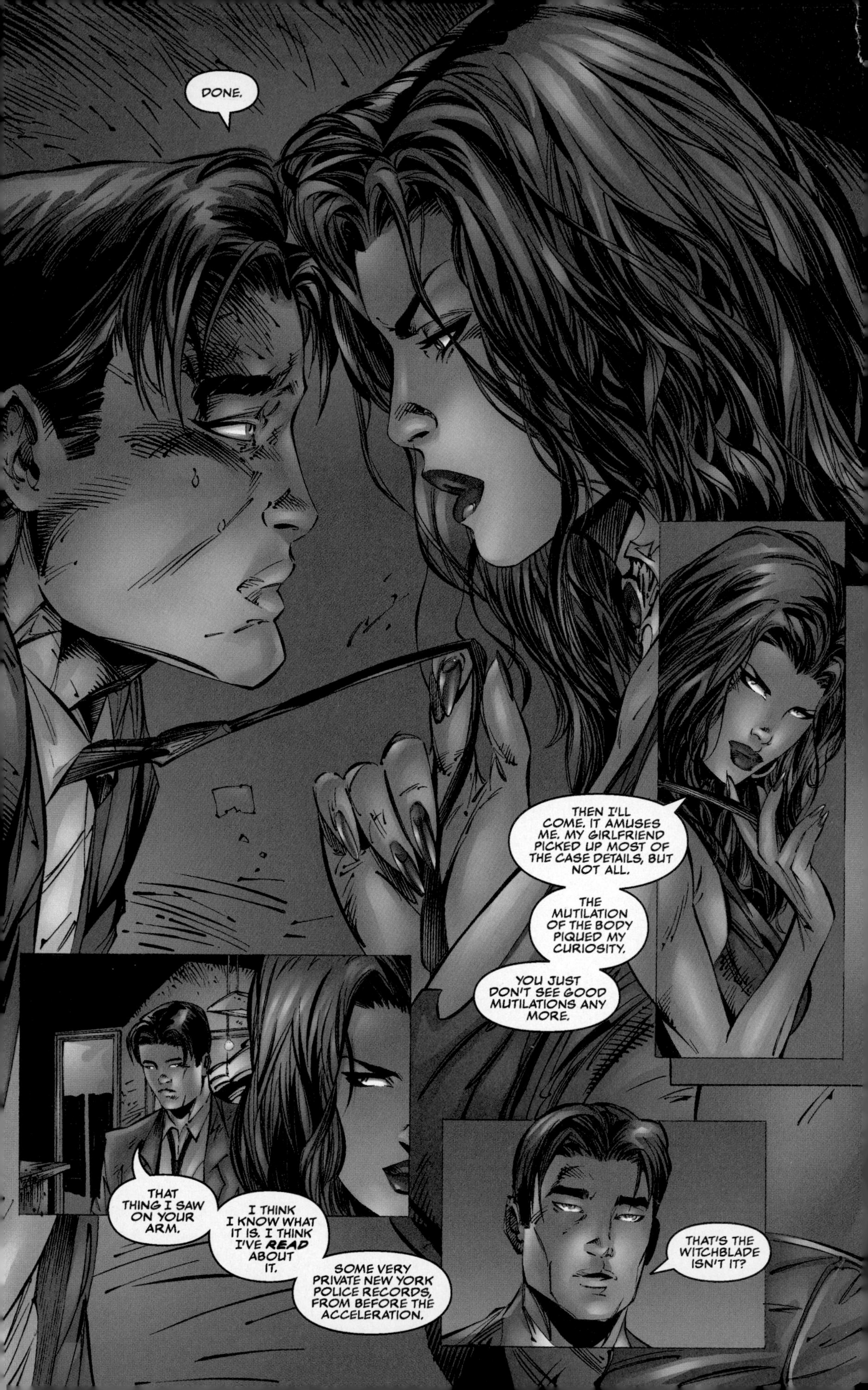
DONE.
THEN I'LL COME. IT AMUSES ME. MY GIRLFRIEND PICKED UP MOST OF THE CASE DETAILS, BUT NOT ALL.
THE MUTILATION OF THE BODY PIQUED MY CURIOSITY.
YOU JUST DON'T SEE GOOD MUTILATIONS ANY MORE.
THAT THING I SAW ON YOUR ARM.
I THINK I KNOW WHAT IT IS. I THINK I'VE *READ* ABOUT IT.
SOME VERY PRIVATE NEW YORK POLICE RECORDS, FROM BEFORE THE ACCELERATION.
THAT'S THE WITCHBLADE ISN'T IT?

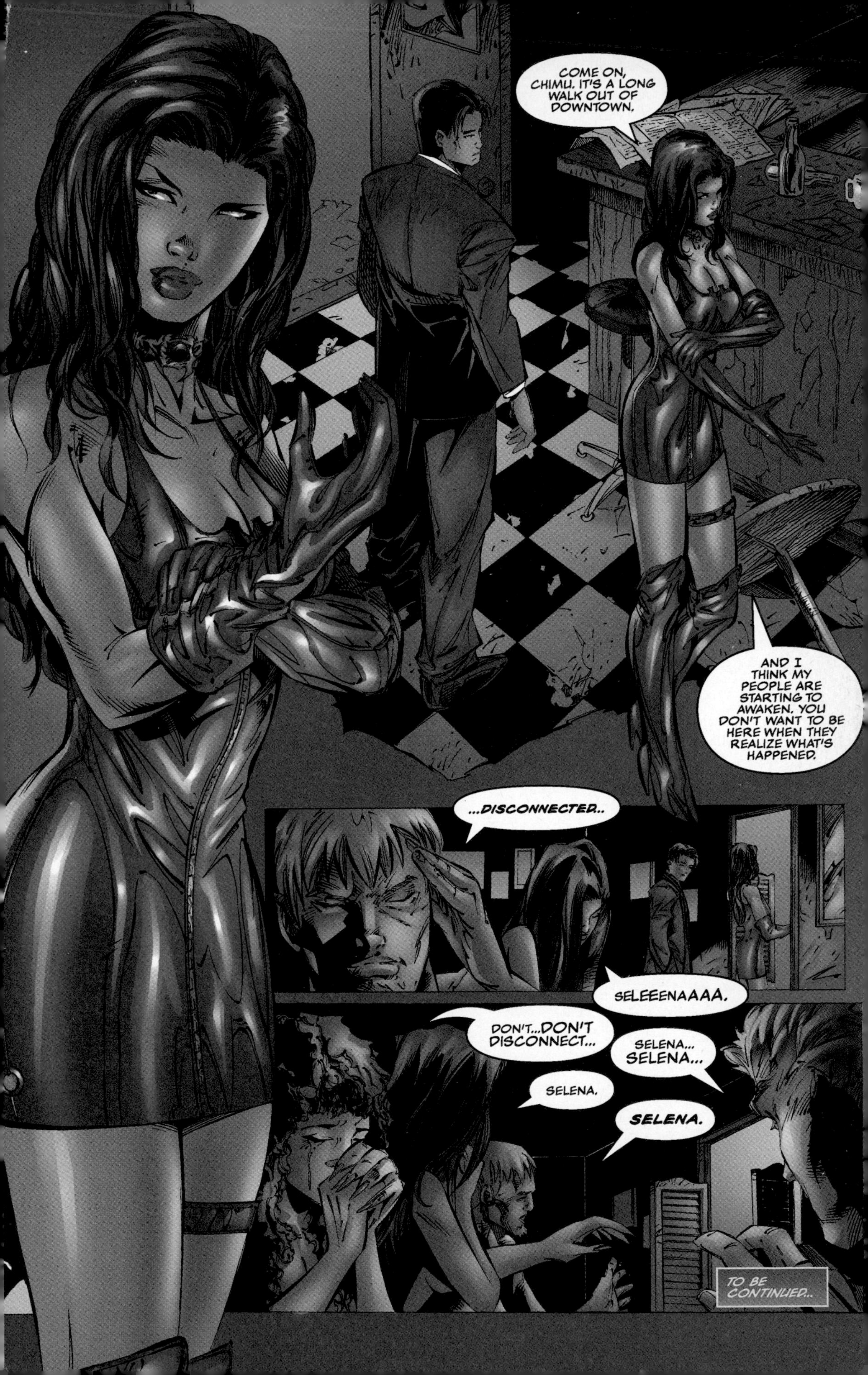
COME ON, CHIMU. IT'S A LONG WALK OUT OF DOWNTOWN.
AND I THINK MY PEOPLE ARE STARTING TO AWAKEN. YOU DON'T WANT TO BE HERE WHEN THEY REALIZE WHAT'S HAPPENED.
...DISCONNECTED..
SELEEENAAAA.
DON'T...DON'T DISCONNECT...
SELENA... SELENA...
SELENA.
SELENA.
TO BE CONTINUED..

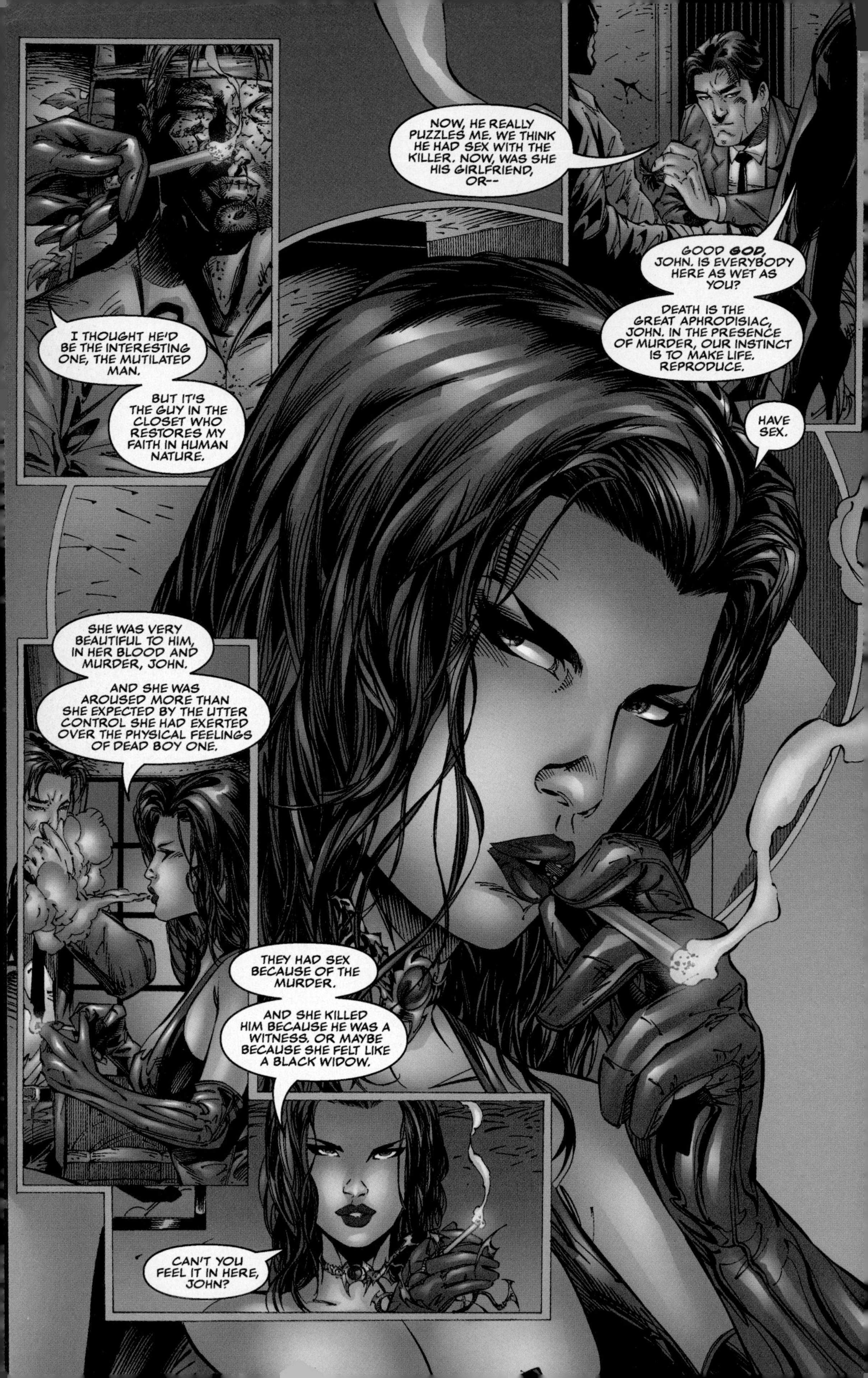
I THOUGHT HE'D BE THE INTERESTING ONE, THE MUTILATED MAN.
BUT IT'S THE GUY IN THE CLOSET WHO RESTORES MY FAITH IN HUMAN NATURE.
NOW, HE REALLY PUZZLES ME. WE THINK HE HAD SEX WITH THE KILLER. NOW, WAS SHE HIS GIRLFRIEND, OR--
GOOD GOD, JOHN. IS EVERYBODY HERE AS WET AS YOU?
DEATH IS THE GREAT APHRODISIAC, JOHN. IN THE PRESENCE OF MURDER, OUR INSTINCT IS TO MAKE LIFE. REPRODUCE.
HAVE SEX.
SHE WAS VERY BEAUTIFUL TO HIM, IN HER BLOOD AND MURDER, JOHN.
AND SHE WAS AROUSED MORE THAN SHE EXPECTED BY THE UTTER CONTROL SHE HAD EXERTED OVER THE PHYSICAL FEELINGS OF DEAD BOY ONE.
THEY HAD SEX BECAUSE OF THE MURDER.
AND SHE KILLED HIM BECAUSE HE WAS A WITNESS. OR MAYBE BECAUSE SHE FELT LIKE A BLACK WIDOW.
CAN'T YOU FEEL IT IN HERE, JOHN?

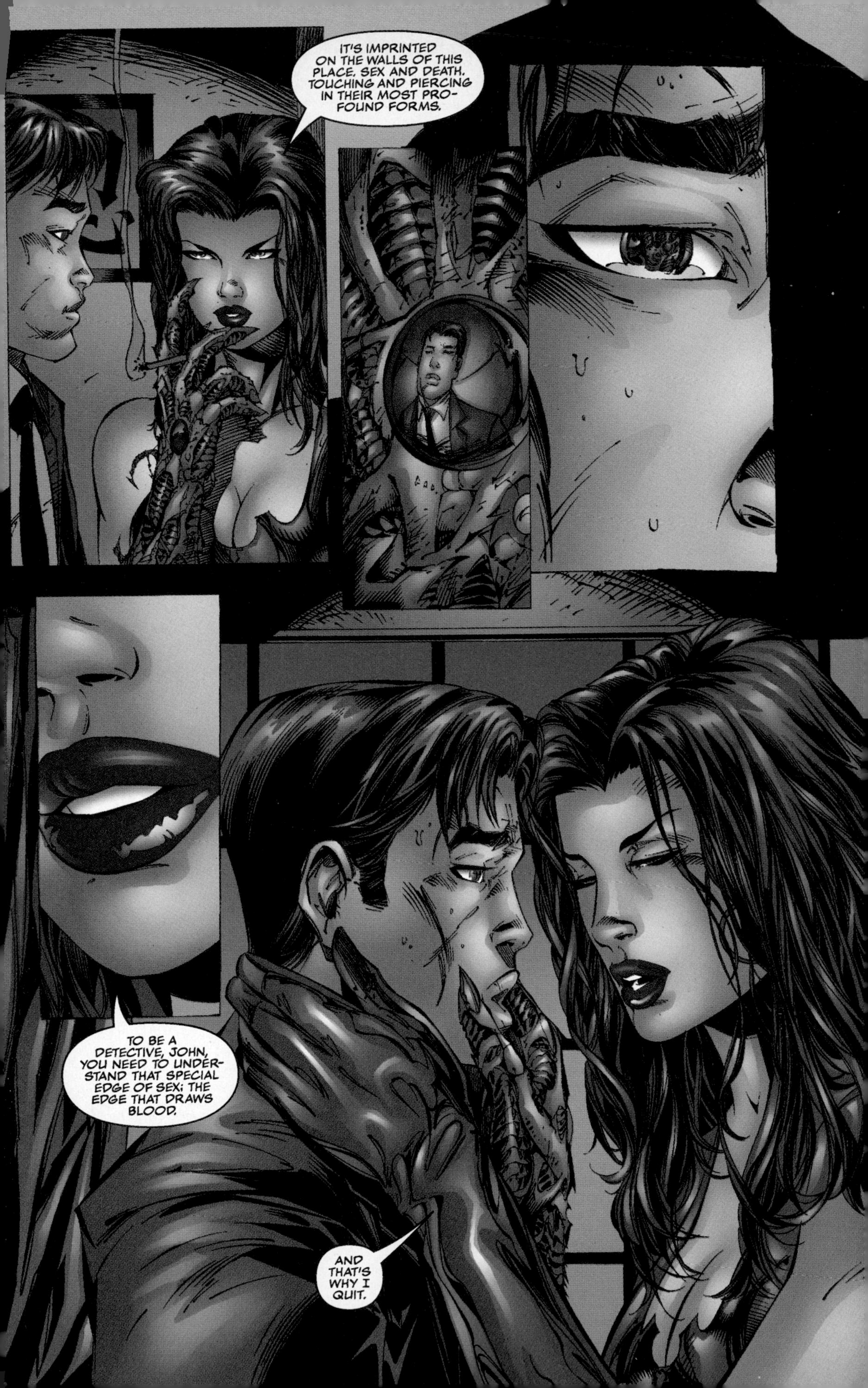
IT'S IMPRINTED ON THE WALLS OF THIS PLACE. SEX AND DEATH. TOUCHING AND PIERCING IN THEIR MOST PRO-FOUND FORMS.
TO BE A DETECTIVE, JOHN, YOU NEED TO UNDER-STAND THAT SPECIAL EDGE OF SEX; THE EDGE THAT DRAWS BLOOD.
AND THAT'S WHY I QUIT.

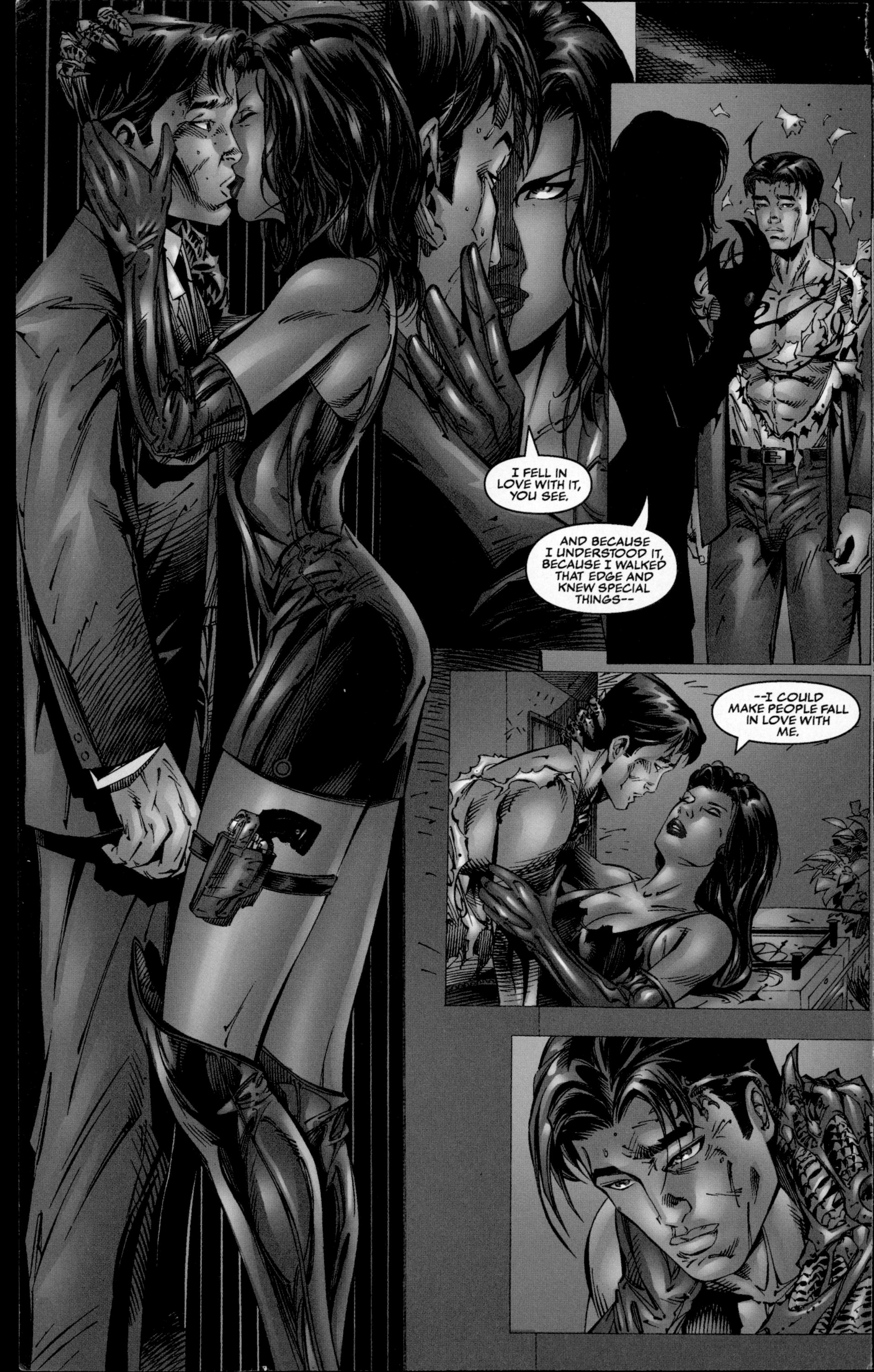
I FELL IN LOVE WITH IT, YOU SEE.
AND BECAUSE I UNDERSTOOD IT, BECAUSE I WALKED THAT EDGE AND KNEW SPECIAL THINGS--
--I COULD MAKE PEOPLE FALL IN LOVE WITH ME.

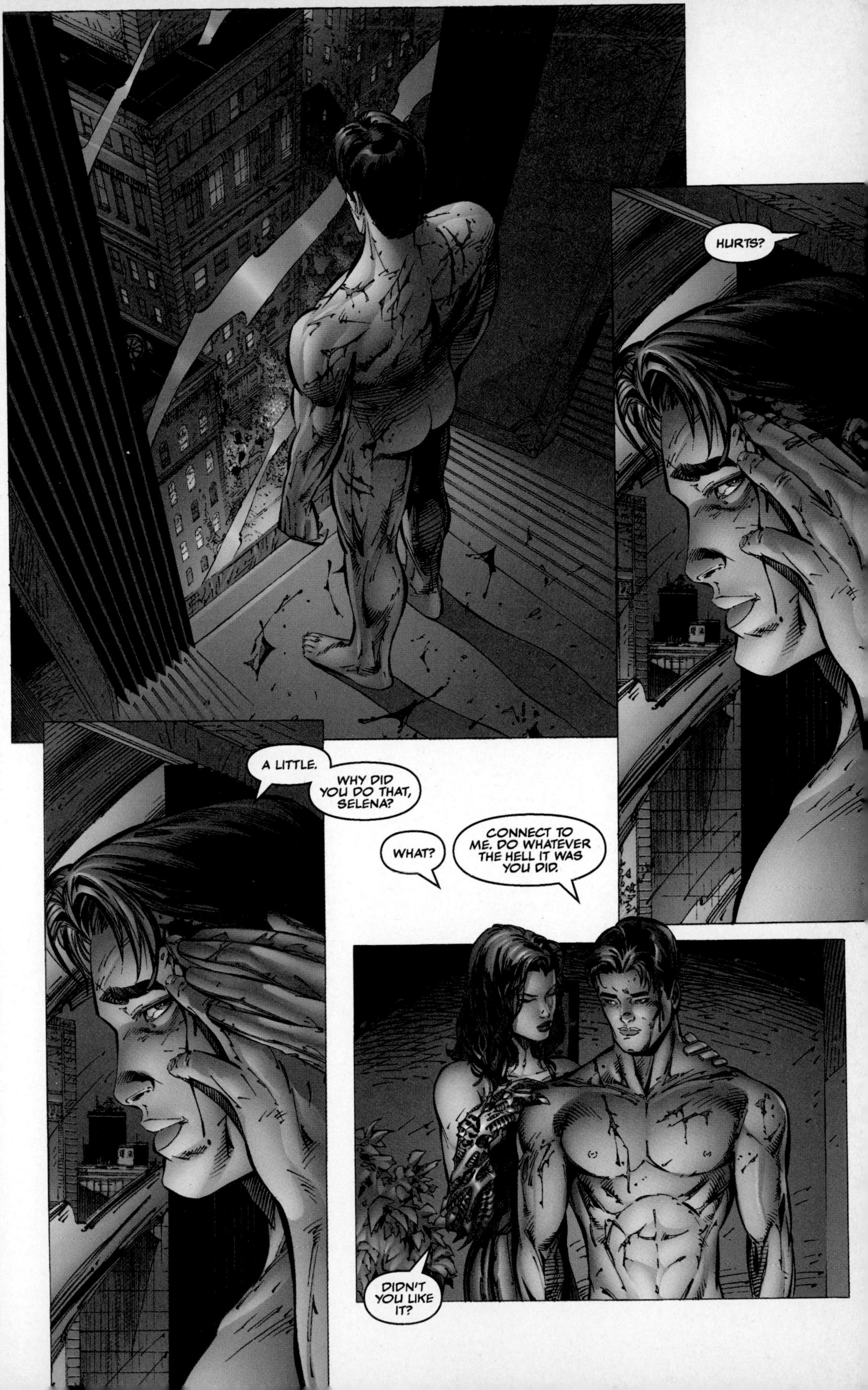
HURTS?
A LITTLE.
WHY DID YOU DO THAT, SELENA?
WHAT?
CONNECT TO ME. DO WHATEVER THE HELL IT WAS YOU DID.
DIDN'T YOU LIKE IT?

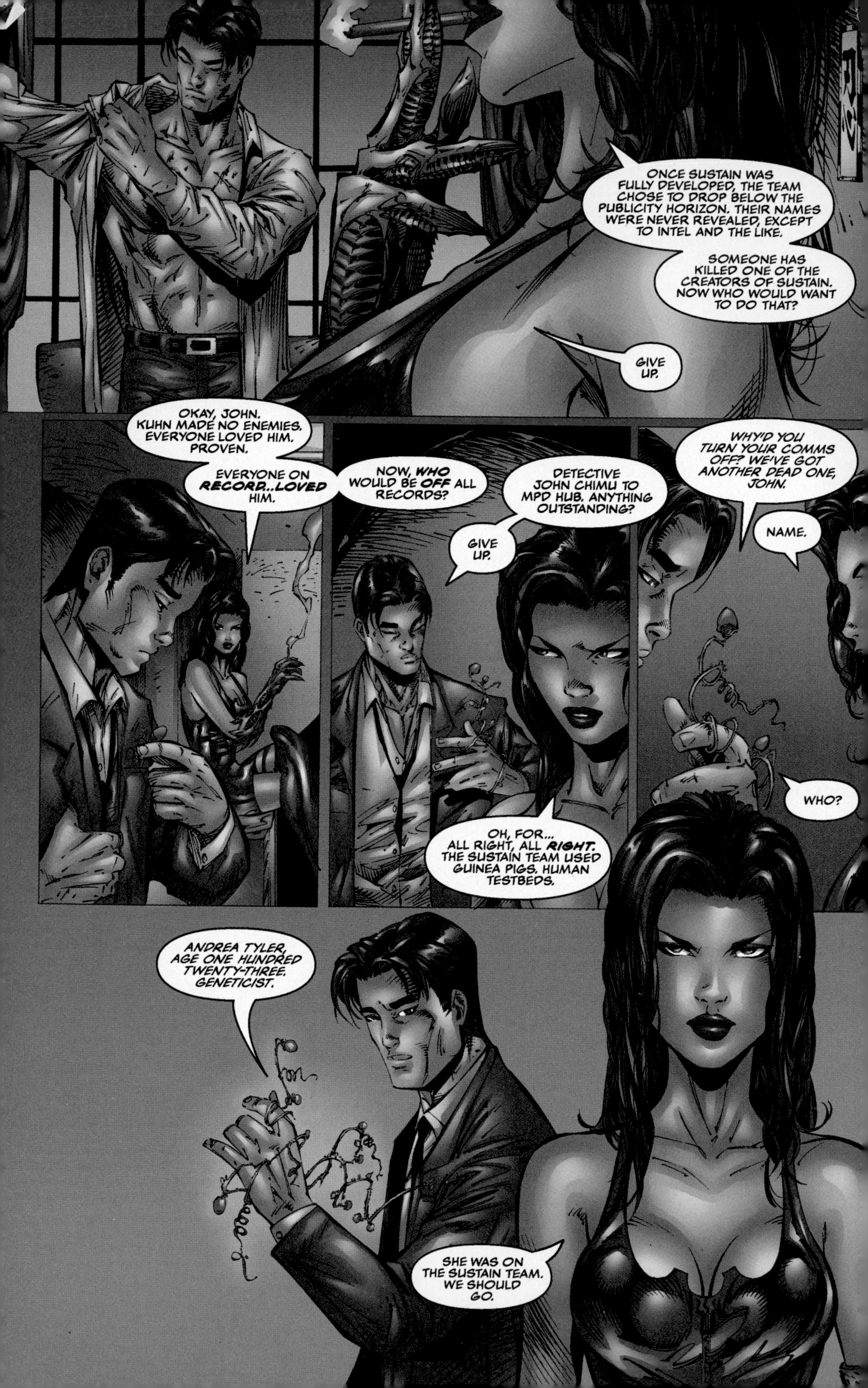
ONCE SUSTAIN WAS FULLY DEVELOPED, THE TEAM CHOSE TO DROP BELOW THE PUBLICITY HORIZON. THEIR NAMES WERE NEVER REVEALED, EXCEPT TO INTEL AND THE LIKE.
SOMEONE HAS KILLED ONE OF THE CREATORS OF SUSTAIN. NOW WHO WOULD WANT TO DO THAT?
GIVE UP.
OKAY, JOHN. KUHN MADE NO ENEMIES. EVERYONE LOVED HIM. PROVEN.
EVERYONE ON RECORD...LOVED HIM.
NOW, WHO WOULD BE OFF ALL RECORDS?
GIVE UP.
DETECTIVE JOHN CHIMU TO MPD HUB. ANYTHING OUTSTANDING?
OH, FOR... ALL RIGHT, ALL RIGHT. THE SUSTAIN TEAM USED GUINEA PIGS. HUMAN TESTBEDS.
WHY'D YOU TURN YOUR COMMS OFF? WE'VE GOT ANOTHER DEAD ONE, JOHN.
NAME.
WHO?
ANDREA TYLER, AGE ONE HUNDRED TWENTY-THREE. GENETICIST.
SHE WAS ON THE SUSTAIN TEAM. WE SHOULD GO.

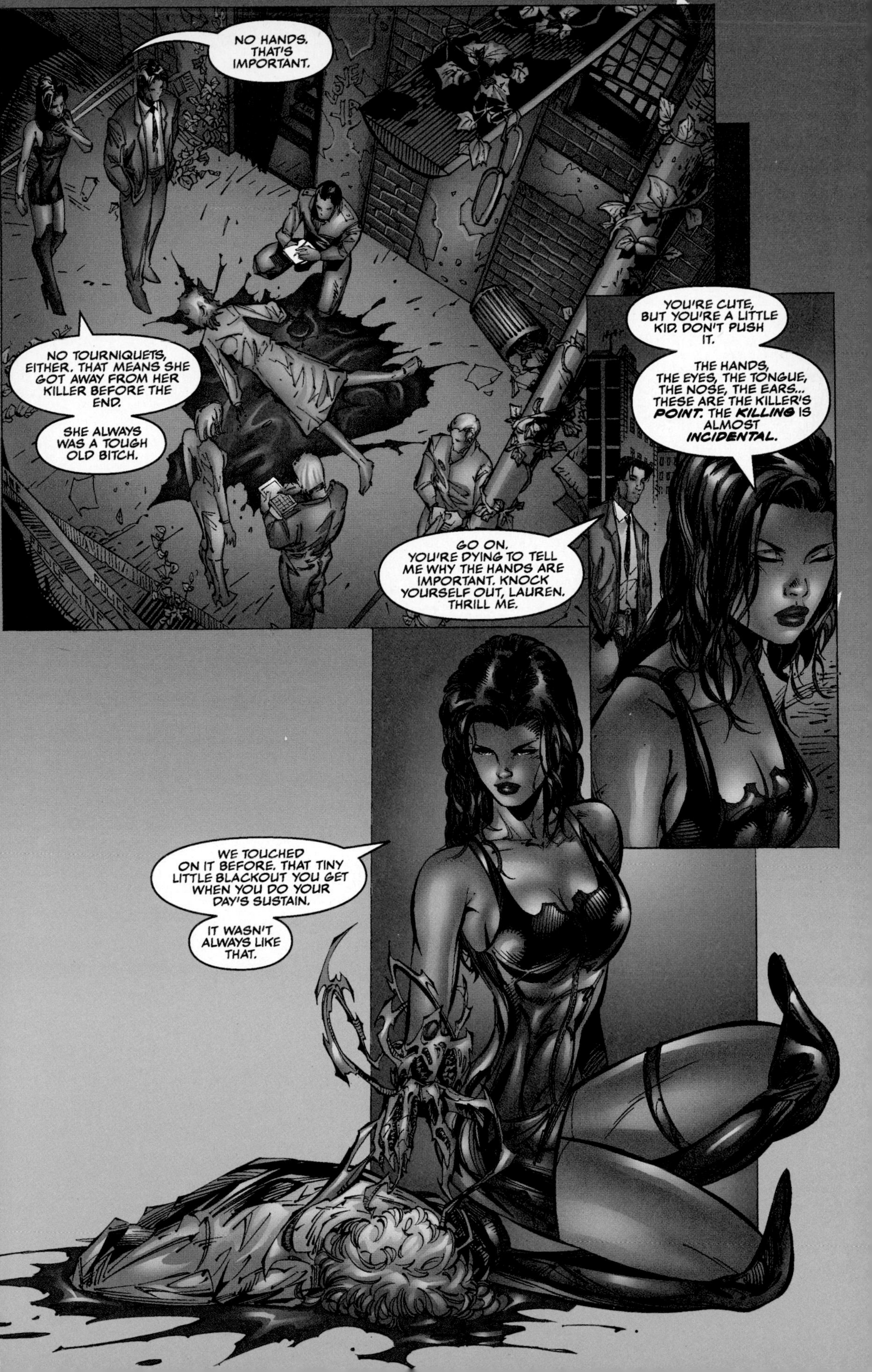
NO HANDS. THAT'S IMPORTANT.
NO TOURNIQUETS, EITHER. THAT MEANS SHE GOT AWAY FROM HER KILLER BEFORE THE END.
SHE ALWAYS WAS A TOUGH OLD BITCH.
GO ON. YOU'RE DYING TO TELL ME WHY THE HANDS ARE IMPORTANT. KNOCK YOURSELF OUT, LAUREN. THRILL ME.
YOU'RE CUTE, BUT YOU'RE A LITTLE KID. DON'T PUSH IT.
THE HANDS, THE EYES, THE TONGUE, THE NOSE, THE EARS... THESE ARE THE KILLER'S POINT. THE KILLING IS ALMOST INCIDENTAL.
WE TOUCHED ON IT BEFORE. THAT TINY LITTLE BLACKOUT YOU GET WHEN YOU DO YOUR DAY'S SUSTAIN.
IT WASN'T ALWAYS LIKE THAT.

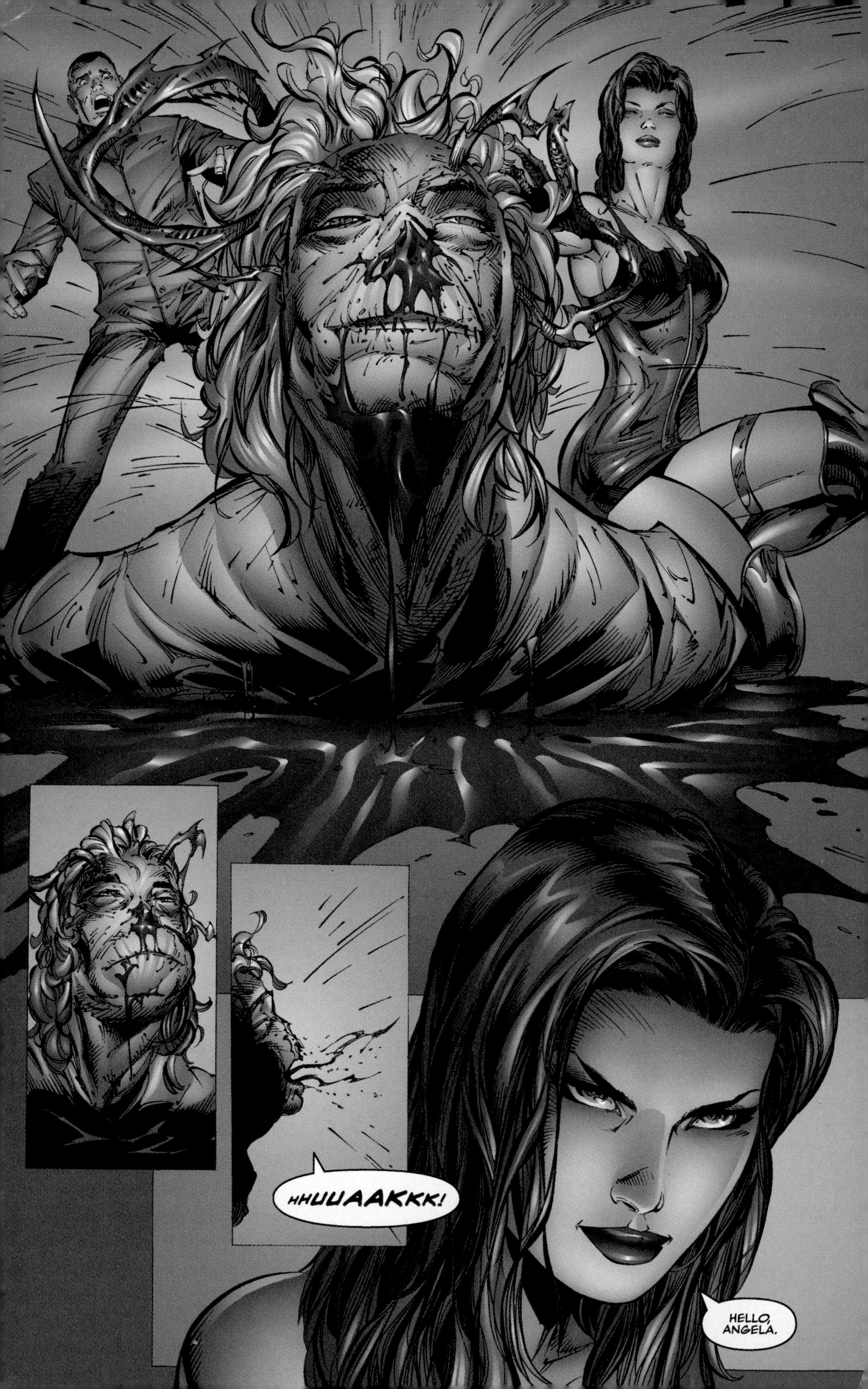
HHUUAAKKK!
HELLO, ANGELA.

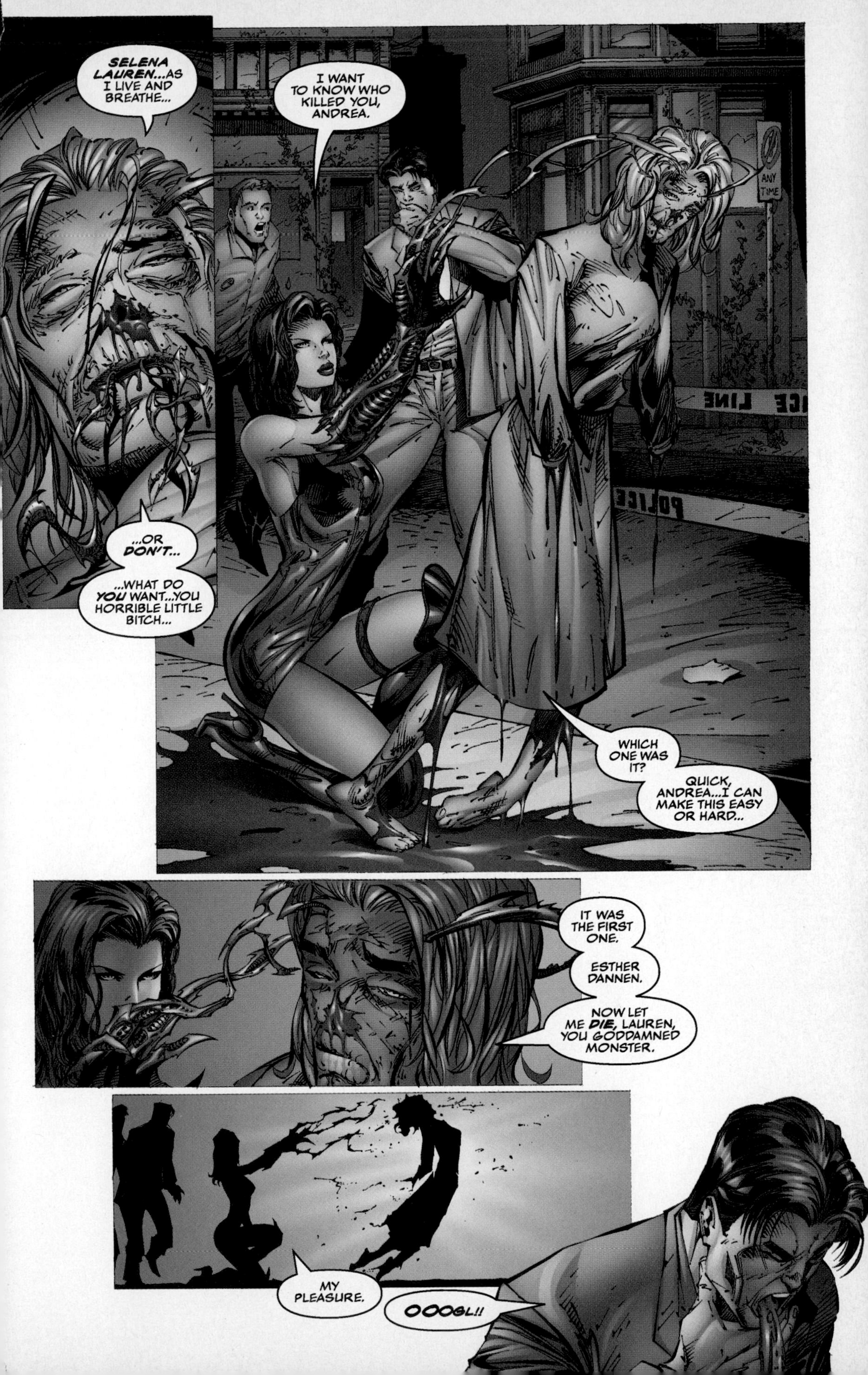
SELENA LAUREN...AS I LIVE AND BREATHE...
I WANT TO KNOW WHO KILLED YOU, ANDREA.
...OR DON'T...
...WHAT DO YOU WANT...YOU HORRIBLE LITTLE BITCH...
ANY TIME
LINE
POLICE
WHICH ONE WAS IT?
QUICK, ANDREA...I CAN MAKE THIS EASY OR HARD...
IT WAS THE FIRST ONE.
ESTHER DANNEN.
NOW LET ME DIE, LAUREN, YOU GODDAMNED MONSTER.
MY PLEASURE.
OOOGL!!

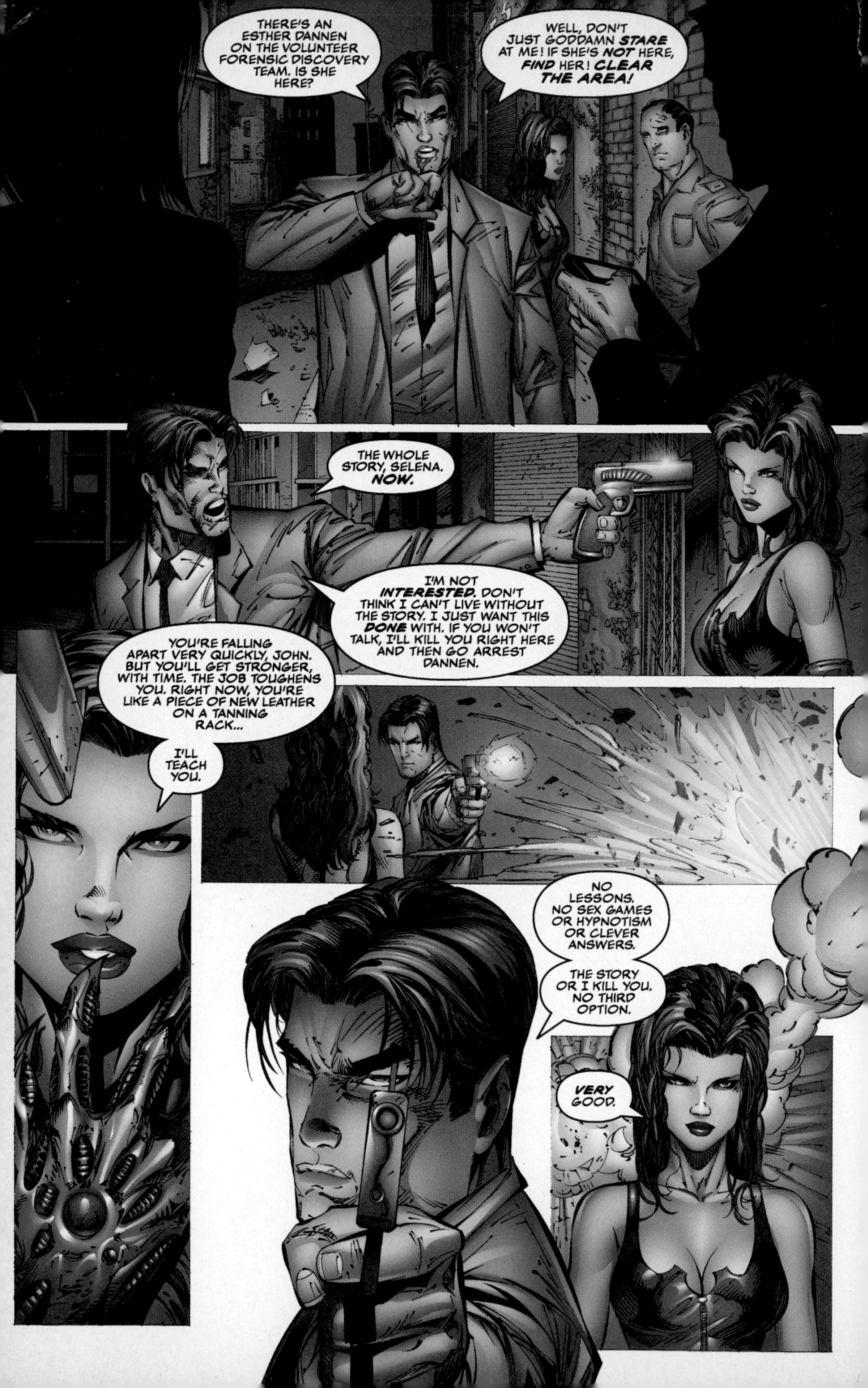
THERE'S AN ESTHER DANNEN ON THE VOLUNTEER FORENSIC DISCOVERY TEAM. IS SHE HERE?
WELL, DON'T JUST GODDAMN **STARE** AT ME! IF SHE'S **NOT** HERE, **FIND** HER! **CLEAR THE AREA!**
THE WHOLE STORY, SELENA. **NOW.**
I'M NOT **INTERESTED.** DON'T THINK I CAN'T LIVE WITHOUT THE STORY. I JUST WANT THIS **DONE** WITH. IF YOU WON'T TALK, I'LL KILL YOU RIGHT HERE AND THEN GO ARREST DANNEN.
YOU'RE FALLING APART VERY QUICKLY, JOHN. BUT YOU'LL GET STRONGER, WITH TIME. THE JOB TOUGHENS YOU. RIGHT NOW, YOU'RE LIKE A PIECE OF NEW LEATHER ON A TANNING RACK...
I'LL TEACH YOU.
NO LESSONS. NO SEX GAMES OR HYPNOTISM OR CLEVER ANSWERS.
THE STORY OR I KILL YOU. NO THIRD OPTION.
VERY GOOD.

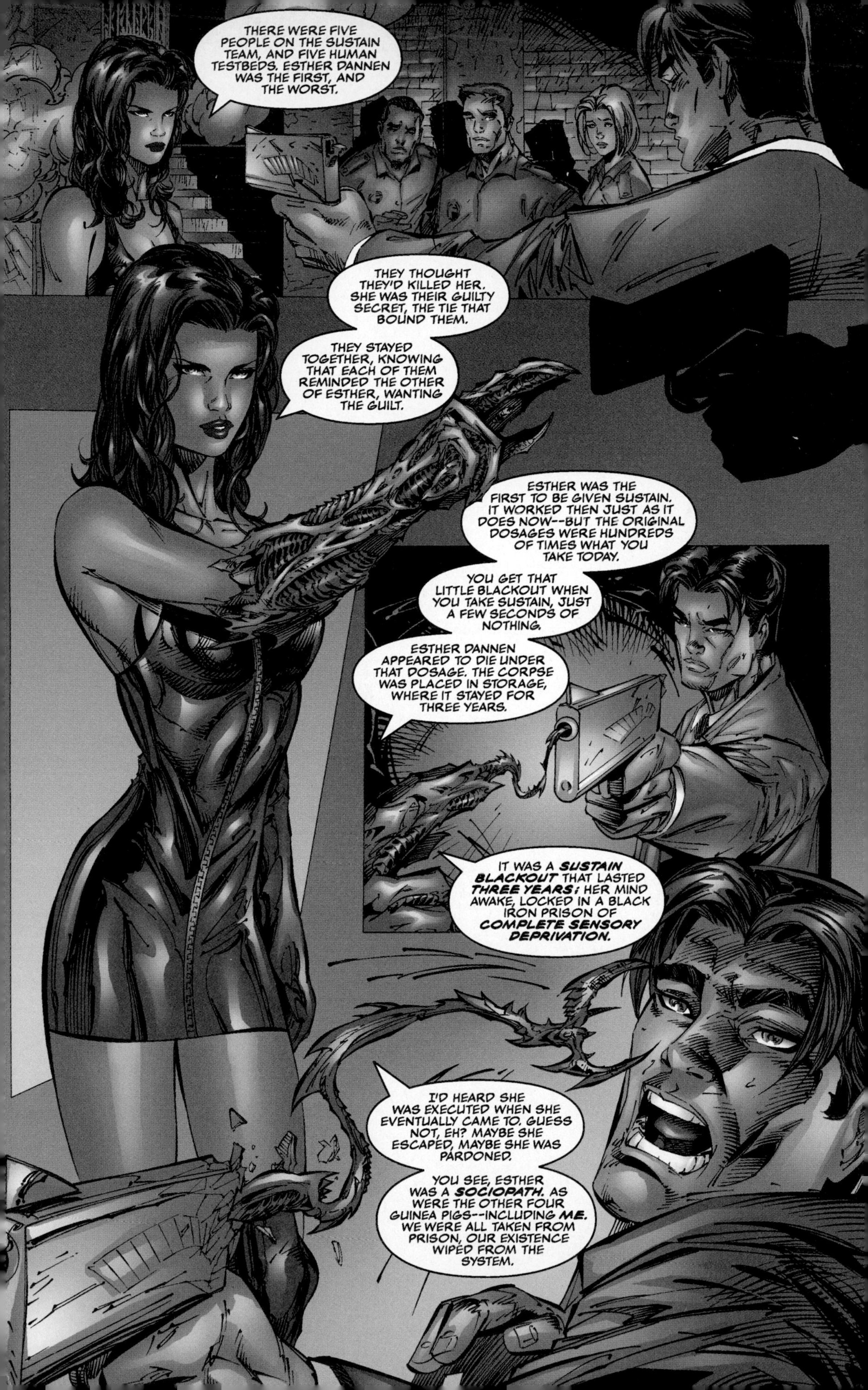
THERE WERE FIVE PEOPLE ON THE SUSTAIN TEAM, AND FIVE HUMAN TESTBEDS. ESTHER DANNEN WAS THE FIRST, AND THE WORST.
THEY THOUGHT THEY'D KILLED HER. SHE WAS THEIR GUILTY SECRET, THE TIE THAT BOUND THEM.
THEY STAYED TOGETHER, KNOWING THAT EACH OF THEM REMINDED THE OTHER OF ESTHER, WANTING THE GUILT.
ESTHER WAS THE FIRST TO BE GIVEN SUSTAIN. IT WORKED THEN JUST AS IT DOES NOW--BUT THE ORIGINAL DOSAGES WERE HUNDREDS OF TIMES WHAT YOU TAKE TODAY.
YOU GET THAT LITTLE BLACKOUT WHEN YOU TAKE SUSTAIN, JUST A FEW SECONDS OF NOTHING.
ESTHER DANNEN APPEARED TO DIE UNDER THAT DOSAGE. THE CORPSE WAS PLACED IN STORAGE, WHERE IT STAYED FOR THREE YEARS.
IT WAS A ***SUSTAIN BLACKOUT*** THAT LASTED ***THREE YEARS;*** HER MIND AWAKE, LOCKED IN A BLACK IRON PRISON OF ***COMPLETE SENSORY DEPRIVATION.***
I'D HEARD SHE WAS EXECUTED WHEN SHE EVENTUALLY CAME TO. GUESS NOT, EH? MAYBE SHE ESCAPED, MAYBE SHE WAS PARDONED.
YOU SEE, ESTHER WAS A ***SOCIOPATH.*** AS WERE THE OTHER FOUR GUINEA PIGS--INCLUDING ***ME.*** WE WERE ALL TAKEN FROM PRISON, OUR EXISTENCE WIPED FROM THE SYSTEM.

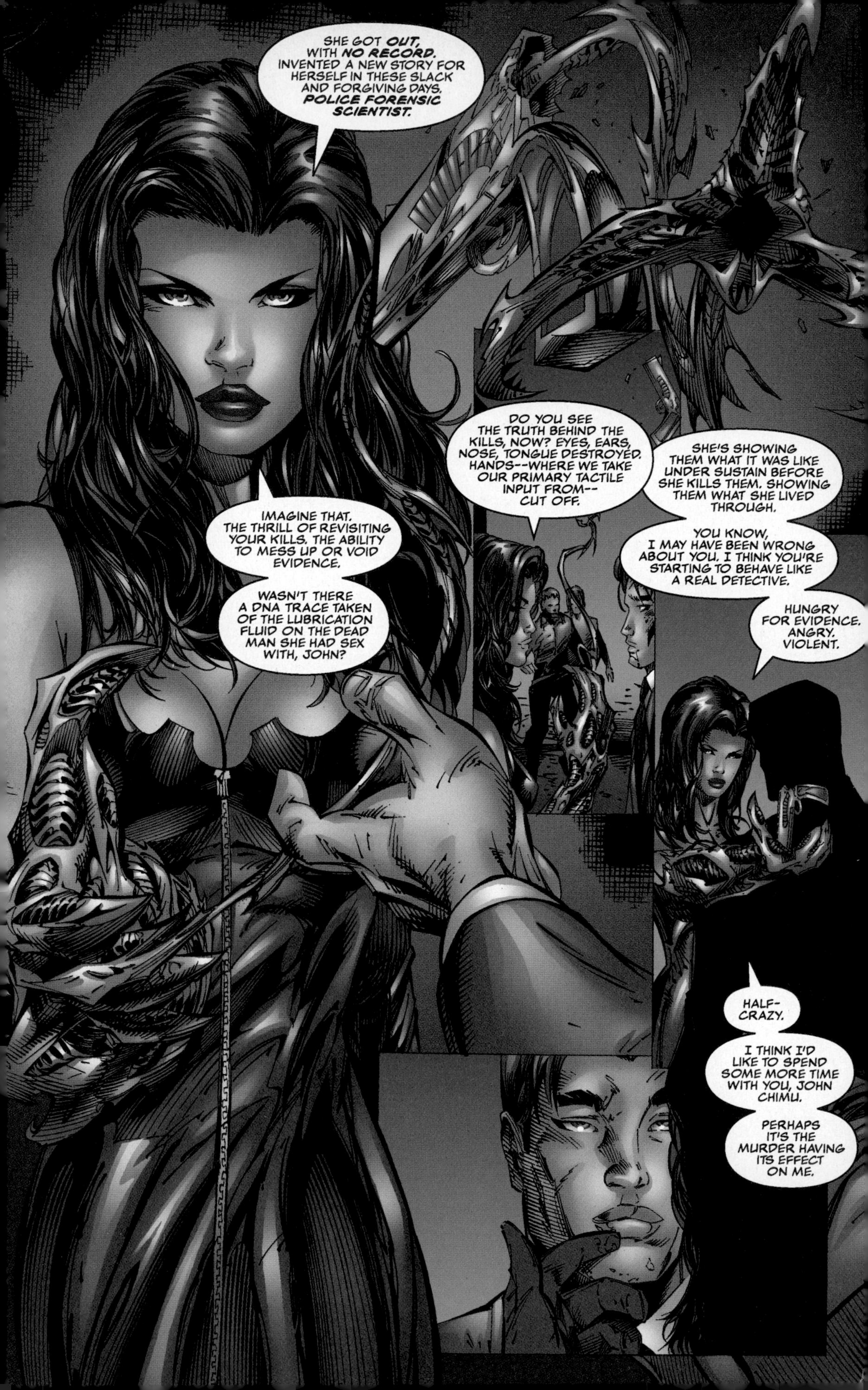
SHE GOT OUT, WITH NO RECORD. INVENTED A NEW STORY FOR HERSELF IN THESE SLACK AND FORGIVING DAYS. POLICE FORENSIC SCIENTIST.
IMAGINE THAT. THE THRILL OF REVISITING YOUR KILLS. THE ABILITY TO MESS UP OR VOID EVIDENCE.
WASN'T THERE A DNA TRACE TAKEN OF THE LUBRICATION FLUID ON THE DEAD MAN SHE HAD SEX WITH, JOHN?
DO YOU SEE THE TRUTH BEHIND THE KILLS, NOW? EYES, EARS, NOSE, TONGUE DESTROYED. HANDS--WHERE WE TAKE OUR PRIMARY TACTILE INPUT FROM--CUT OFF.
SHE'S SHOWING THEM WHAT IT WAS LIKE UNDER SUSTAIN BEFORE SHE KILLS THEM. SHOWING THEM WHAT SHE LIVED THROUGH.
YOU KNOW, I MAY HAVE BEEN WRONG ABOUT YOU. I THINK YOU'RE STARTING TO BEHAVE LIKE A REAL DETECTIVE.
HUNGRY FOR EVIDENCE. ANGRY. VIOLENT.
HALF-CRAZY.
I THINK I'D LIKE TO SPEND SOME MORE TIME WITH YOU, JOHN CHIMU.
PERHAPS IT'S THE MURDER HAVING ITS EFFECT ON ME.

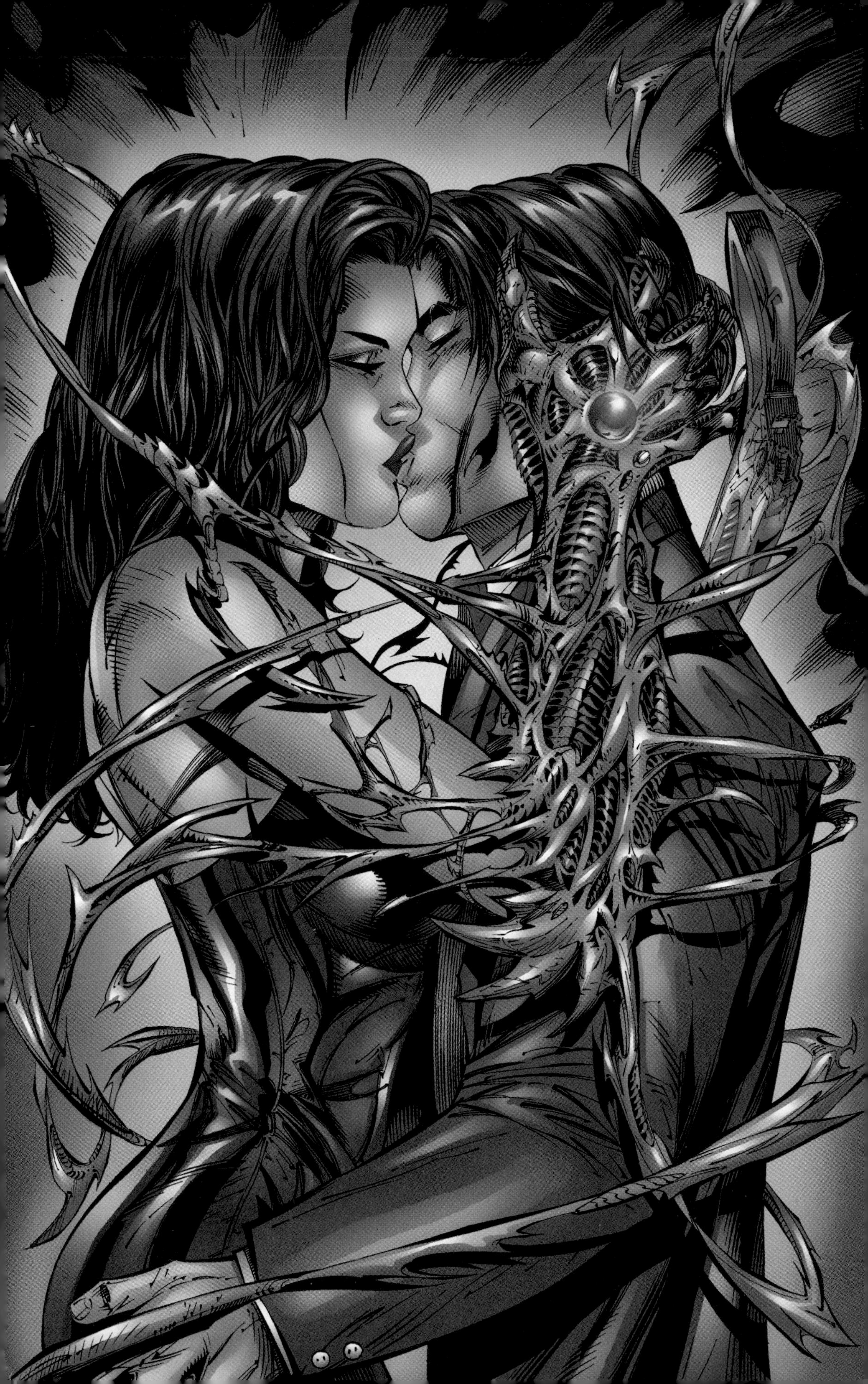

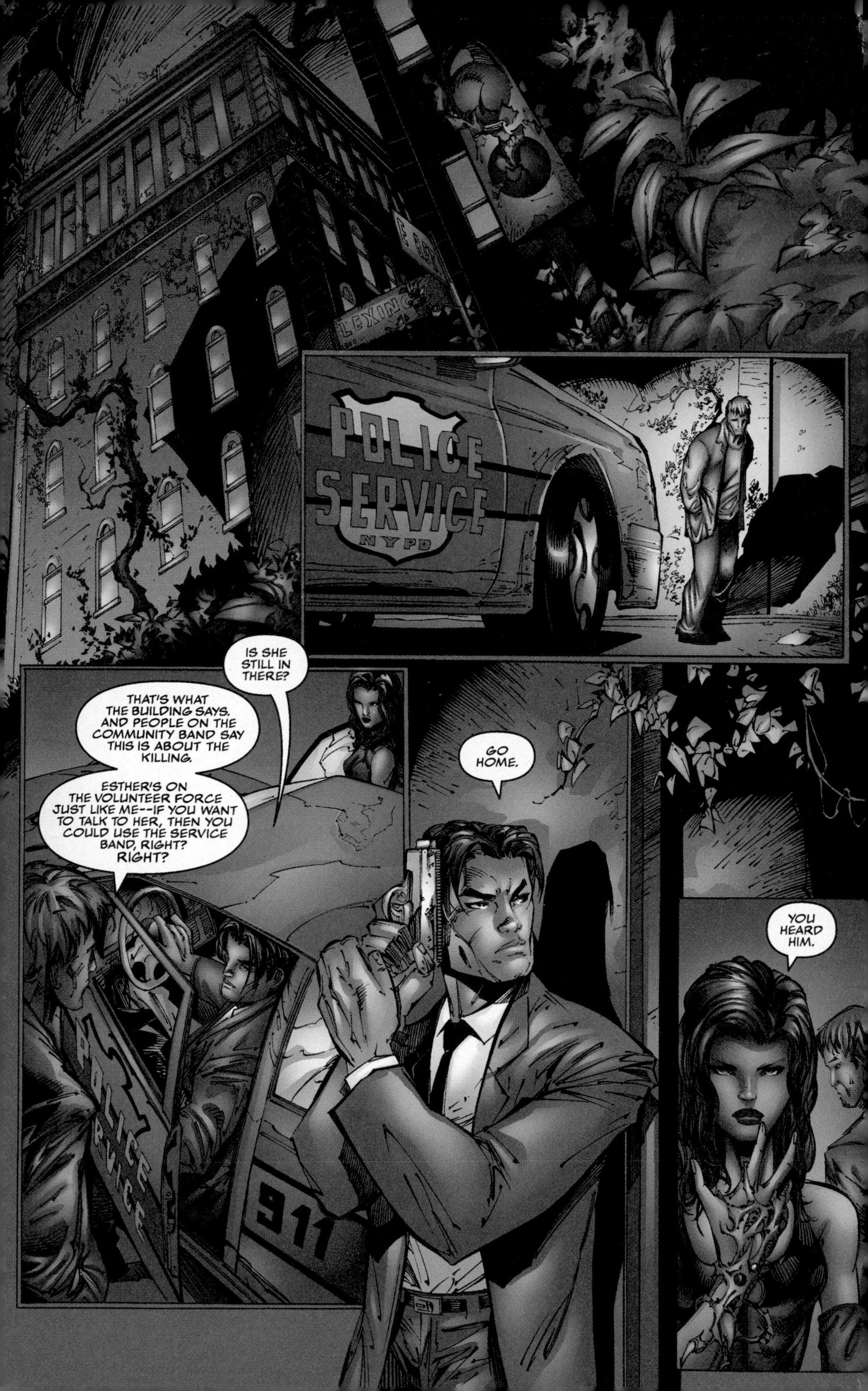
LEXING
POLICE SERVICE
NYPD
IS SHE STILL IN THERE?
THAT'S WHAT THE BUILDING SAYS. AND PEOPLE ON THE COMMUNITY BAND SAY THIS IS ABOUT THE KILLING.
ESTHER'S ON THE VOLUNTEER FORCE JUST LIKE ME--IF YOU WANT TO TALK TO HER, THEN YOU COULD USE THE SERVICE BAND, RIGHT? RIGHT?
POLICE SERVICE
911
GO HOME.
YOU HEARD HIM.

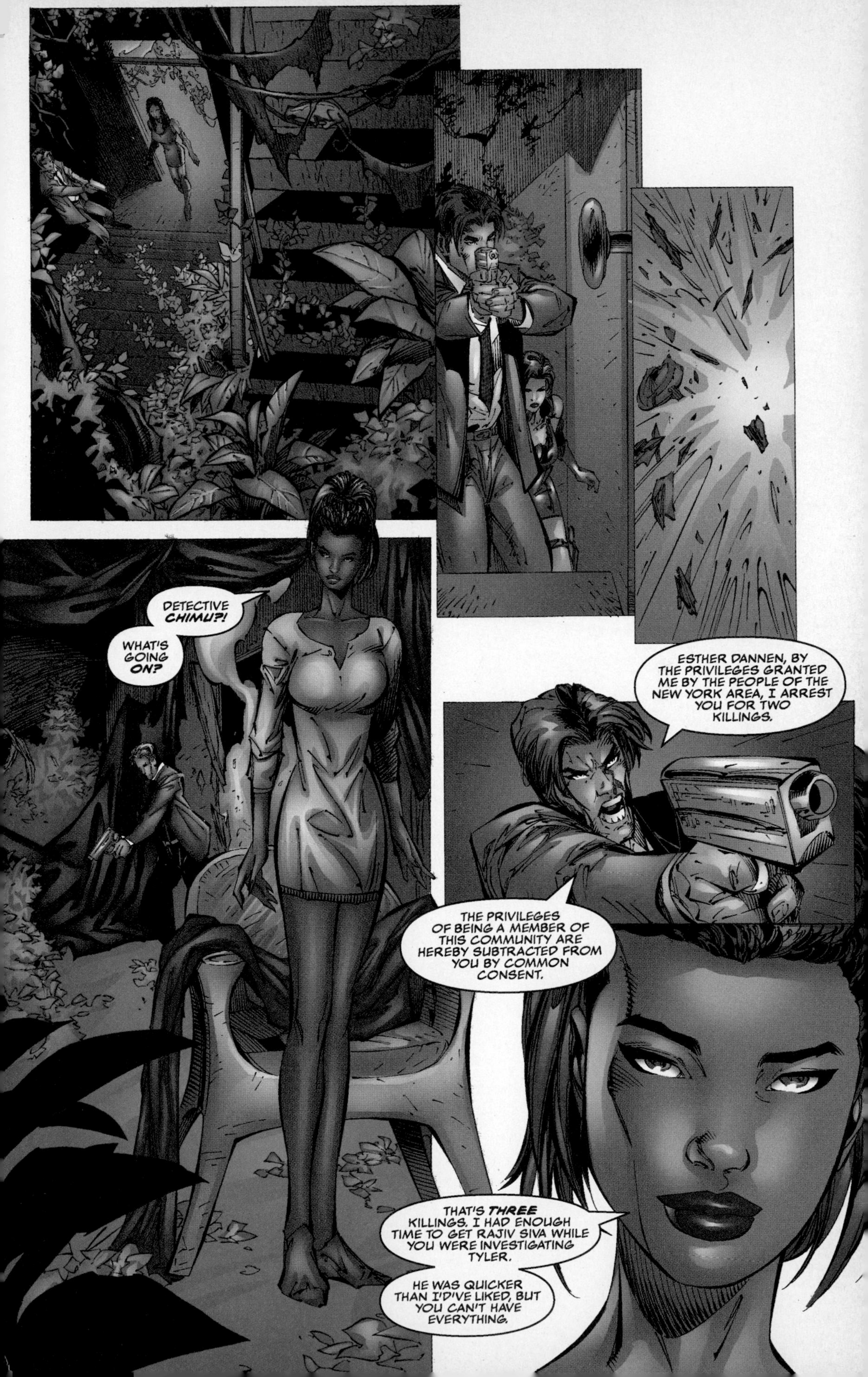
DETECTIVE CHIMU?!
WHAT'S GOING ON?
ESTHER DANNEN, BY THE PRIVILEGES GRANTED ME BY THE PEOPLE OF THE NEW YORK AREA, I ARREST YOU FOR TWO KILLINGS.
THE PRIVILEGES OF BEING A MEMBER OF THIS COMMUNITY ARE HEREBY SUBTRACTED FROM YOU BY COMMON CONSENT.
THAT'S THREE KILLINGS. I HAD ENOUGH TIME TO GET RAJIV SIVA WHILE YOU WERE INVESTIGATING TYLER.
HE WAS QUICKER THAN I'D'VE LIKED, BUT YOU CAN'T HAVE EVERYTHING.

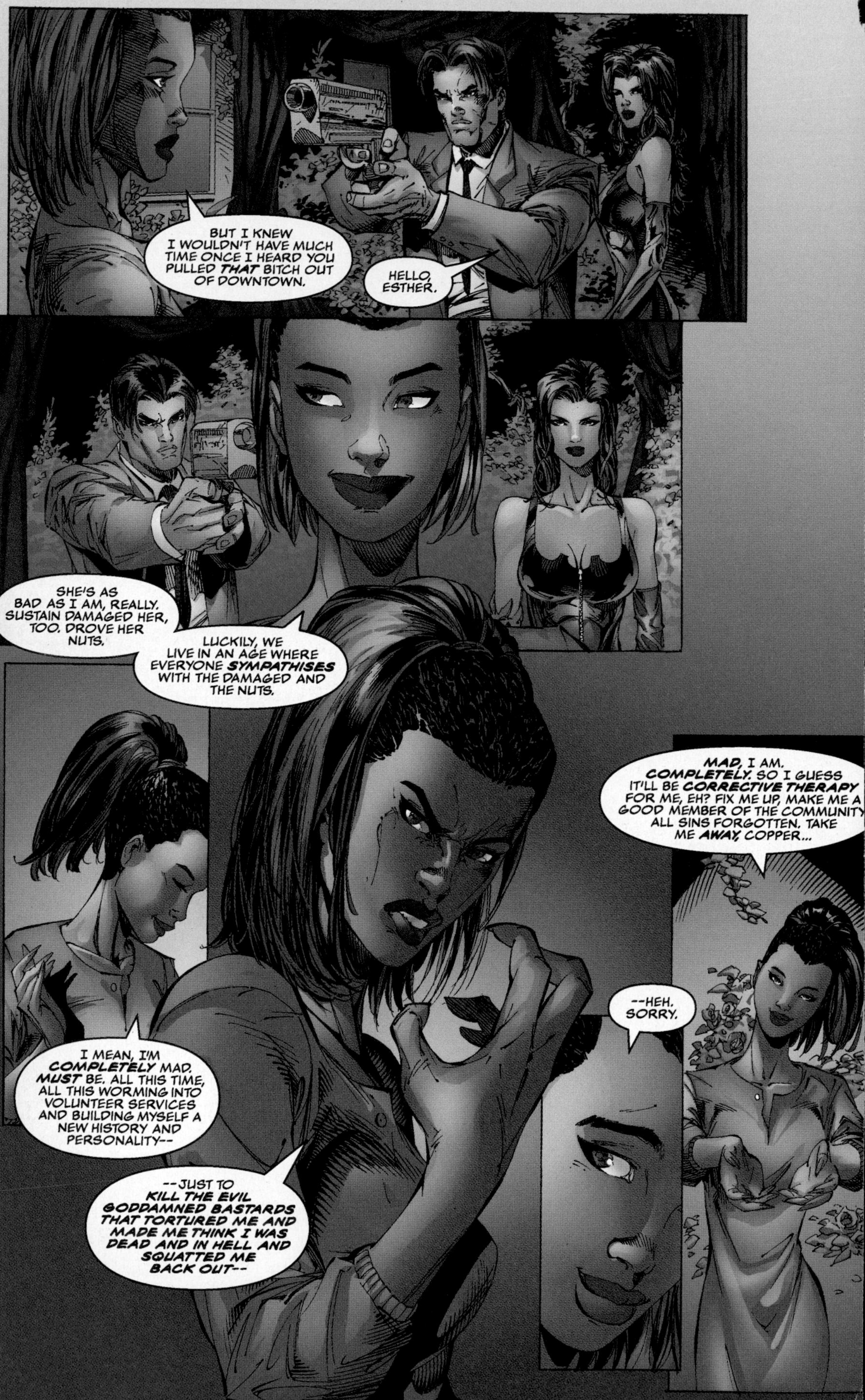
BUT I KNEW I WOULDN'T HAVE MUCH TIME ONCE I HEARD YOU PULLED THAT BITCH OUT OF DOWNTOWN.
HELLO, ESTHER.
SHE'S AS BAD AS I AM, REALLY. SUSTAIN DAMAGED HER, TOO. DROVE HER NUTS.
LUCKILY, WE LIVE IN AN AGE WHERE EVERYONE SYMPATHISES WITH THE DAMAGED AND THE NUTS.
I MEAN, I'M COMPLETELY MAD. MUST BE. ALL THIS TIME, ALL THIS WORMING INTO VOLUNTEER SERVICES AND BUILDING MYSELF A NEW HISTORY AND PERSONALITY--
--JUST TO KILL THE EVIL GODDAMNED BASTARDS THAT TORTURED ME AND MADE ME THINK I WAS DEAD AND IN HELL AND SQUATTED ME BACK OUT--
--HEH. SORRY.
MAD, I AM. COMPLETELY. SO I GUESS IT'LL BE CORRECTIVE THERAPY FOR ME, EH? FIX ME UP, MAKE ME A GOOD MEMBER OF THE COMMUNITY. ALL SINS FORGOTTEN. TAKE ME AWAY, COPPER...

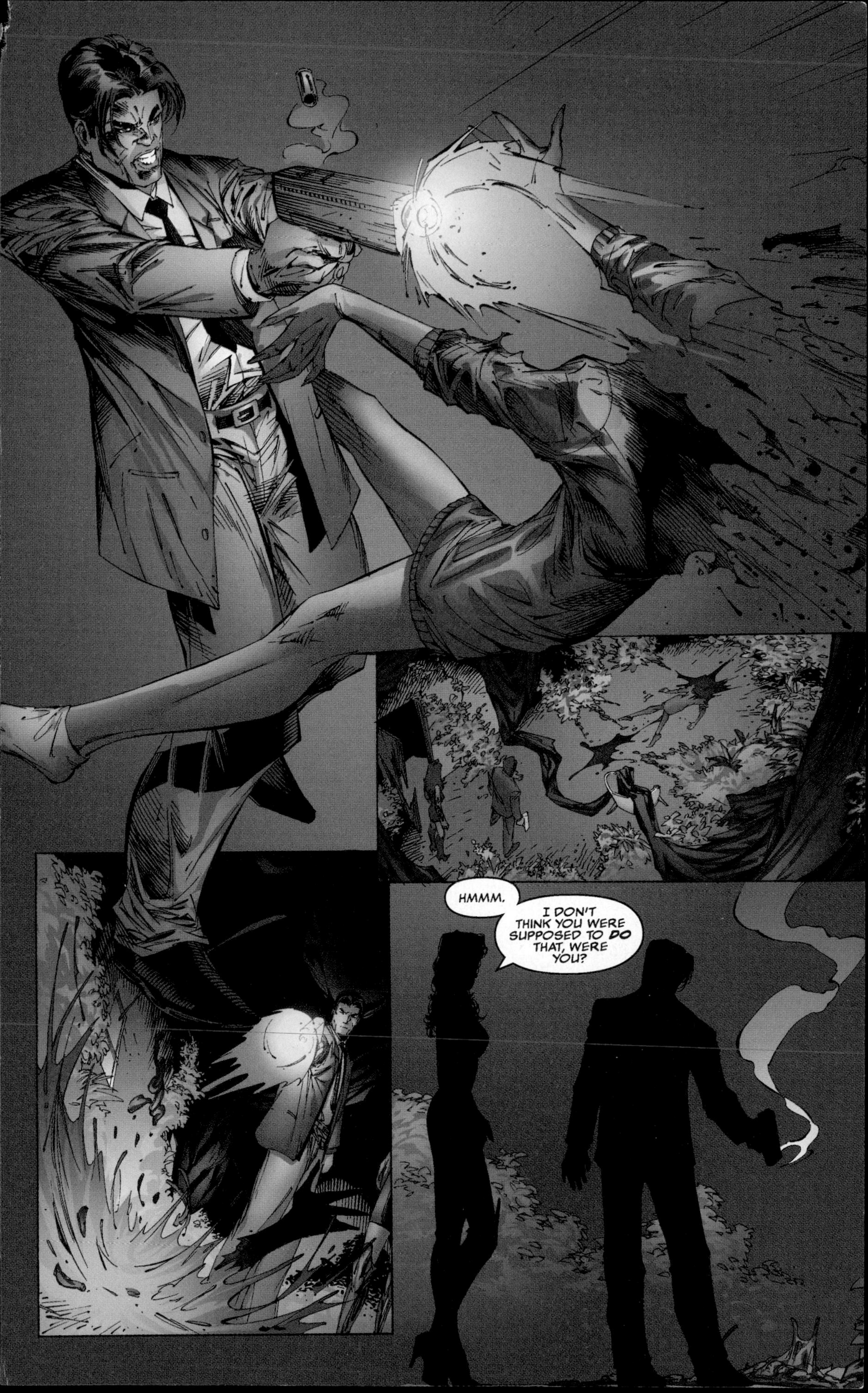
HMMM.
I DON'T THINK YOU WERE SUPPOSED TO DO THAT, WERE YOU?

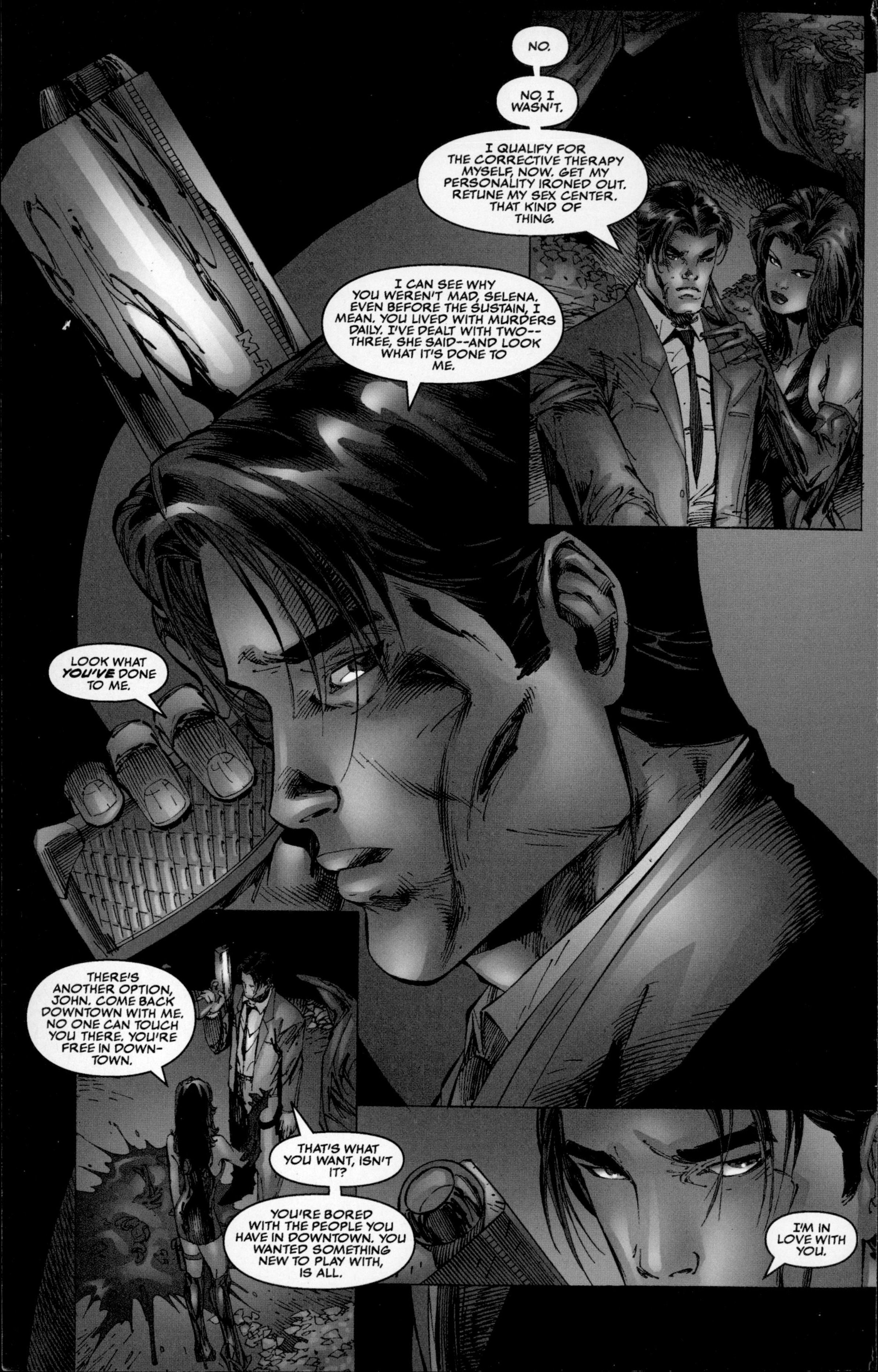
NO.
NO, I WASN'T.
I QUALIFY FOR THE CORRECTIVE THERAPY MYSELF, NOW. GET MY PERSONALITY IRONED OUT. RETUNE MY SEX CENTER. THAT KIND OF THING.
I CAN SEE WHY YOU WEREN'T MAD, SELENA. EVEN BEFORE THE SUSTAIN, I MEAN. YOU LIVED WITH MURDERS DAILY. I'VE DEALT WITH TWO-- THREE, SHE SAID--AND LOOK WHAT IT'S DONE TO ME.
LOOK WHAT ***YOU'VE*** DONE TO ME.
THERE'S ANOTHER OPTION, JOHN. COME BACK DOWNTOWN WITH ME. NO ONE CAN TOUCH YOU THERE. YOU'RE FREE IN DOWN-TOWN.
THAT'S WHAT YOU WANT, ISN'T IT?
YOU'RE BORED WITH THE PEOPLE YOU HAVE IN DOWNTOWN. YOU WANTED SOMETHING NEW TO PLAY WITH, IS ALL.
I'M IN LOVE WITH YOU.

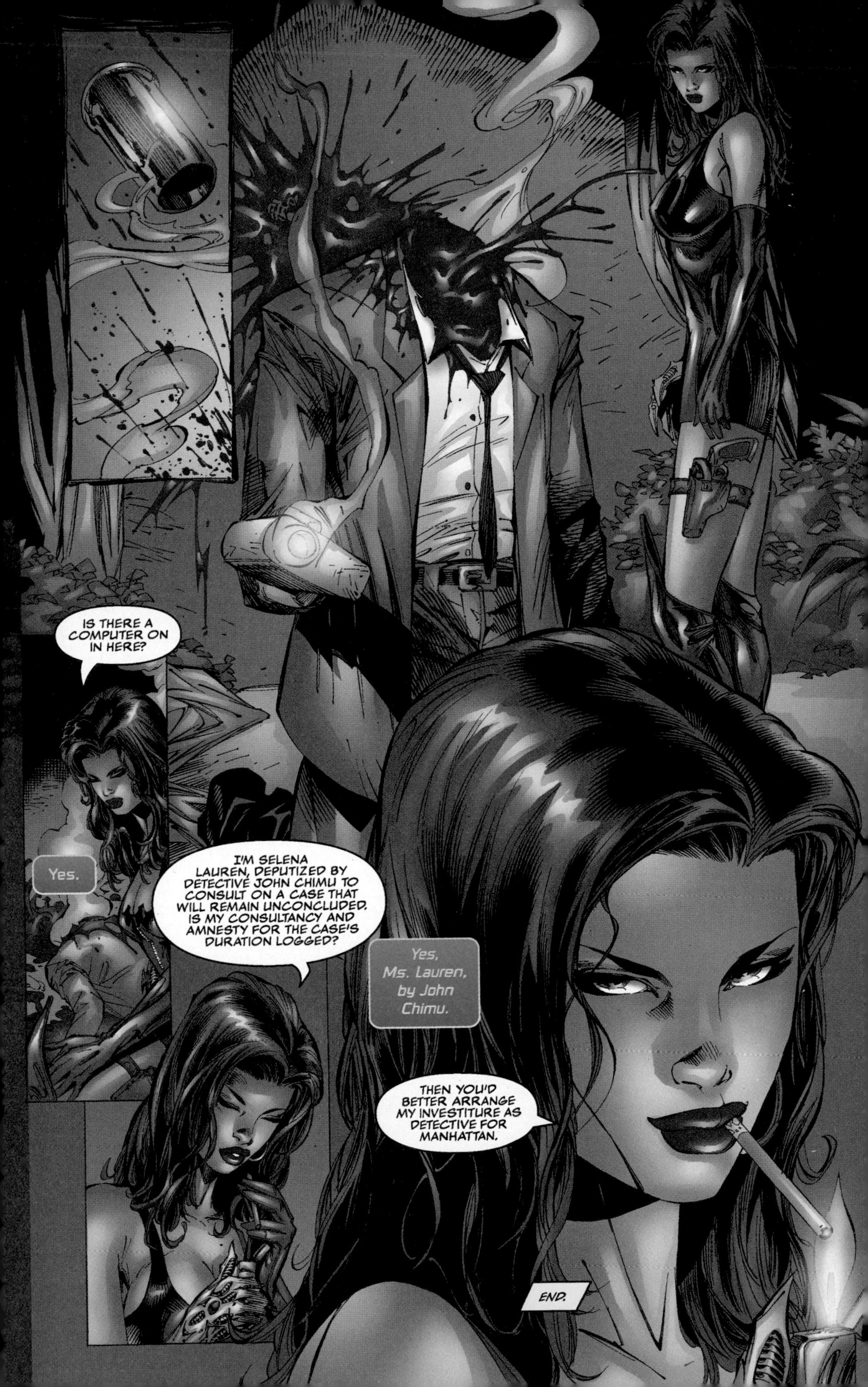
IS THERE A COMPUTER ON IN HERE?
Yes.
I'M SELENA LAUREN, DEPUTIZED BY DETECTIVE JOHN CHIMU TO CONSULT ON A CASE THAT WILL REMAIN UNCONCLUDED. IS MY CONSULTANCY AND AMNESTY FOR THE CASE'S DURATION LOGGED?
Yes, Ms. Lauren, by John Chimu.
THEN YOU'D BETTER ARRANGE MY INVESTITURE AS DETECTIVE FOR MANHATTAN.
END.

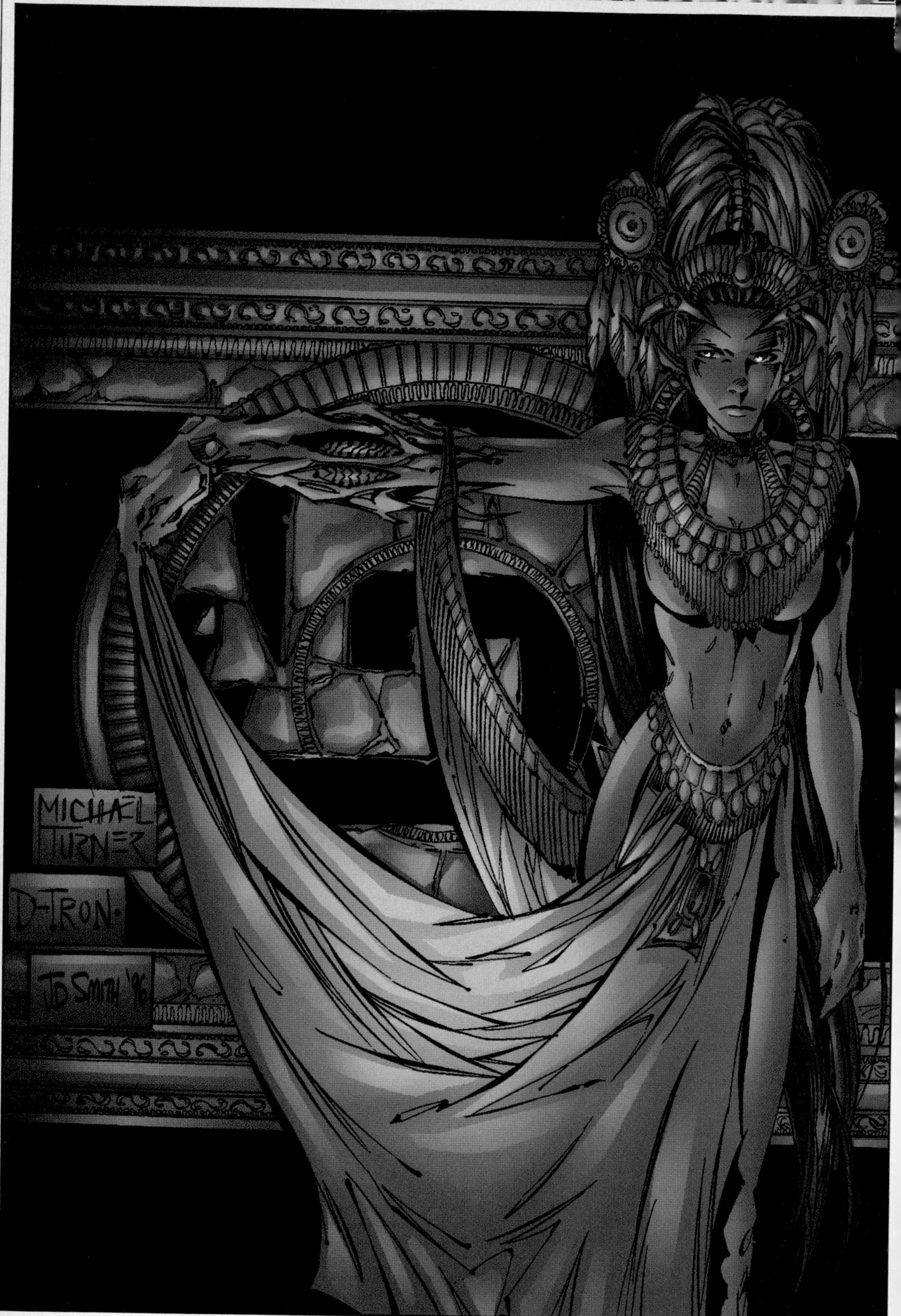
MICHAEL TURNER
D-TRON.
JD SMITH '96

A Z T E C
WITCHBLADE
Michael Turner, D-Tron & Jonathan D. Smith

TALES of the WITCHBLADE

05

STORY by
Christina Z.
David Wohl

PENCILED and INKED by
Richard Bennett

COLORED by
Matt Nelson

LETTERED by
Dennis Heisler

SPECIAL THANKS
Monica Bennett
Scott Gordon

COVER by
Richard Bennett
and
Matt Nelson

MAITEA

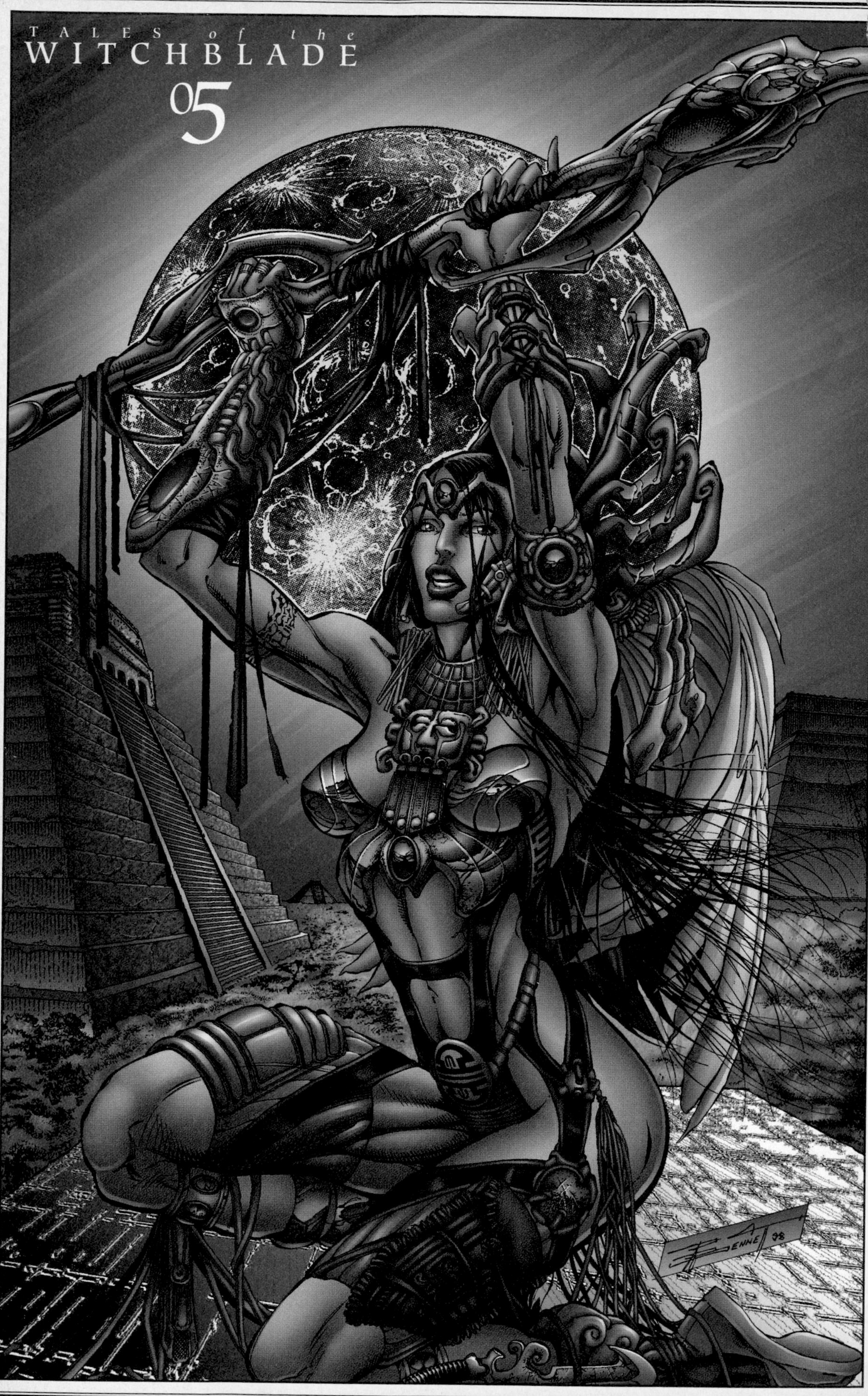
TALES of the
WITCHBLADE
05
BENNETT '98

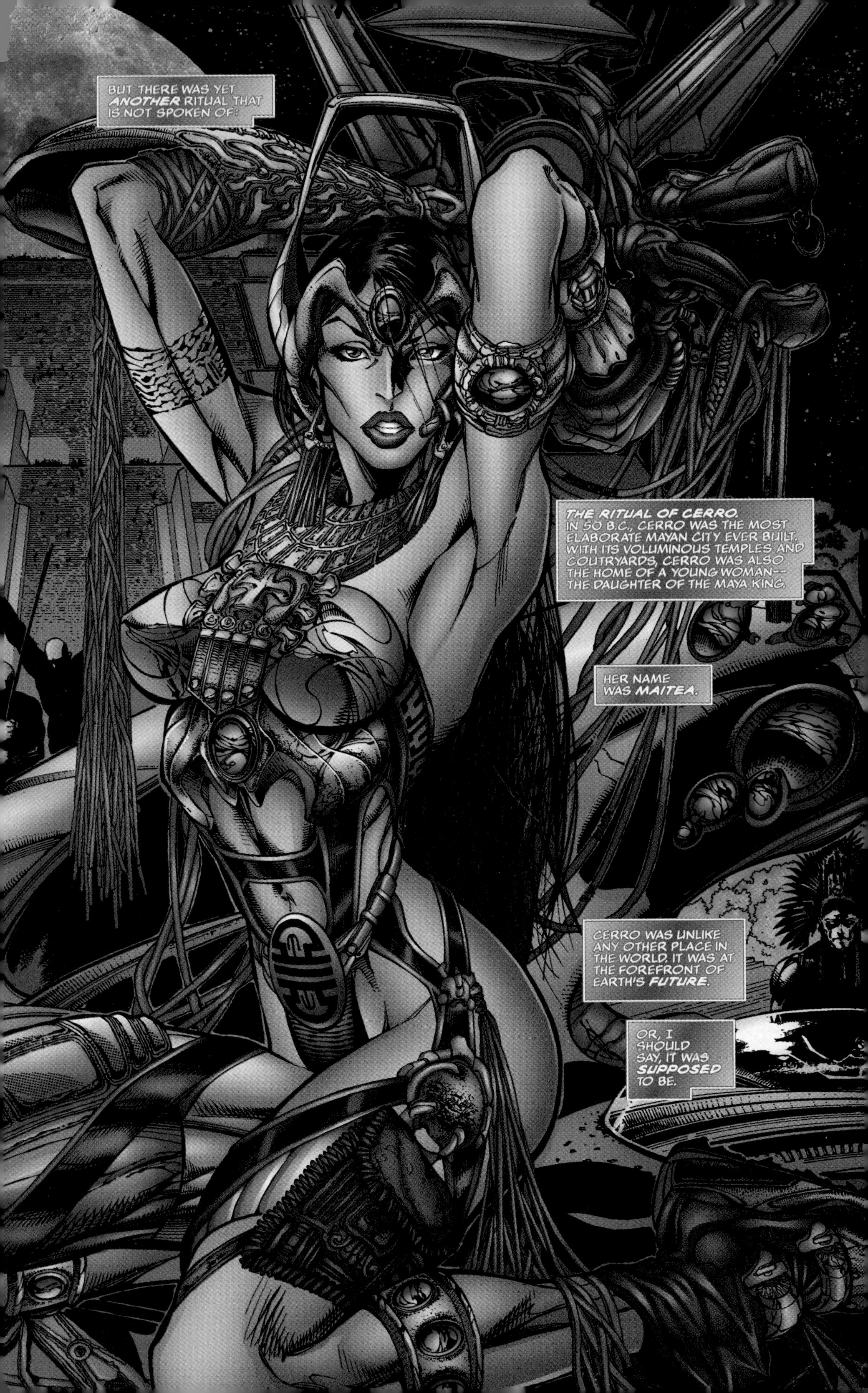
BUT THERE WAS YET ANOTHER RITUAL THAT IS NOT SPOKEN OF:
THE RITUAL OF CERRO. IN 50 B.C., CERRO WAS THE MOST ELABORATE MAYAN CITY EVER BUILT. WITH ITS VOLUMINOUS TEMPLES AND COUTRYARDS, CERRO WAS ALSO THE HOME OF A YOUNG WOMAN-- THE DAUGHTER OF THE MAYA KING.
HER NAME WAS MAITEA.
CERRO WAS UNLIKE ANY OTHER PLACE IN THE WORLD. IT WAS AT THE FOREFRONT OF EARTH'S FUTURE.
OR, I SHOULD SAY, IT WAS SUPPOSED TO BE.

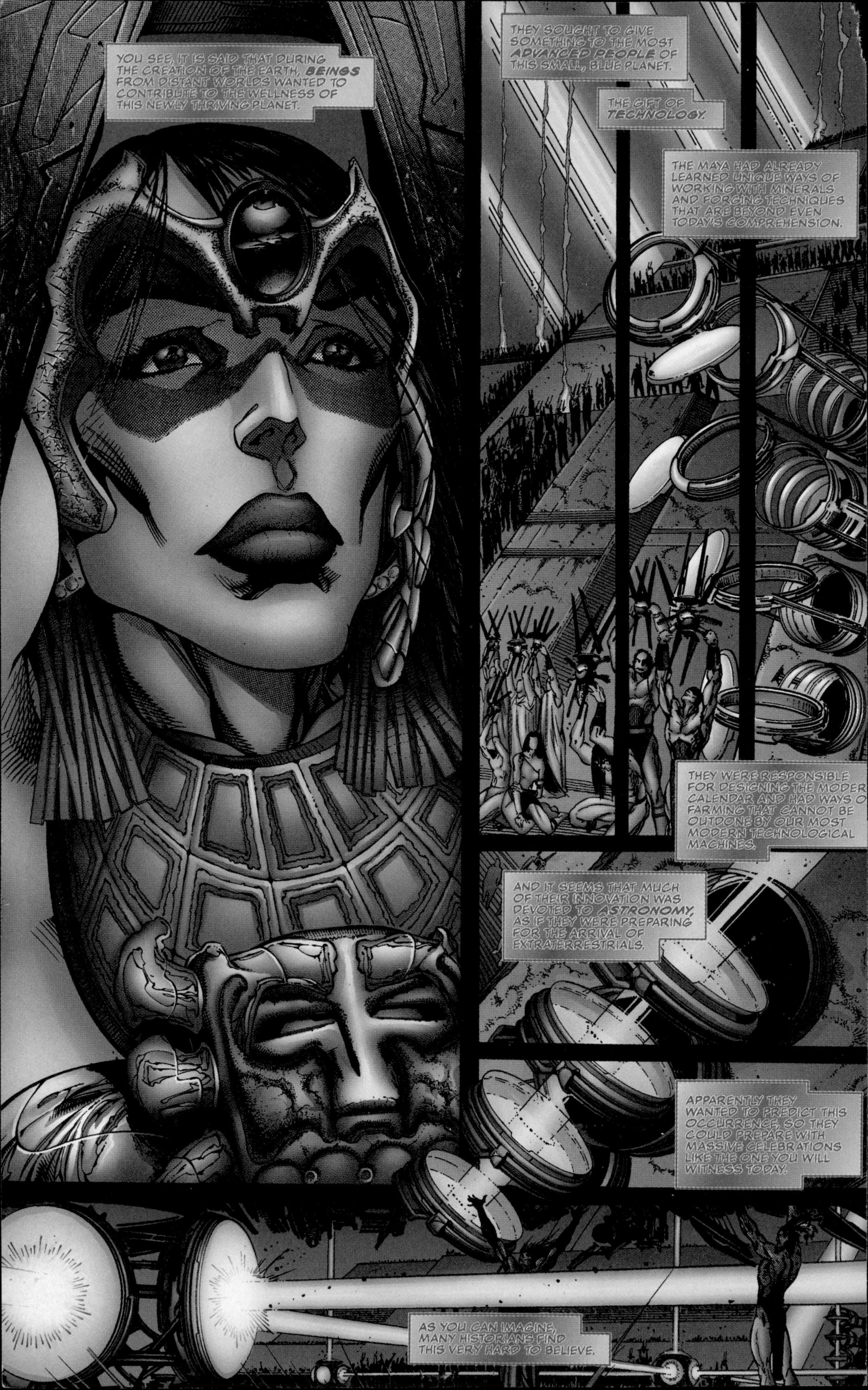
YOU SEE, IT IS SAID THAT DURING THE CREATION OF THE EARTH, BEINGS FROM DISTANT WORLDS WANTED TO CONTRIBUTE TO THE WELLNESS OF THIS NEWLY THRIVING PLANET.
THEY SOUGHT TO GIVE SOMETHING TO THE MOST ADVANCED PEOPLE OF THIS SMALL, BLUE PLANET.
THE GIFT OF TECHNOLOGY.
THE MAYA HAD ALREADY LEARNED UNIQUE WAYS OF WORKING WITH MINERALS AND FORGING TECHNIQUES THAT ARE BEYOND EVEN TODAY'S COMPREHENSION.
THEY WERE RESPONSIBLE FOR DESIGNING THE MODER CALENDAR AND HAD WAYS O FARMING THAT CANNOT BE OUTDONE BY OUR MOST MODERN TECHNOLOGICAL MACHINES.
AND IT SEEMS THAT MUCH OF THEIR INNOVATION WAS DEVOTED TO ASTRONOMY, AS IF THEY WERE PREPARING FOR THE ARRIVAL OF EXTRATERRESTRIALS.
APPARENTLY THEY WANTED TO PREDICT THIS OCCURRENCE, SO THEY COULD PREPARE WITH MASSIVE CELEBRATIONS LIKE THE ONE YOU WILL WITNESS TODAY.
AS YOU CAN IMAGINE, MANY HISTORIANS FIND THIS VERY HARD TO BELIEVE.

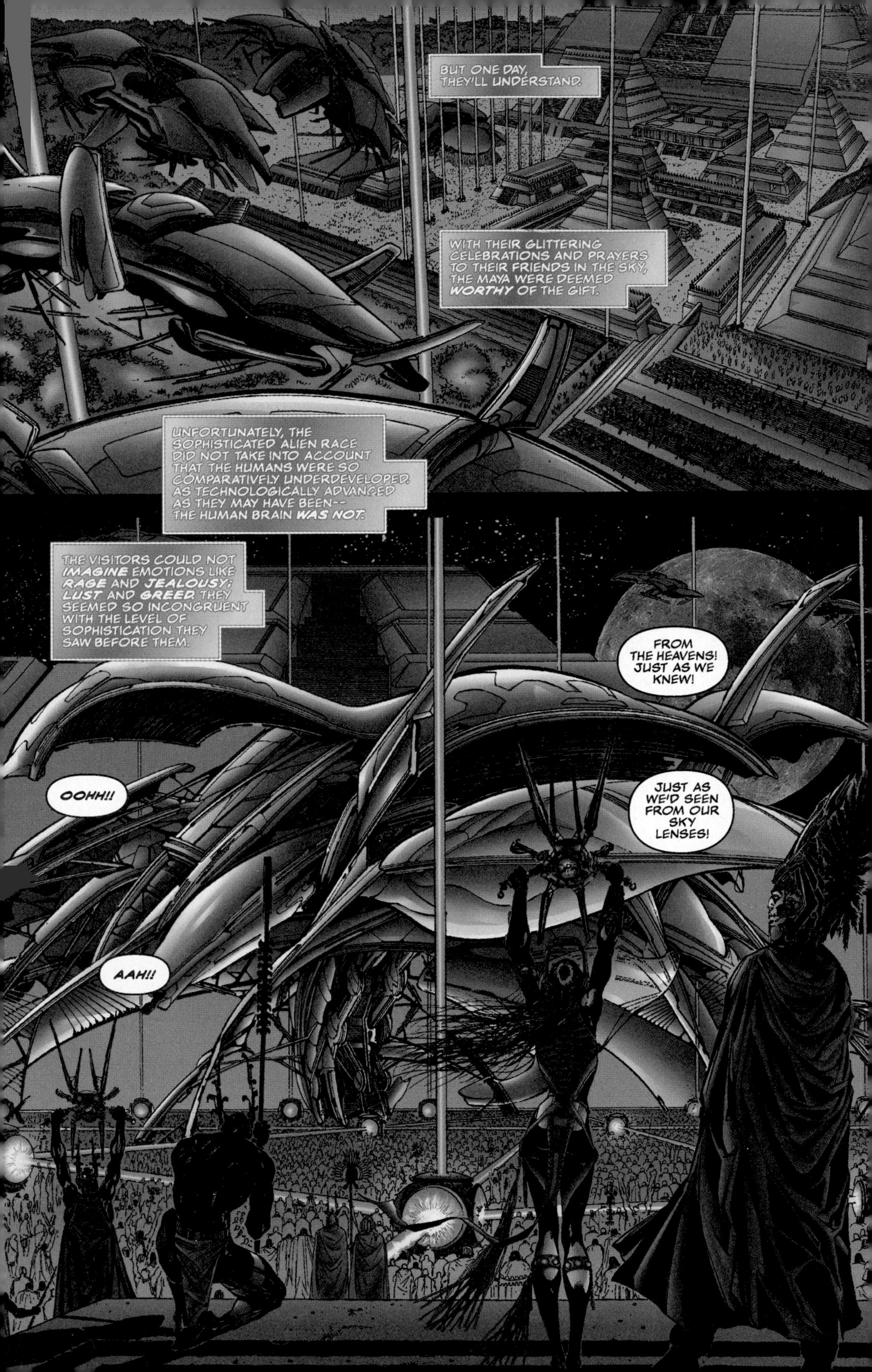

BUT ONE DAY, THEY'LL UNDERSTAND.
WITH THEIR GLITTERING CELEBRATIONS AND PRAYERS TO THEIR FRIENDS IN THE SKY, THE MAYA WERE DEEMED WORTHY OF THE GIFT.
UNFORTUNATELY, THE SOPHISTICATED ALIEN RACE DID NOT TAKE INTO ACCOUNT THAT THE HUMANS WERE SO COMPARATIVELY UNDERDEVELOPED. AS TECHNOLOGICALLY ADVANCED AS THEY MAY HAVE BEEN-- THE HUMAN BRAIN WAS NOT.
THE VISITORS COULD NOT IMAGINE EMOTIONS LIKE RAGE AND JEALOUSY; LUST AND GREED. THEY SEEMED SO INCONGRUENT WITH THE LEVEL OF SOPHISTICATION THEY SAW BEFORE THEM.
FROM THE HEAVENS! JUST AS WE KNEW!
OOHH!!
JUST AS WE'D SEEN FROM OUR SKY LENSES!
AAH!!

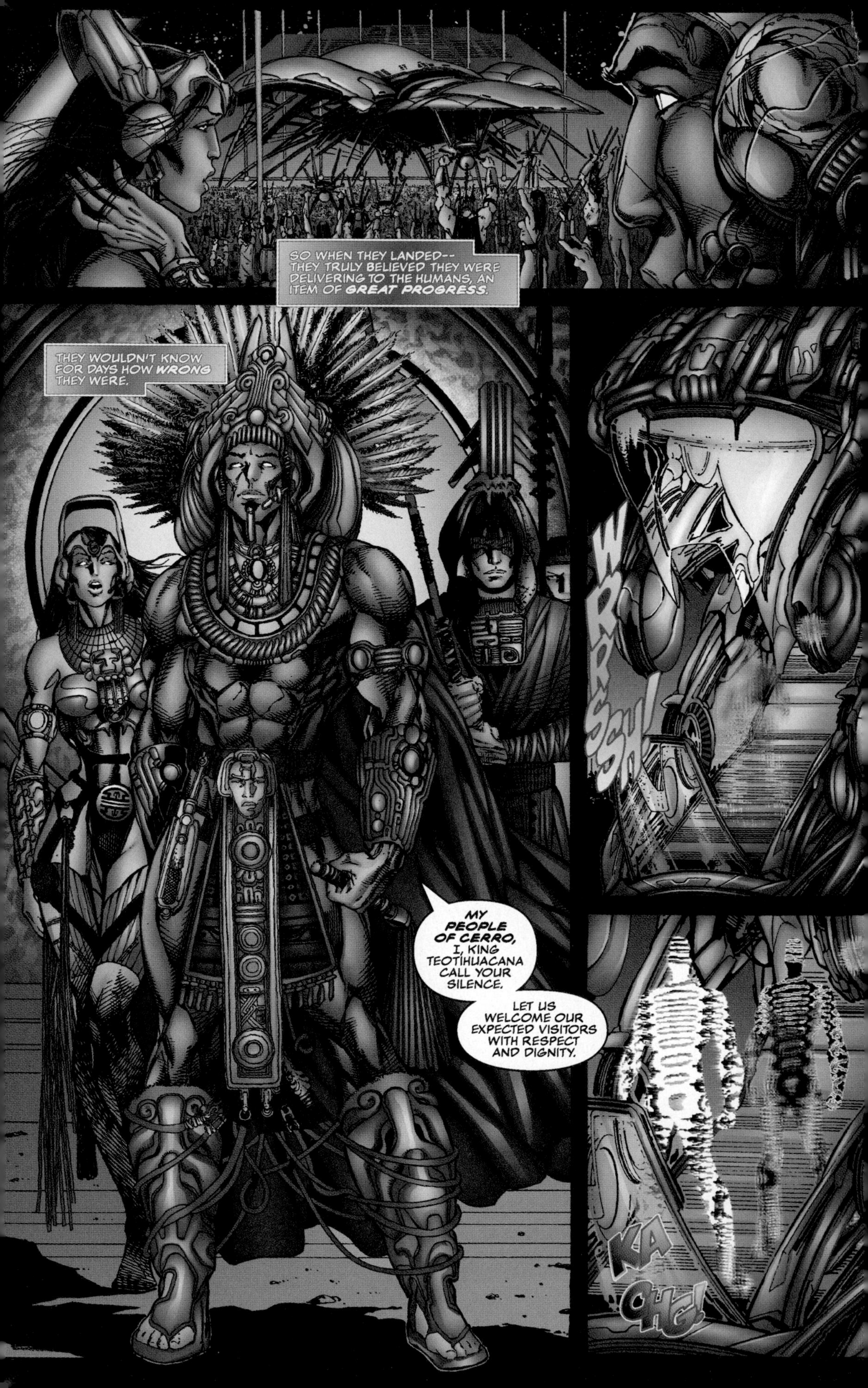
SO WHEN THEY LANDED-- THEY TRULY BELIEVED THEY WERE DELIVERING TO THE HUMANS, AN ITEM OF GREAT PROGRESS.
THEY WOULDN'T KNOW FOR DAYS HOW WRONG THEY WERE.
WRRSSH!
MY PEOPLE OF CERRO, I, KING TEOTIHUACANA CALL YOUR SILENCE.
LET US WELCOME OUR EXPECTED VISITORS WITH RESPECT AND DIGNITY.
KA CHG!

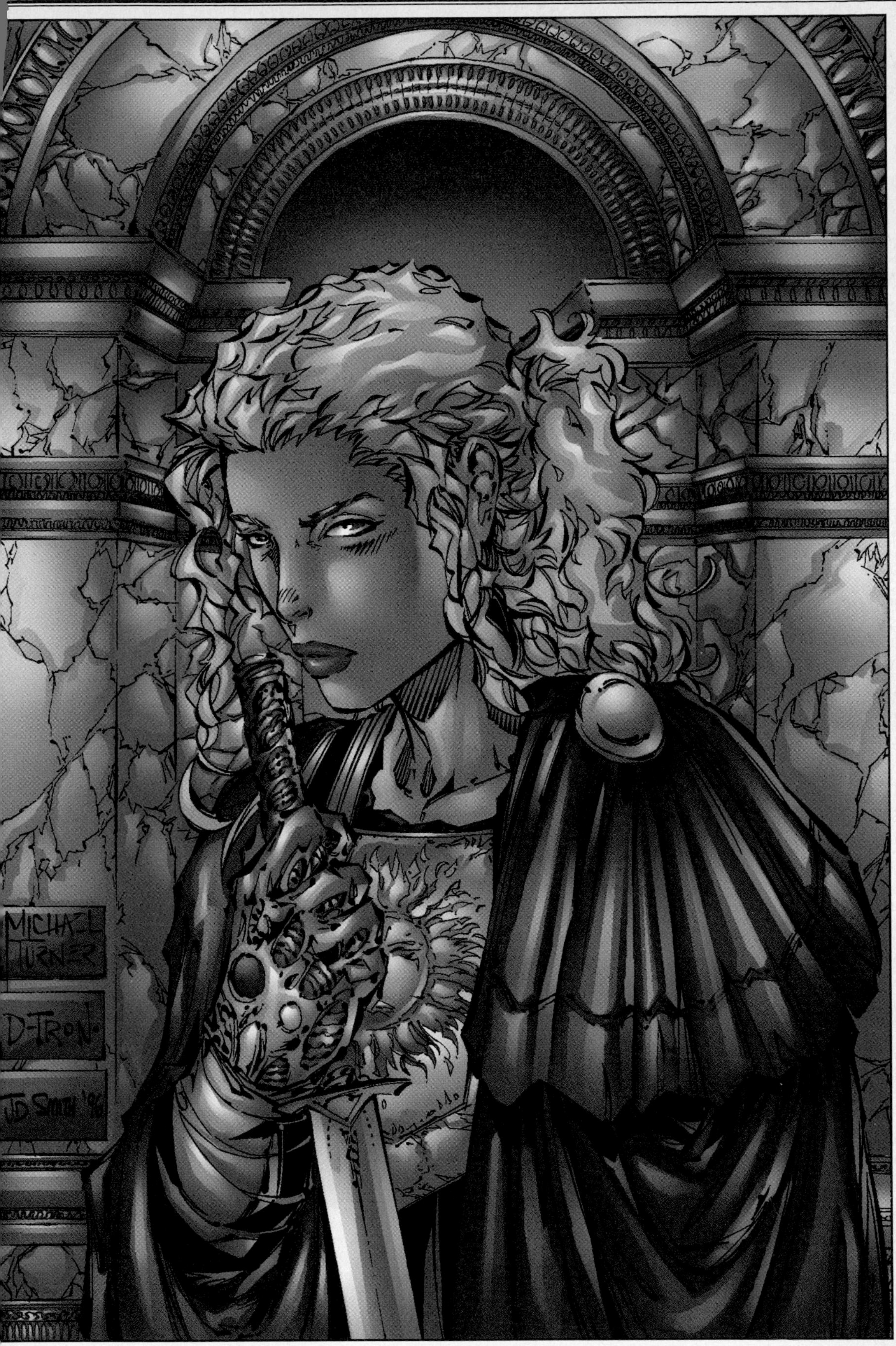
MICHAEL TURNER
D-TRON
JD SMITH '96

R O M A N
WITCHBLADE
Michael Turner, D-Tron & Jonathan D. Smith

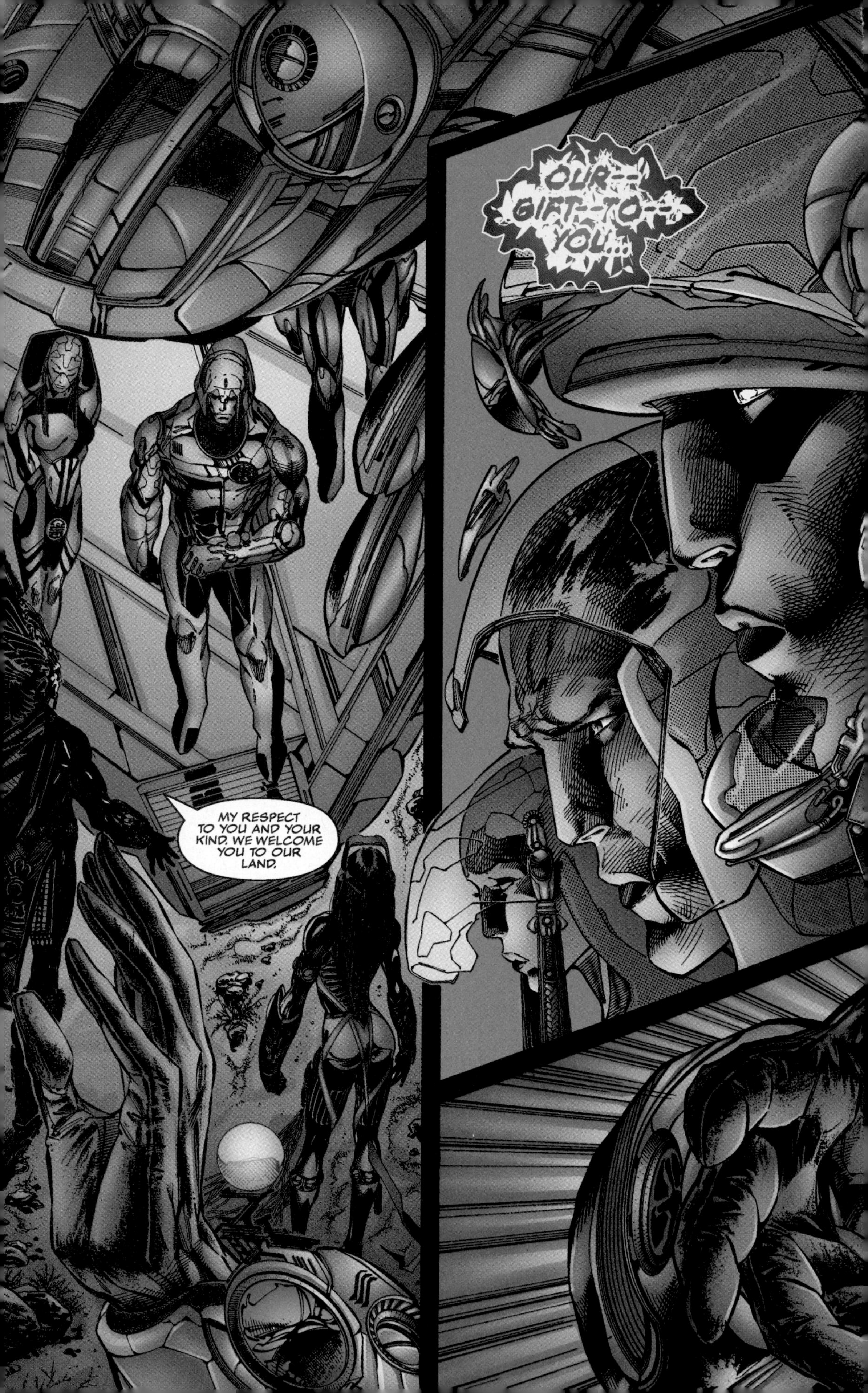
MY RESPECT TO YOU AND YOUR KIND. WE WELCOME YOU TO OUR LAND.
OUR-- GIFT--TO-- YOU...

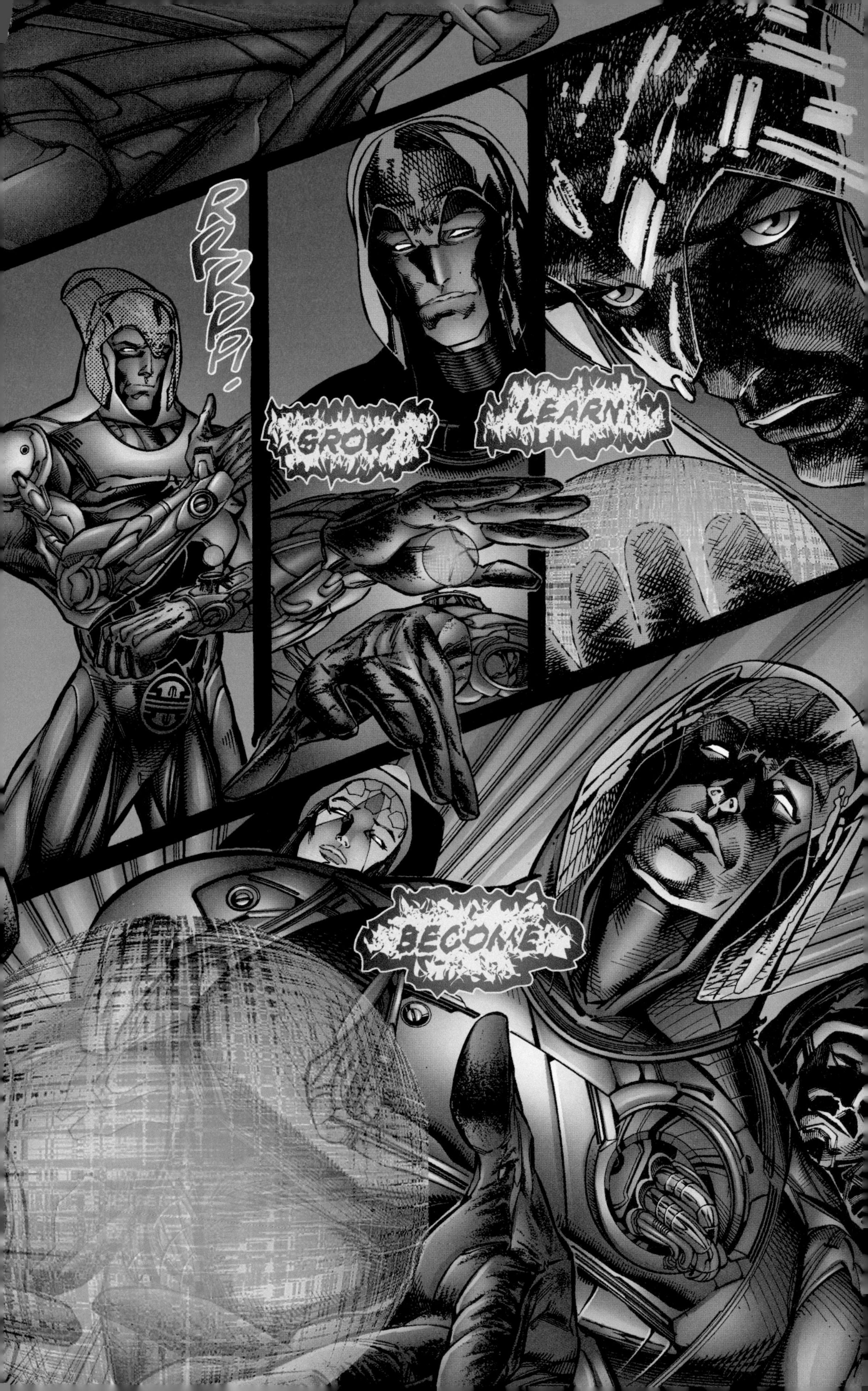
RRRRRP!
GROW
LEARN
BECOME

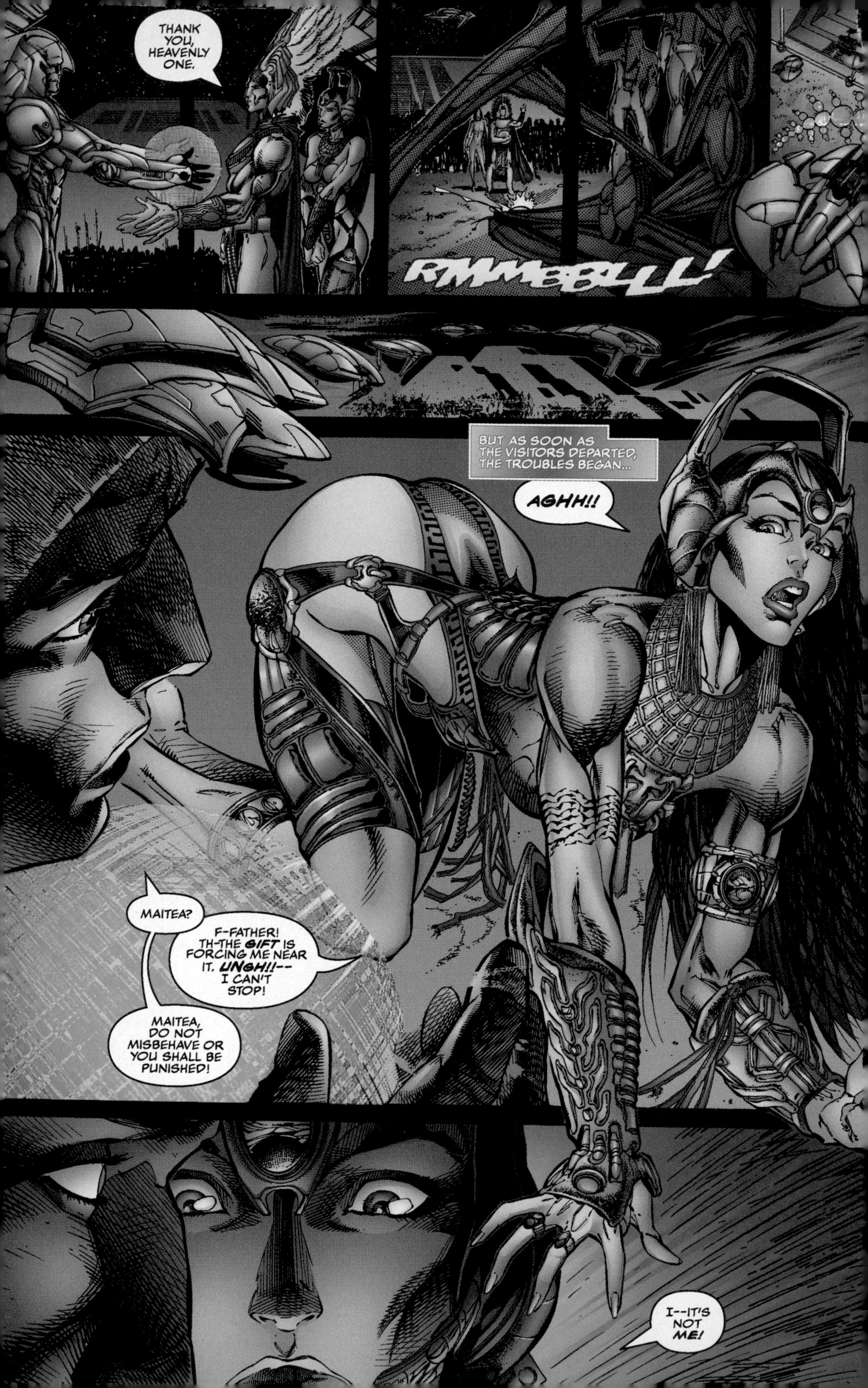
THANK YOU, HEAVENLY ONE.
RMMBLLL!
BUT AS SOON AS THE VISITORS DEPARTED, THE TROUBLES BEGAN...
AGHH!!
MAITEA?
F-FATHER! TH-THE GIFT IS FORCING ME NEAR IT. UNGH!!-- I CAN'T STOP!
MAITEA, DO NOT MISBEHAVE OR YOU SHALL BE PUNISHED!
I--IT'S NOT ME!

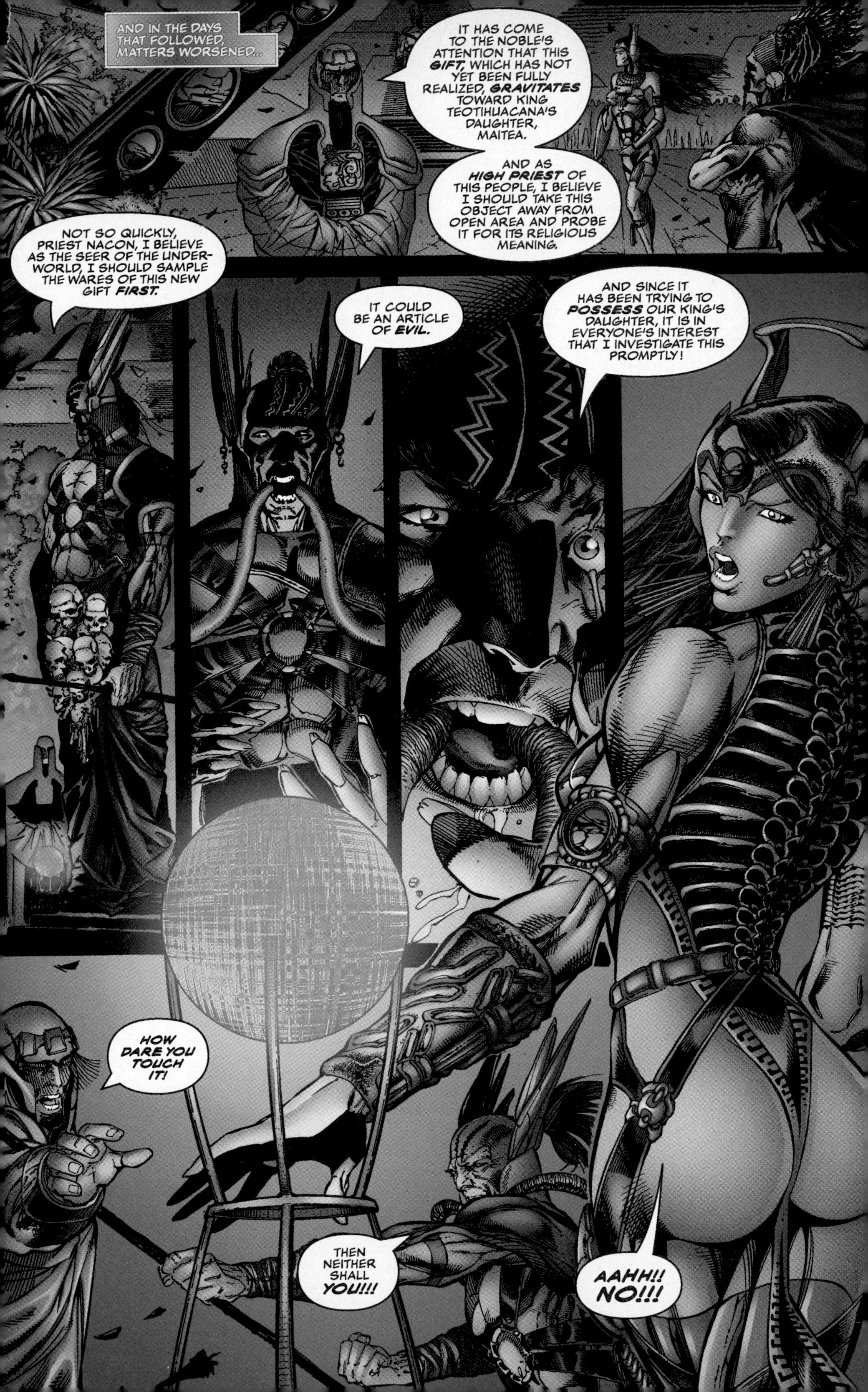
AND IN THE DAYS THAT FOLLOWED, MATTERS WORSENED...
IT HAS COME TO THE NOBLE'S ATTENTION THAT THIS GIFT, WHICH HAS NOT YET BEEN FULLY REALIZED, GRAVITATES TOWARD KING TEOTIHUACANA'S DAUGHTER, MAITEA.
AND AS HIGH PRIEST OF THIS PEOPLE, I BELIEVE I SHOULD TAKE THIS OBJECT AWAY FROM OPEN AREA AND PROBE IT FOR ITS RELIGIOUS MEANING.
NOT SO QUICKLY, PRIEST NACON, I BELIEVE AS THE SEER OF THE UNDER-WORLD, I SHOULD SAMPLE THE WARES OF THIS NEW GIFT FIRST.
IT COULD BE AN ARTICLE OF EVIL.
AND SINCE IT HAS BEEN TRYING TO POSSESS OUR KING'S DAUGHTER, IT IS IN EVERYONE'S INTEREST THAT I INVESTIGATE THIS PROMPTLY!
HOW DARE YOU TOUCH IT!
THEN NEITHER SHALL YOU!!!
AAHH!! NO!!!

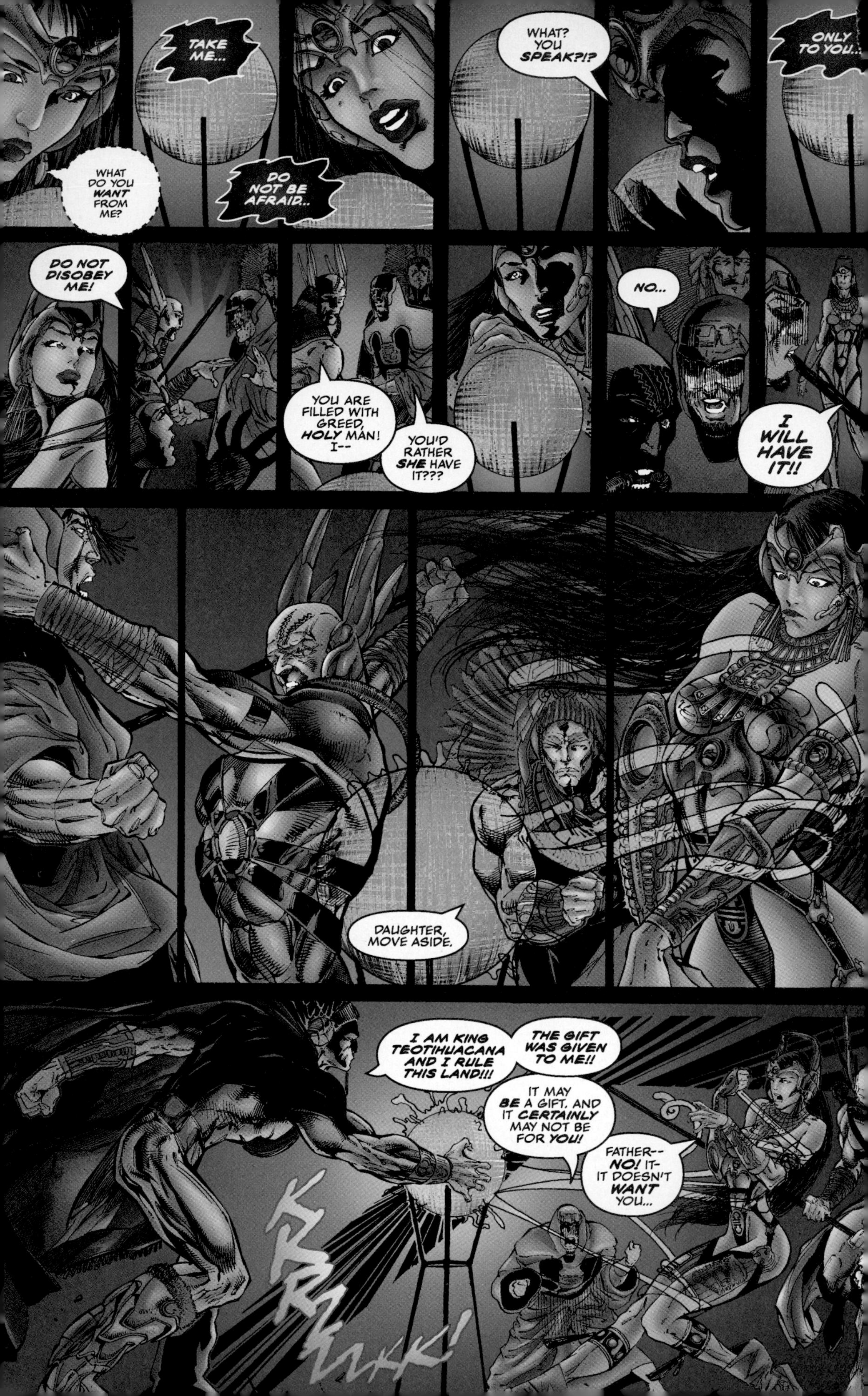

TAKE ME...
WHAT DO YOU WANT FROM ME?
DO NOT BE AFRAID...
WHAT? YOU SPEAK?!?
ONLY TO YOU...
DO NOT DISOBEY ME!
YOU ARE FILLED WITH GREED, HOLY MAN! I--
YOU'D RATHER SHE HAVE IT???
NO...
I WILL HAVE IT!!
DAUGHTER, MOVE ASIDE.
I AM KING TEOTIHUACANA AND I RULE THIS LAND!!!
THE GIFT WAS GIVEN TO ME!!
IT MAY BE A GIFT, AND IT CERTAINLY MAY NOT BE FOR YOU!
FATHER-- NO! IT-- IT DOESN'T WANT YOU...
KRRAKK!

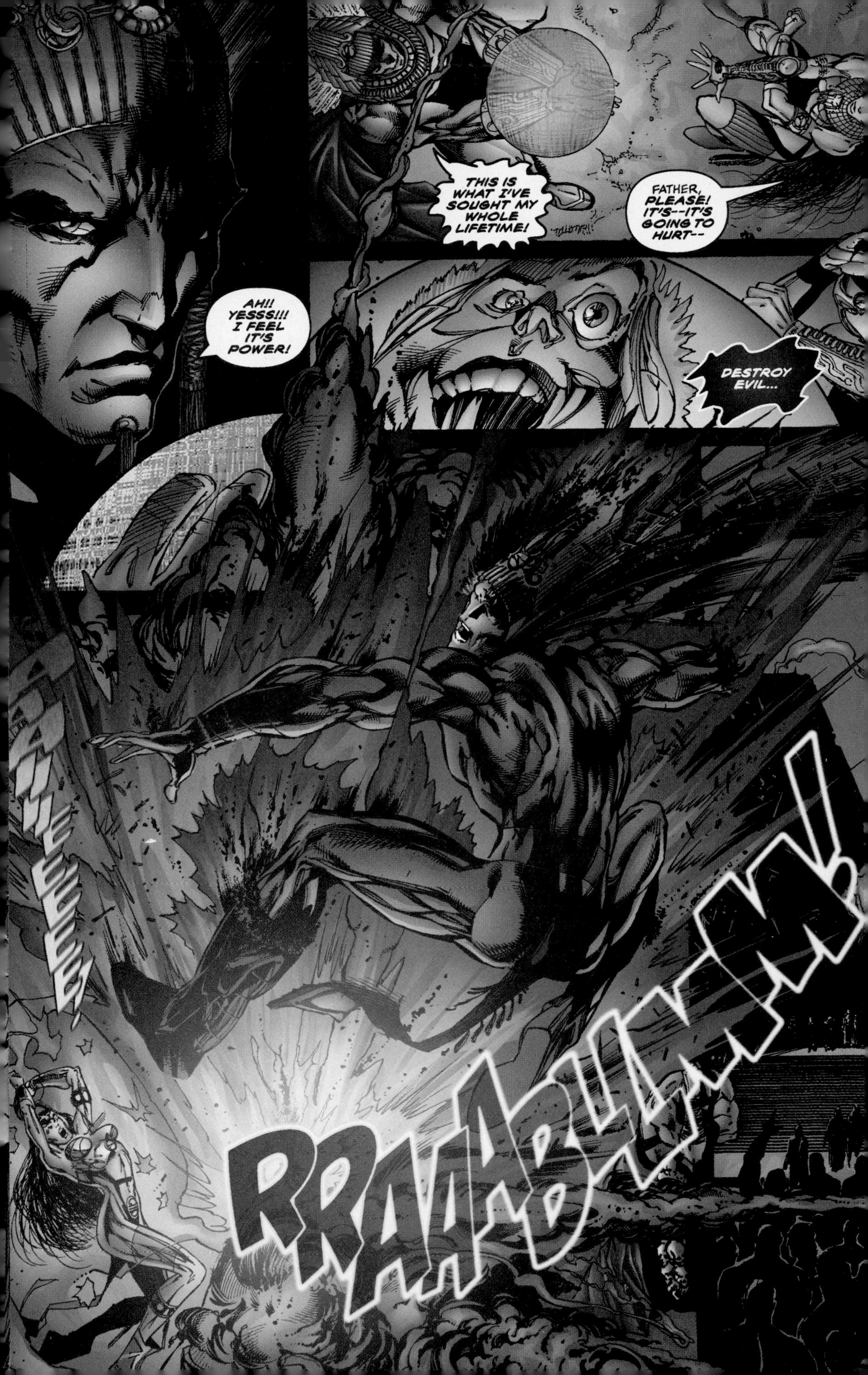
THIS IS WHAT I'VE SOUGHT MY WHOLE LIFETIME!
FATHER, PLEASE! IT'S--IT'S GOING TO HURT--
AH!! YESSS!!! I FEEL IT'S POWER!
DESTROY EVIL...
RRAABLAMM!

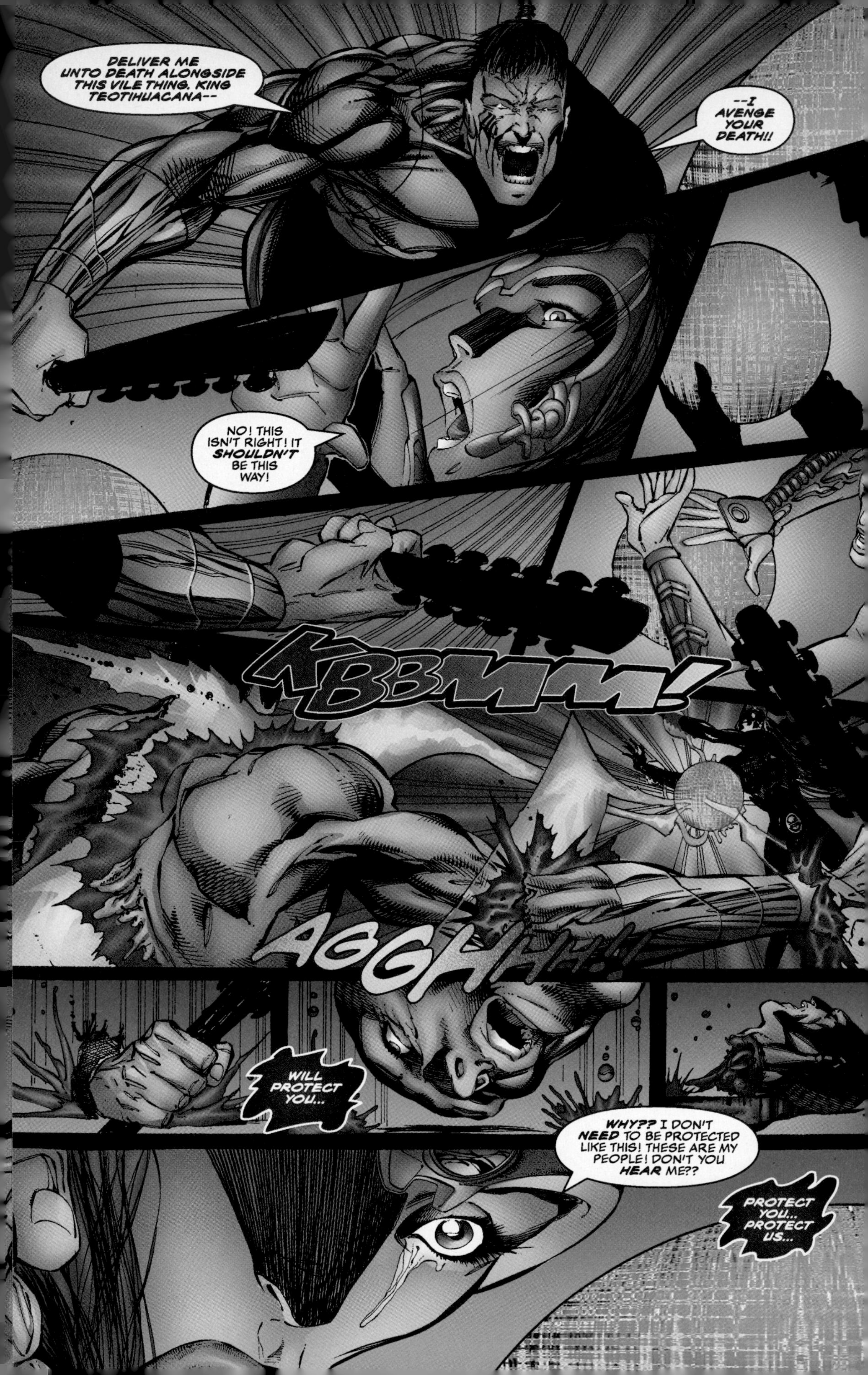
DELIVER ME UNTO DEATH ALONGSIDE THIS VILE THING. KING TEOTIHUACANA--
--I AVENGE YOUR DEATH!!
NO! THIS ISN'T RIGHT! IT SHOULDN'T BE THIS WAY!
KBBMMM!
AGGHHH!!
WILL PROTECT YOU...
WHY?? I DON'T NEED TO BE PROTECTED LIKE THIS! THESE ARE MY PEOPLE! DON'T YOU HEAR ME??
PROTECT YOU... PROTECT US...

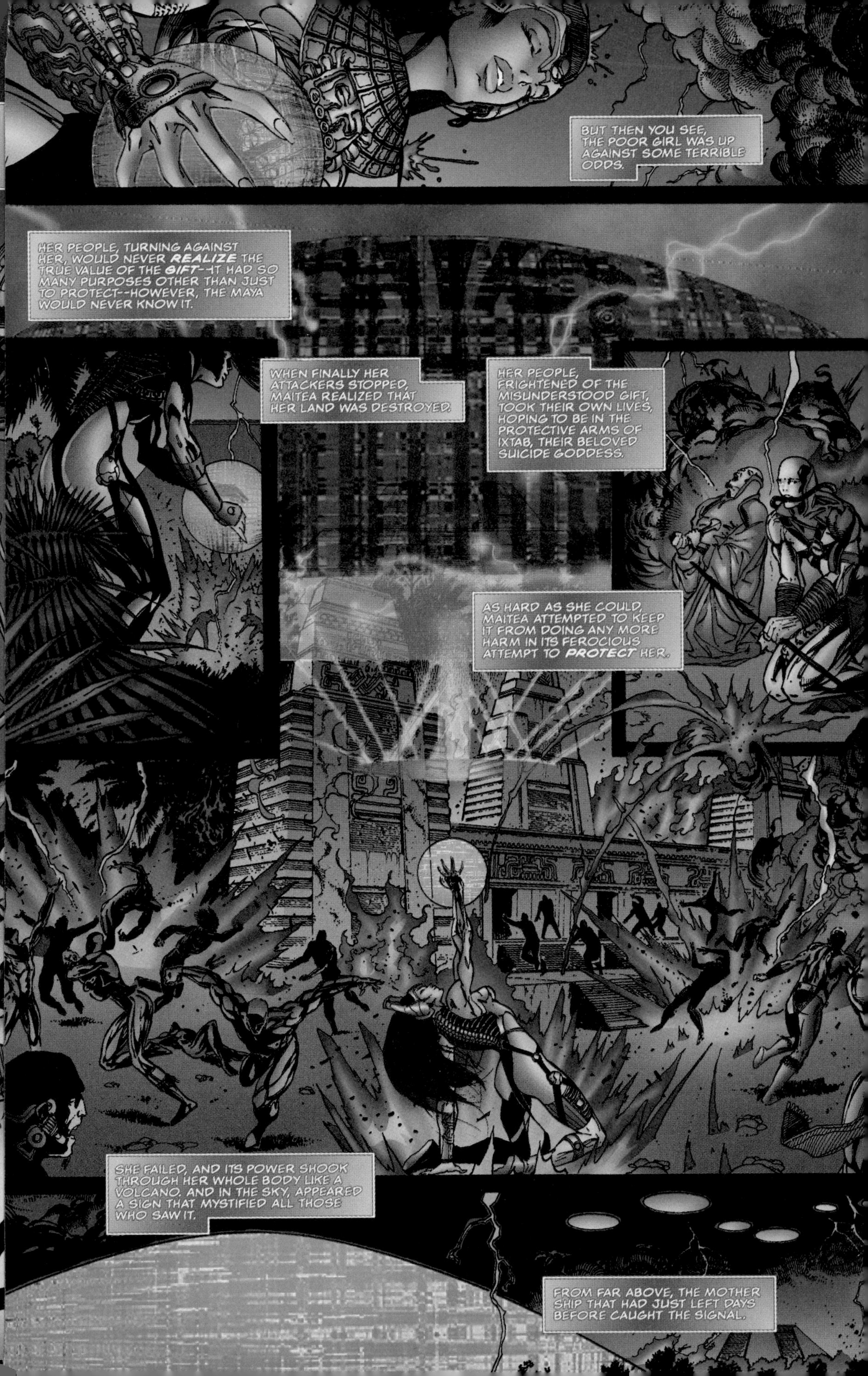
BUT THEN YOU SEE, THE POOR GIRL WAS UP AGAINST SOME TERRIBLE ODDS.
HER PEOPLE, TURNING AGAINST HER, WOULD NEVER REALIZE THE TRUE VALUE OF THE GIFT--IT HAD SO MANY PURPOSES OTHER THAN JUST TO PROTECT--HOWEVER, THE MAYA WOULD NEVER KNOW IT.
WHEN FINALLY HER ATTACKERS STOPPED, MAITEA REALIZED THAT HER LAND WAS DESTROYED.
HER PEOPLE, FRIGHTENED OF THE MISUNDERSTOOD GIFT, TOOK THEIR OWN LIVES, HOPING TO BE IN THE PROTECTIVE ARMS OF IXTAB, THEIR BELOVED SUICIDE GODDESS.
AS HARD AS SHE COULD, MAITEA ATTEMPTED TO KEEP IT FROM DOING ANY MORE HARM IN ITS FEROCIOUS ATTEMPT TO PROTECT HER.
SHE FAILED, AND ITS POWER SHOOK THROUGH HER WHOLE BODY LIKE A VOLCANO. AND IN THE SKY, APPEARED A SIGN THAT MYSTIFIED ALL THOSE WHO SAW IT.
FROM FAR ABOVE, THE MOTHER SHIP THAT HAD JUST LEFT DAYS BEFORE CAUGHT THE SIGNAL.

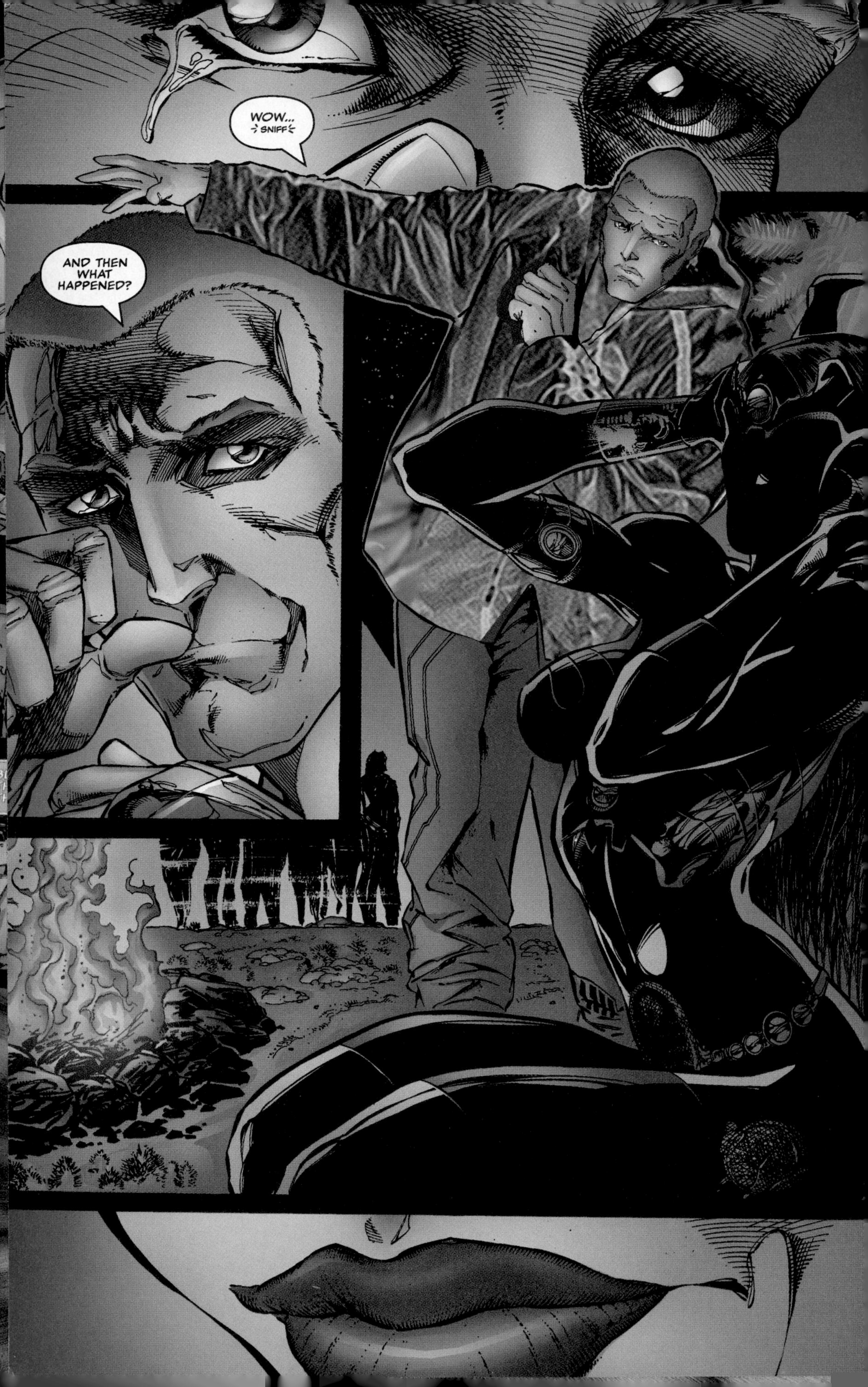
WOW...
SNIFF
AND THEN WHAT HAPPENED?

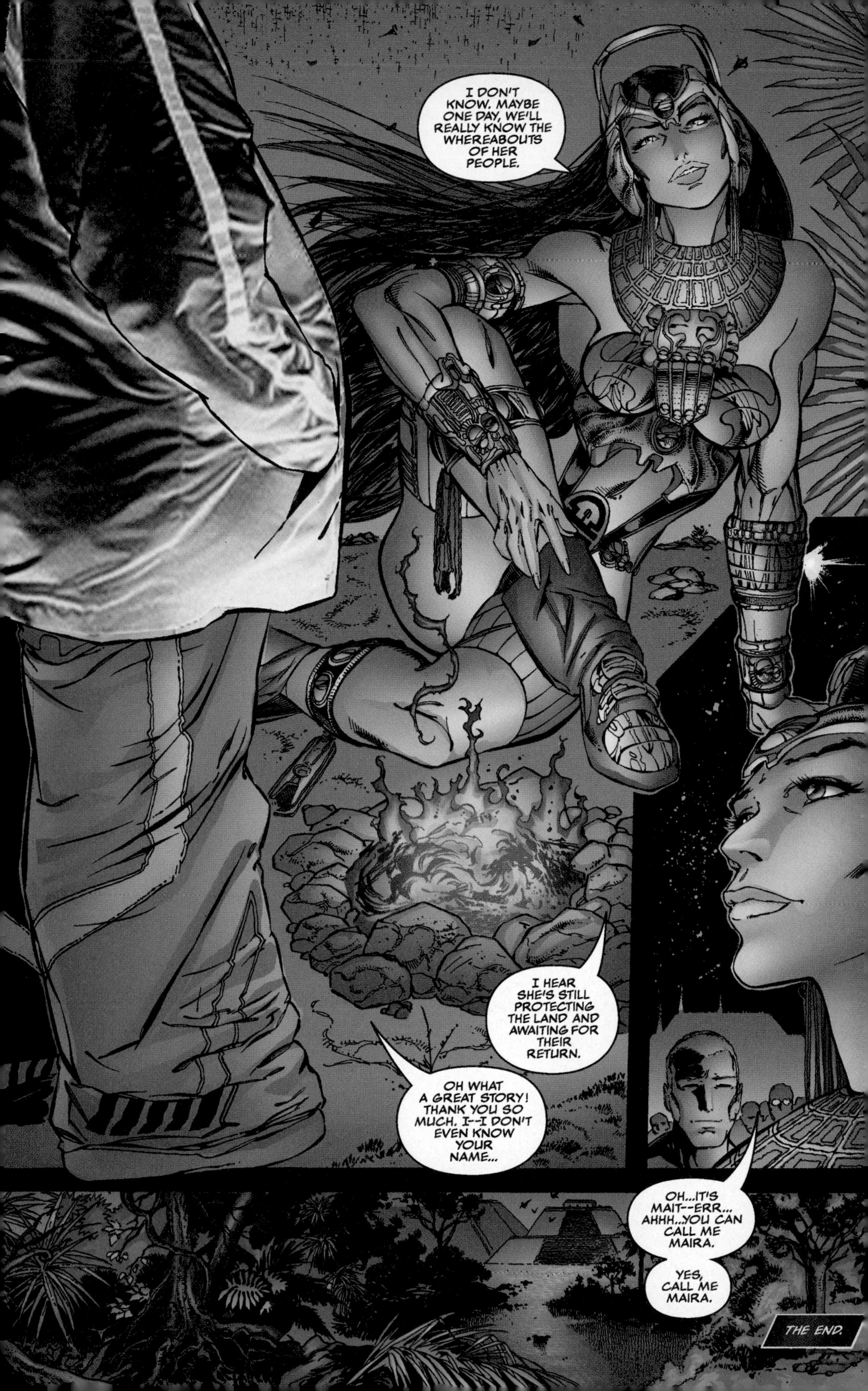
I DON'T KNOW. MAYBE ONE DAY, WE'LL REALLY KNOW THE WHEREABOUTS OF HER PEOPLE.
I HEAR SHE'S STILL PROTECTING THE LAND AND AWAITING FOR THEIR RETURN.
OH WHAT A GREAT STORY! THANK YOU SO MUCH. I--I DON'T EVEN KNOW YOUR NAME...
OH...IT'S MAIT--ERR... AHHH...YOU CAN CALL ME MAIRA.
YES, CALL ME MAIRA.
THE END.

TALES of the WITCHBLADE

STORY by
David Finch

PENCILED by
Clarence Lansang
Cedric Nocon
Randy Green
Billy Tan
Dan Fraga

INKED by
Jason Gorder
Jonathan Sibal
Victor Llamas
Marlo Alquiza
Billy Tan

COLORED by
Matt Nelson
Monica Kubina
Quantum Color FX
Brian Buccellato
Scott Gordon

LETTERED by
Dennis Heisler

COVER by
Randy Green,
Jonathan Sibal·
and
Matt Nelson

SAMANTHA

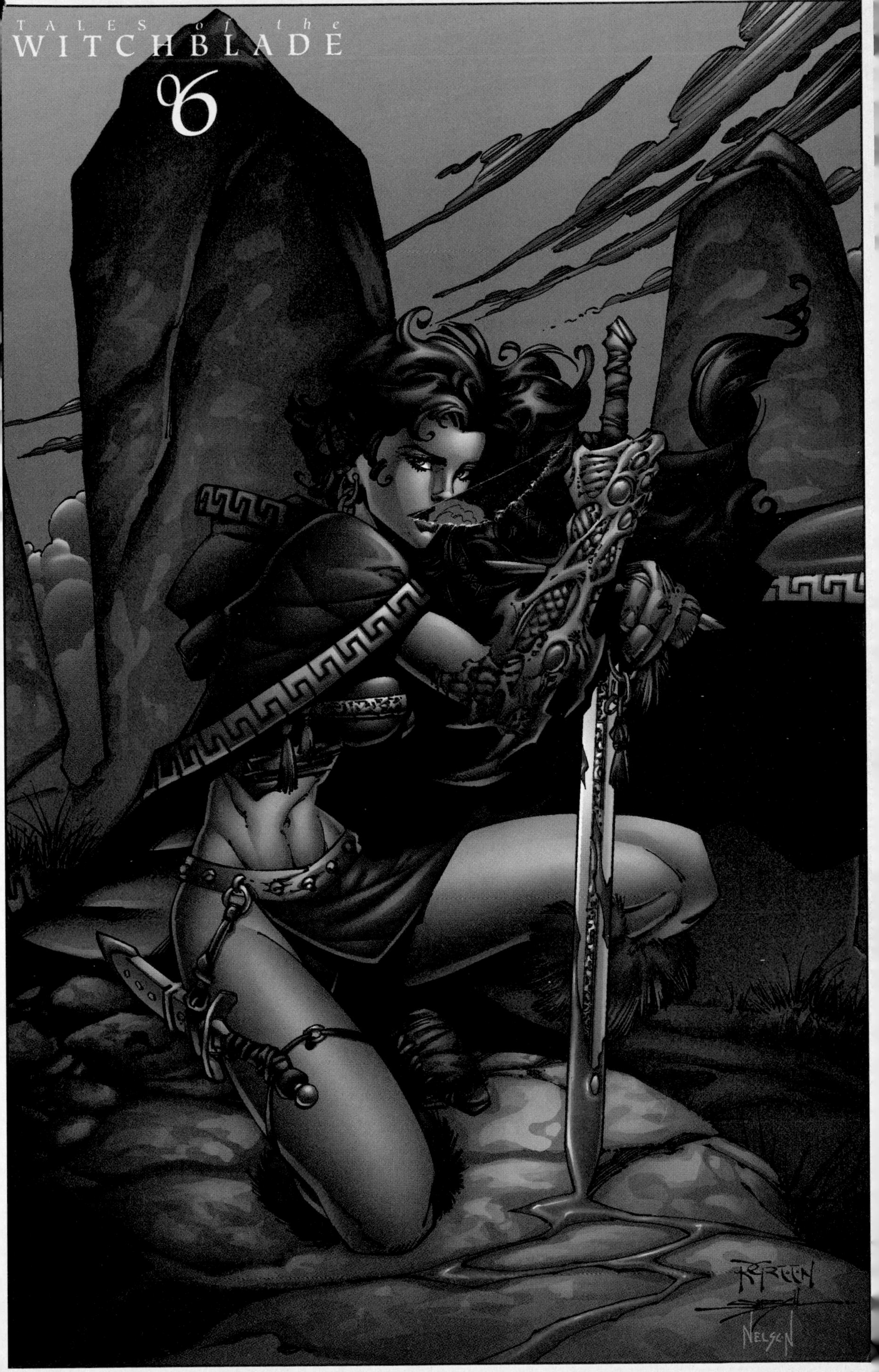
TALES of the
WITCHBLADE
06
NELSON

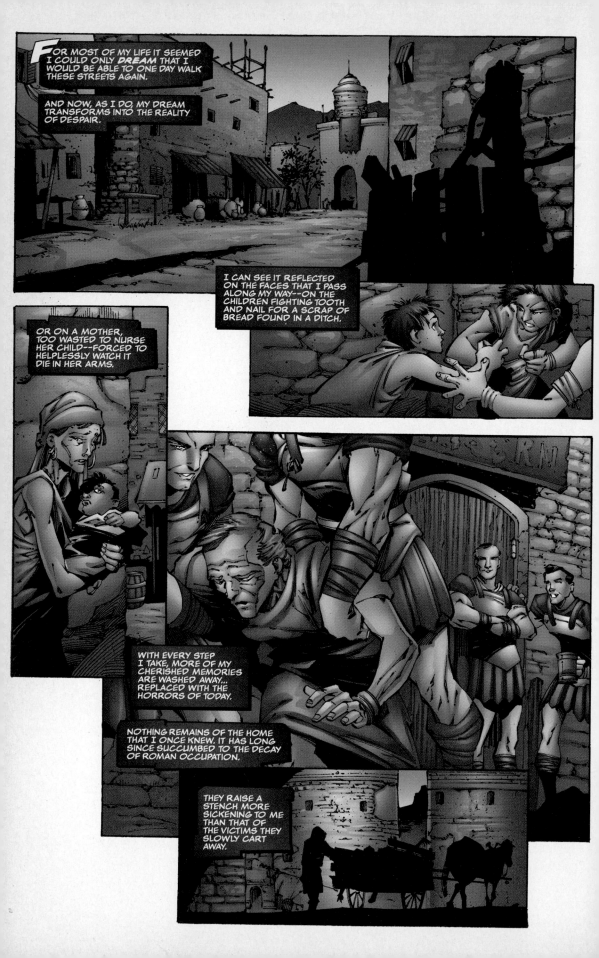

FOR MOST OF MY LIFE IT SEEMED I COULD ONLY *DREAM* THAT I WOULD BE ABLE TO ONE DAY WALK THESE STREETS AGAIN.

AND NOW, AS I DO, MY DREAM TRANSFORMS INTO THE REALITY OF DESPAIR.

I CAN SEE IT REFLECTED ON THE FACES THAT I PASS ALONG MY WAY--ON THE CHILDREN FIGHTING TOOTH AND NAIL FOR A SCRAP OF BREAD FOUND IN A DITCH.

OR ON A MOTHER, TOO WASTED TO NURSE HER CHILD--FORCED TO HELPLESSLY WATCH IT DIE IN HER ARMS.

WITH EVERY STEP I TAKE, MORE OF MY CHERISHED MEMORIES ARE WASHED AWAY... REPLACED WITH THE HORRORS OF TODAY.

NOTHING REMAINS OF THE HOME THAT I ONCE KNEW. IT HAS LONG SINCE SUCCUMBED TO THE DECAY OF ROMAN OCCUPATION.

THEY RAISE A STENCH MORE SICKENING TO ME THAN THAT OF THE VICTIMS THEY SLOWLY CART AWAY.

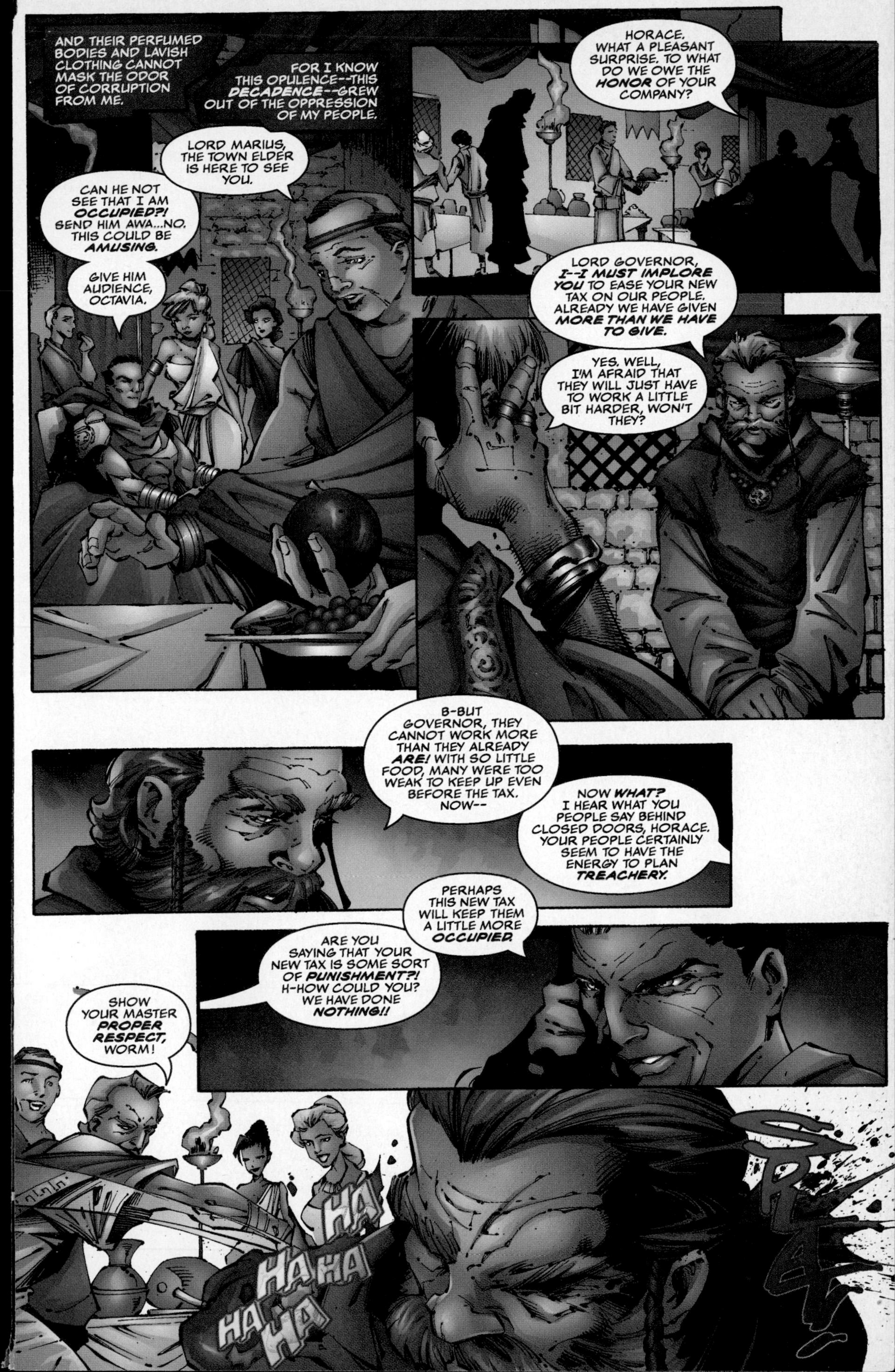
AND THEIR PERFUMED BODIES AND LAVISH CLOTHING CANNOT MASK THE ODOR OF CORRUPTION FROM ME.
FOR I KNOW THIS OPULENCE--THIS DECADENCE--GREW OUT OF THE OPPRESSION OF MY PEOPLE.
LORD MARIUS, THE TOWN ELDER IS HERE TO SEE YOU.
CAN HE NOT SEE THAT I AM OCCUPIED?! SEND HIM AWA...NO. THIS COULD BE AMUSING.
GIVE HIM AUDIENCE, OCTAVIA.
HORACE. WHAT A PLEASANT SURPRISE. TO WHAT DO WE OWE THE HONOR OF YOUR COMPANY?
LORD GOVERNOR, I--I MUST IMPLORE YOU TO EASE YOUR NEW TAX ON OUR PEOPLE. ALREADY WE HAVE GIVEN MORE THAN WE HAVE TO GIVE.
YES. WELL, I'M AFRAID THAT THEY WILL JUST HAVE TO WORK A LITTLE BIT HARDER, WON'T THEY?
B-BUT GOVERNOR, THEY CANNOT WORK MORE THAN THEY ALREADY ARE! WITH SO LITTLE FOOD, MANY WERE TOO WEAK TO KEEP UP EVEN BEFORE THE TAX. NOW--
NOW WHAT? I HEAR WHAT YOU PEOPLE SAY BEHIND CLOSED DOORS, HORACE. YOUR PEOPLE CERTAINLY SEEM TO HAVE THE ENERGY TO PLAN TREACHERY.
PERHAPS THIS NEW TAX WILL KEEP THEM A LITTLE MORE OCCUPIED.
ARE YOU SAYING THAT YOUR NEW TAX IS SOME SORT OF PUNISHMENT?! H-HOW COULD YOU? WE HAVE DONE NOTHING!!
SHOW YOUR MASTER PROPER RESPECT, WORM!
HA HA HA HA HA HA

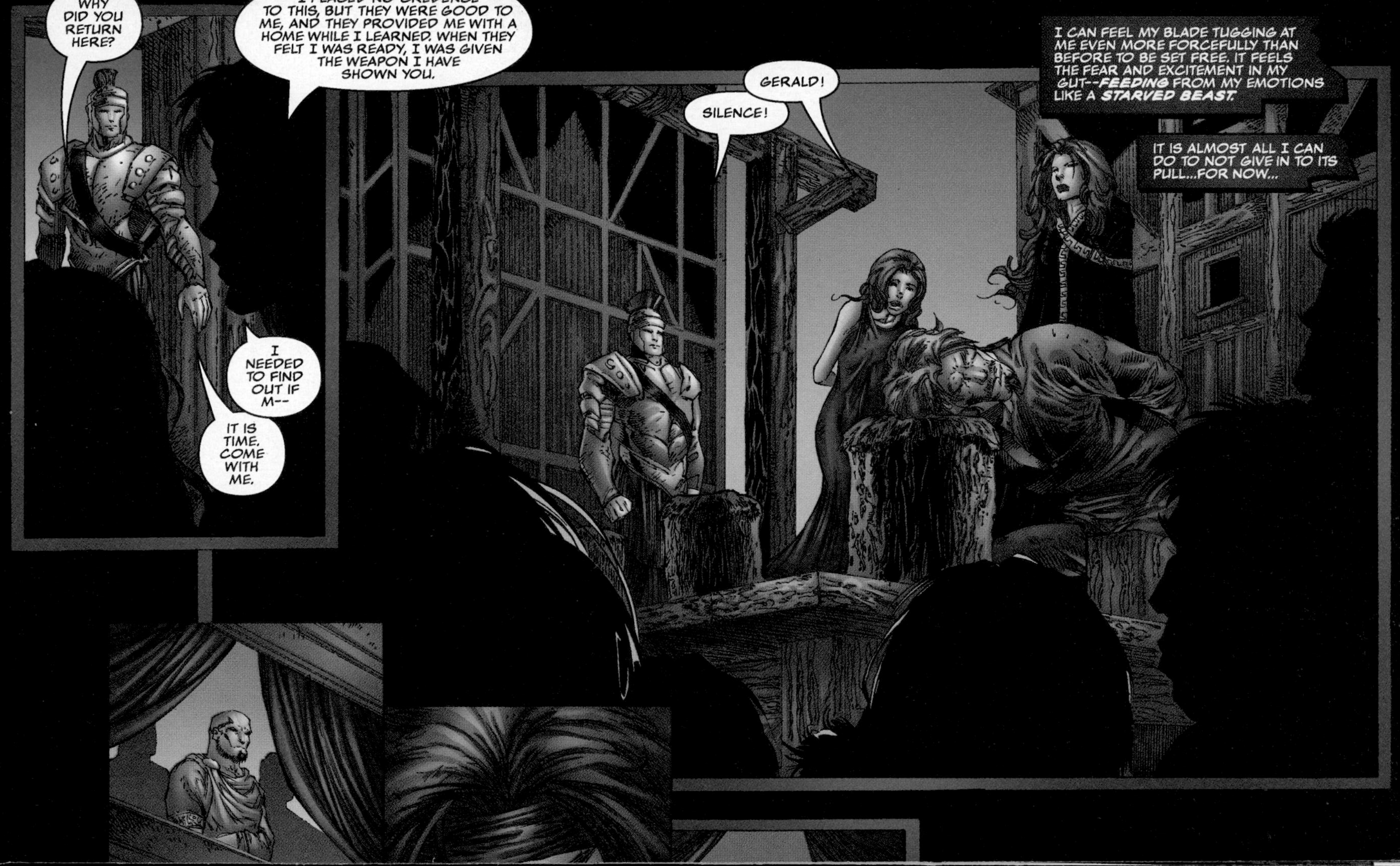
WHY DID YOU RETURN HERE?
I PLACED NO CREDENCE TO THIS, BUT THEY WERE GOOD TO ME, AND THEY PROVIDED ME WITH A HOME WHILE I LEARNED. WHEN THEY FELT I WAS READY, I WAS GIVEN THE WEAPON I HAVE SHOWN YOU.
I NEEDED TO FIND OUT IF M--
IT IS TIME. COME WITH ME.
GERALD!
SILENCE!
I CAN FEEL MY BLADE TUGGING AT ME EVEN MORE FORCEFULLY THAN BEFORE TO BE SET FREE. IT FEELS THE FEAR AND EXCITEMENT IN MY GUT--FEEDING FROM MY EMOTIONS LIKE A STARVED BEAST.
IT IS ALMOST ALL I CAN DO TO NOT GIVE IN TO ITS PULL...FOR NOW...

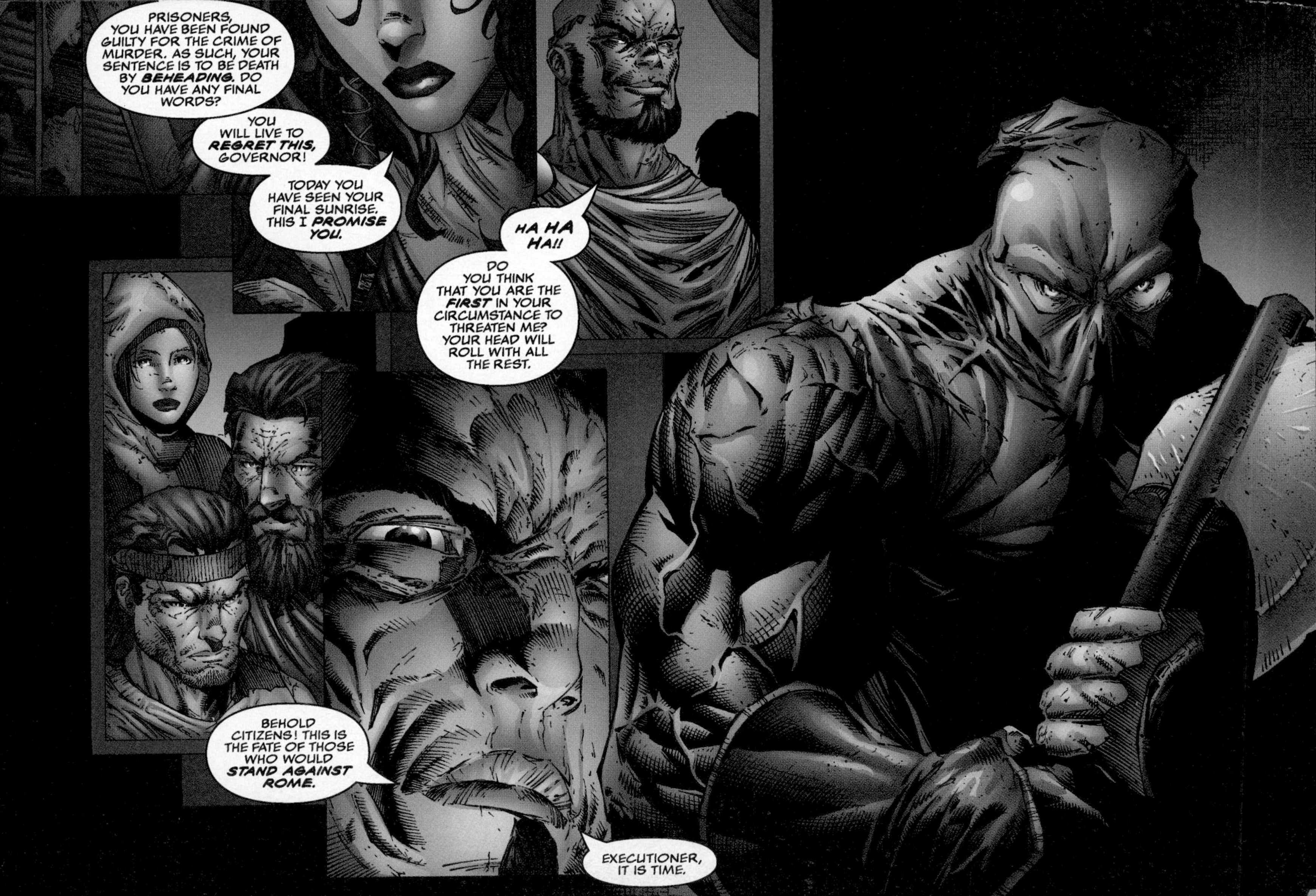
PRISONERS, YOU HAVE BEEN FOUND GUILTY FOR THE CRIME OF MURDER. AS SUCH, YOUR SENTENCE IS TO BE DEATH BY **BEHEADING.** DO YOU HAVE ANY FINAL WORDS?
YOU WILL LIVE TO **REGRET THIS,** GOVERNOR!
TODAY YOU HAVE SEEN YOUR FINAL SUNRISE. THIS I **PROMISE YOU.**
HA HA HA!!
DO YOU THINK THAT YOU ARE THE **FIRST** IN YOUR CIRCUMSTANCE TO THREATEN ME? YOUR HEAD WILL ROLL WITH ALL THE REST.
BEHOLD CITIZENS! THIS IS THE FATE OF THOSE WHO WOULD **STAND AGAINST ROME.**
EXECUTIONER, IT IS TIME.

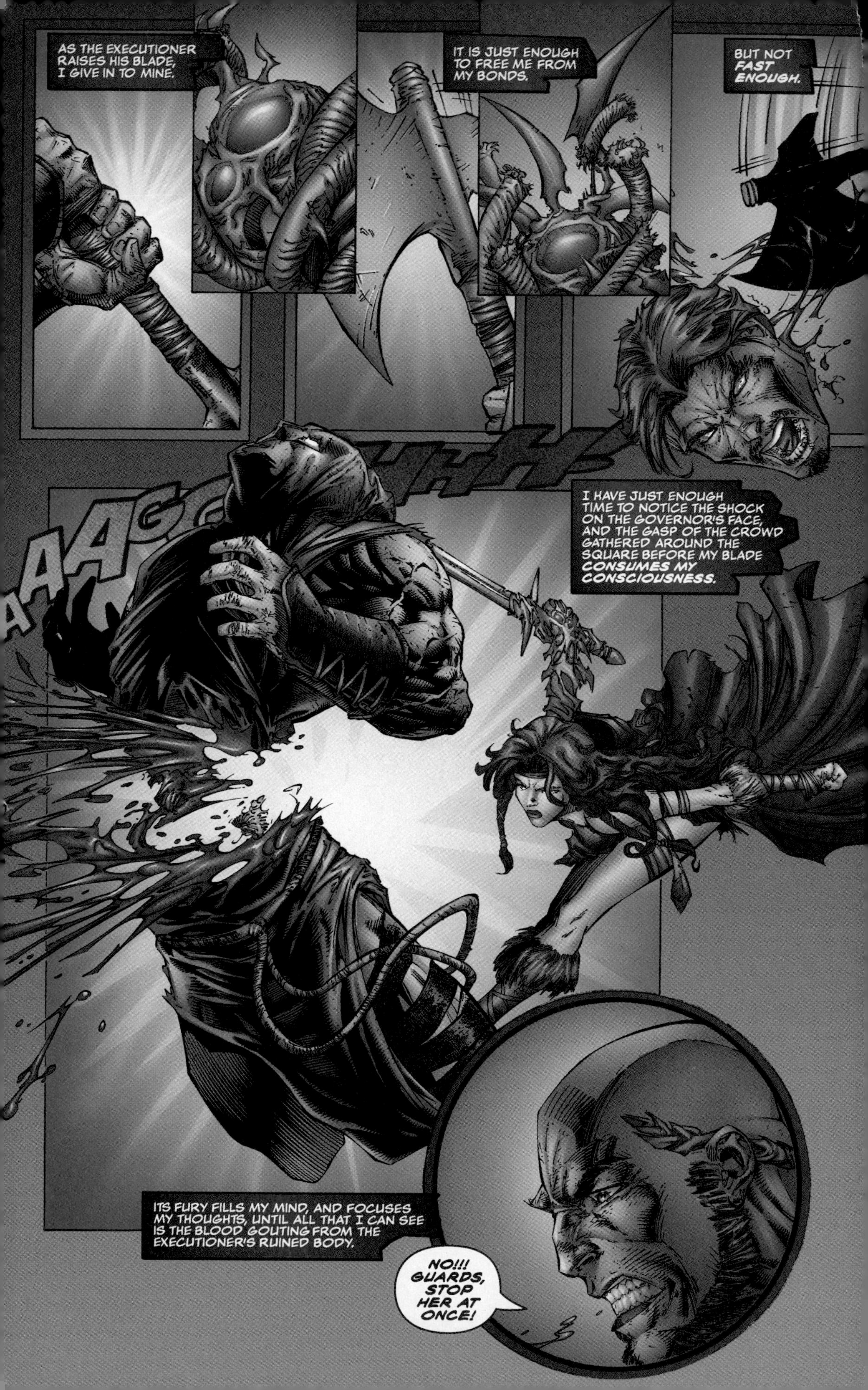

AS THE EXECUTIONER RAISES HIS BLADE, I GIVE IN TO MINE.
IT IS JUST ENOUGH TO FREE ME FROM MY BONDS.
BUT NOT FAST ENOUGH.
I HAVE JUST ENOUGH TIME TO NOTICE THE SHOCK ON THE GOVERNOR'S FACE, AND THE GASP OF THE CROWD GATHERED AROUND THE SQUARE BEFORE MY BLADE CONSUMES MY CONSCIOUSNESS.
ITS FURY FILLS MY MIND, AND FOCUSES MY THOUGHTS, UNTIL ALL THAT I CAN SEE IS THE BLOOD GOUTING FROM THE EXECUTIONER'S RUINED BODY.
NO!!! GUARDS, STOP HER AT ONCE!

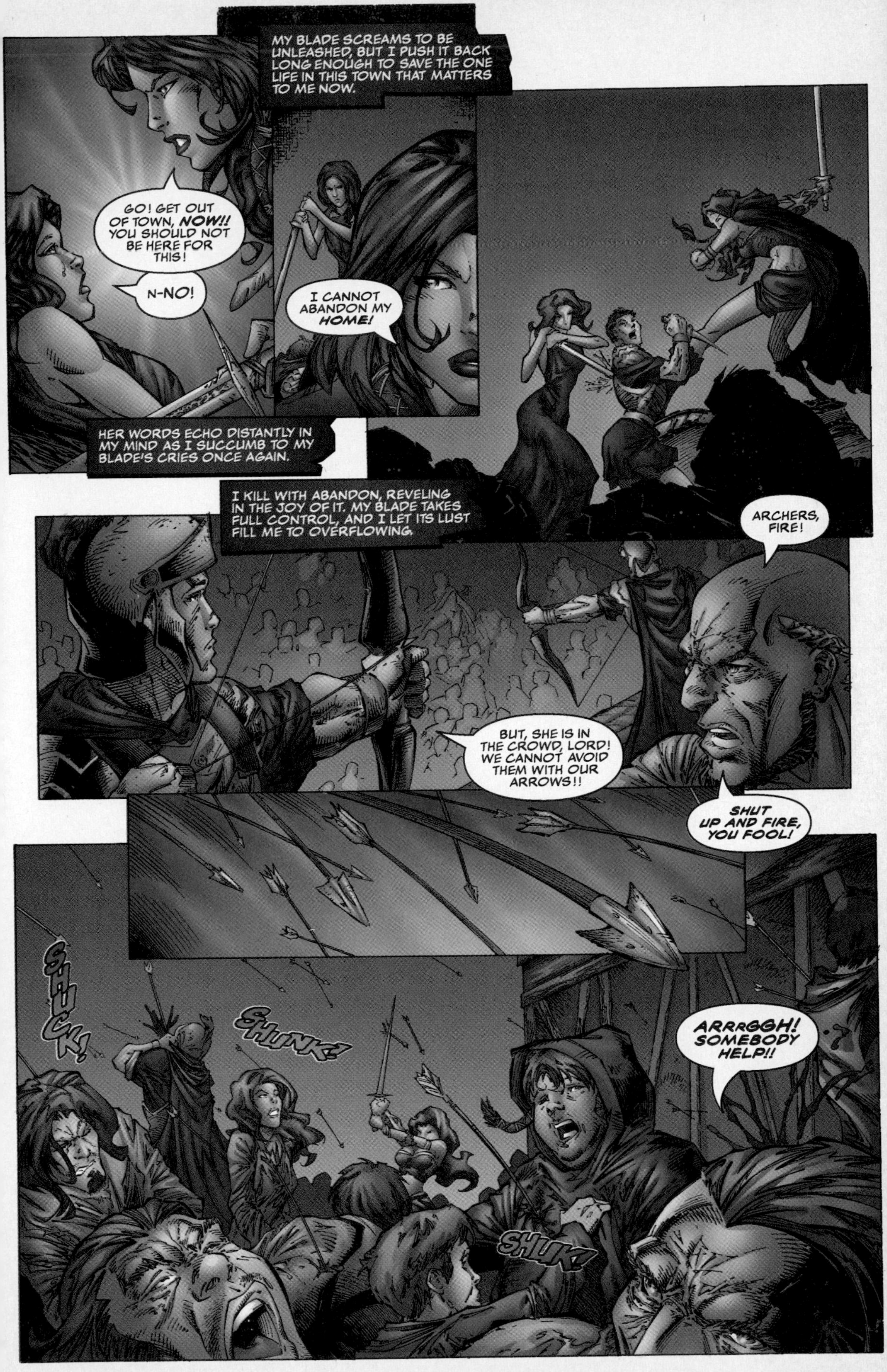
MY BLADE SCREAMS TO BE UNLEASHED, BUT I PUSH IT BACK LONG ENOUGH TO SAVE THE ONE LIFE IN THIS TOWN THAT MATTERS TO ME NOW.
GO! GET OUT OF TOWN, NOW!! YOU SHOULD NOT BE HERE FOR THIS!
N-NO!
I CANNOT ABANDON MY HOME!
HER WORDS ECHO DISTANTLY IN MY MIND AS I SUCCUMB TO MY BLADE'S CRIES ONCE AGAIN.
I KILL WITH ABANDON, REVELING IN THE JOY OF IT. MY BLADE TAKES FULL CONTROL, AND I LET ITS LUST FILL ME TO OVERFLOWING.
ARCHERS, FIRE!
BUT, SHE IS IN THE CROWD, LORD! WE CANNOT AVOID THEM WITH OUR ARROWS!!
SHUT UP AND FIRE, YOU FOOL!
SHUCK!
SHUNK!
ARRRGGH! SOMEBODY HELP!!
SHUK!

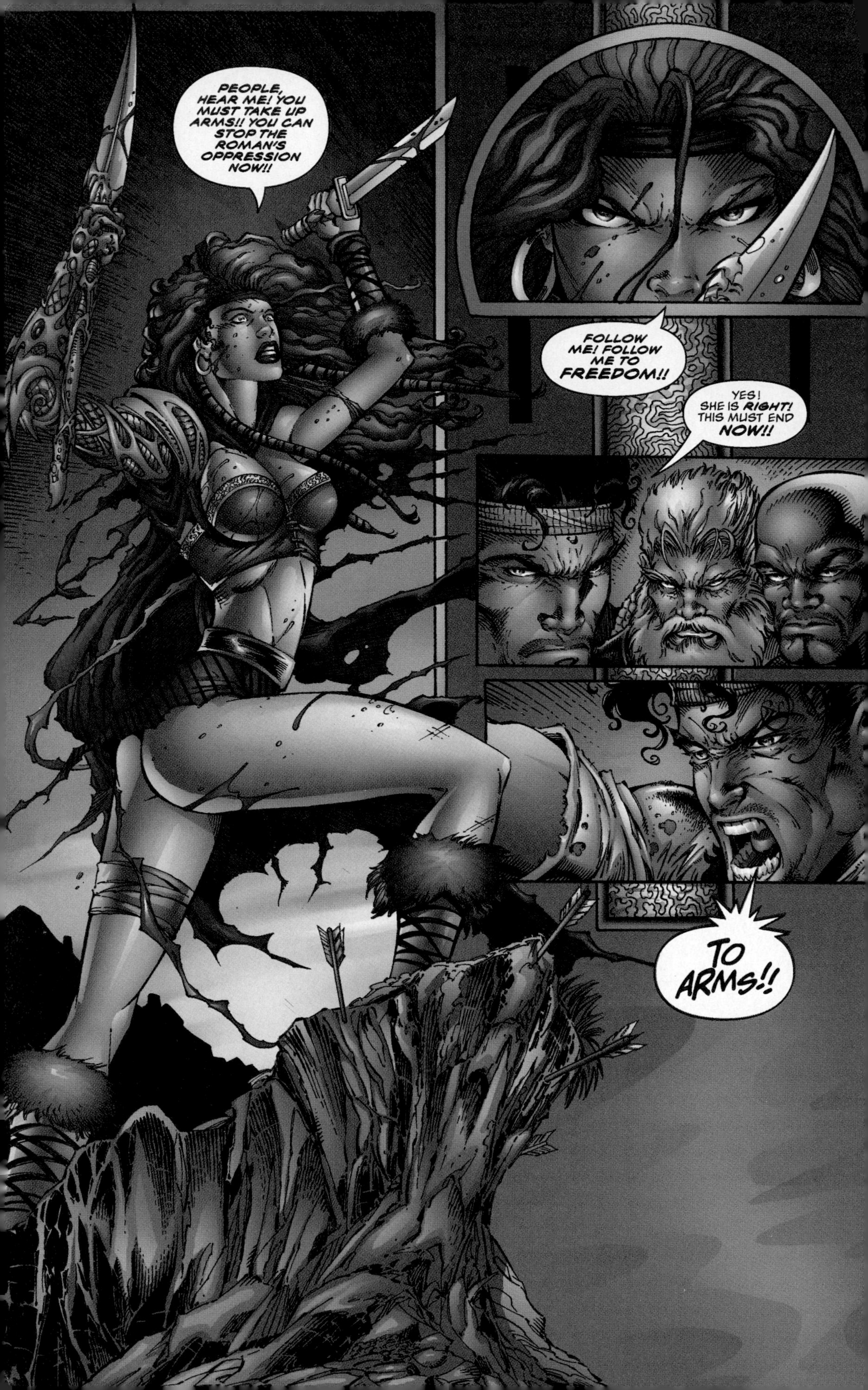
PEOPLE, HEAR ME! YOU MUST TAKE UP ARMS!! YOU CAN STOP THE ROMAN'S OPPRESSION NOW!!
FOLLOW ME! FOLLOW ME TO FREEDOM!!
YES! SHE IS RIGHT! THIS MUST END NOW!!
TO ARMS!!

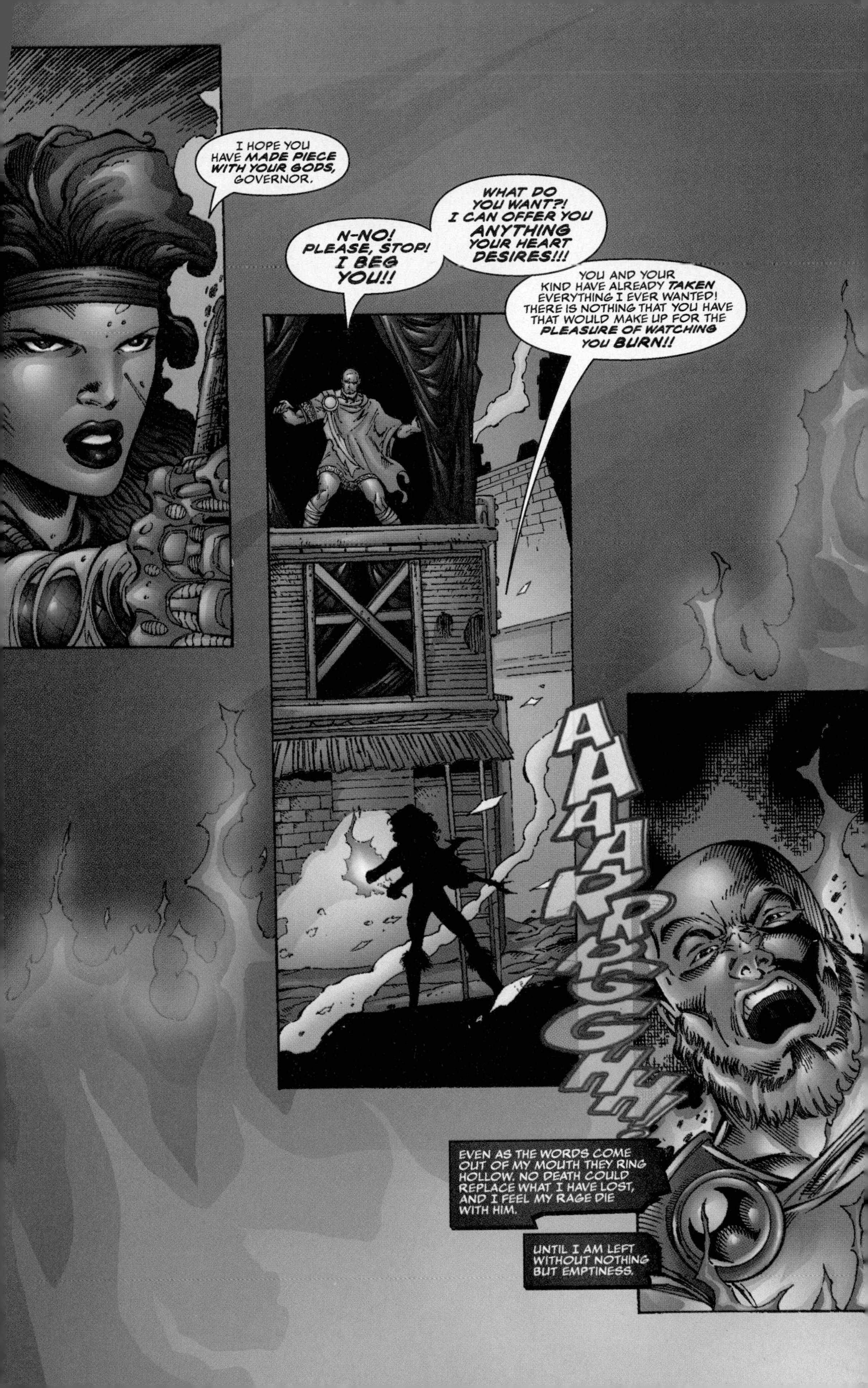
I HOPE YOU HAVE MADE PIECE WITH YOUR GODS, GOVERNOR.
N-NO! PLEASE, STOP! I BEG YOU!!
WHAT DO YOU WANT?! I CAN OFFER YOU ANYTHING YOUR HEART DESIRES!!!
YOU AND YOUR KIND HAVE ALREADY TAKEN EVERYTHING I EVER WANTED! THERE IS NOTHING THAT YOU HAVE THAT WOULD MAKE UP FOR THE PLEASURE OF WATCHING YOU BURN!!
AAAAARRGGHH!
EVEN AS THE WORDS COME OUT OF MY MOUTH THEY RING HOLLOW. NO DEATH COULD REPLACE WHAT I HAVE LOST, AND I FEEL MY RAGE DIE WITH HIM.
UNTIL I AM LEFT WITHOUT NOTHING BUT EMPTINESS.

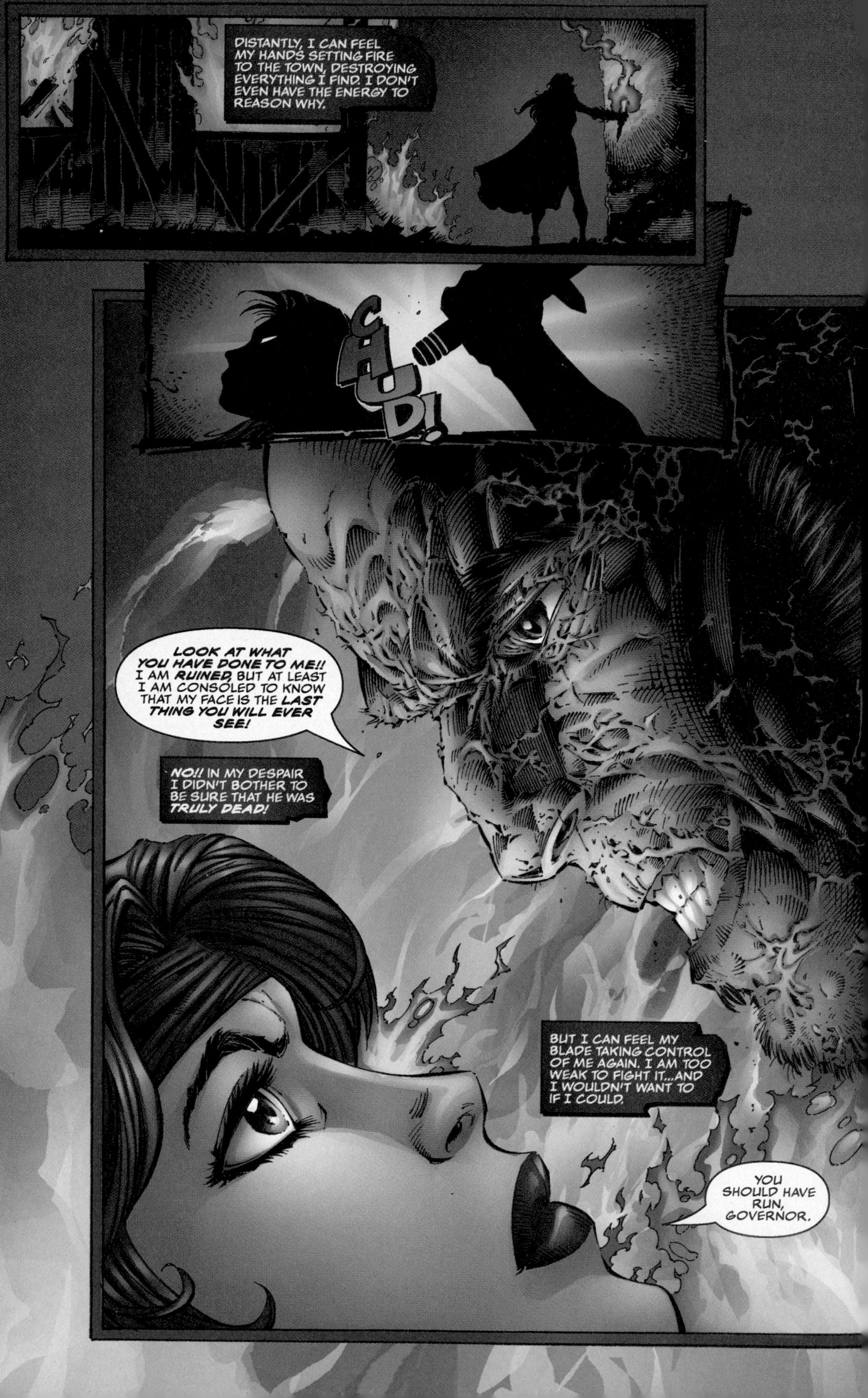
DISTANTLY, I CAN FEEL MY HANDS SETTING FIRE TO THE TOWN, DESTROYING EVERYTHING I FIND. I DON'T EVEN HAVE THE ENERGY TO REASON WHY.
CHUD!
LOOK AT WHAT YOU HAVE DONE TO ME!! I AM RUINED, BUT AT LEAST I AM CONSOLED TO KNOW THAT MY FACE IS THE LAST THING YOU WILL EVER SEE!
NO!! IN MY DESPAIR I DIDN'T BOTHER TO BE SURE THAT HE WAS TRULY DEAD!
BUT I CAN FEEL MY BLADE TAKING CONTROL OF ME AGAIN. I AM TOO WEAK TO FIGHT IT...AND I WOULDN'T WANT TO IF I COULD.
YOU SHOULD HAVE RUN, GOVERNOR.

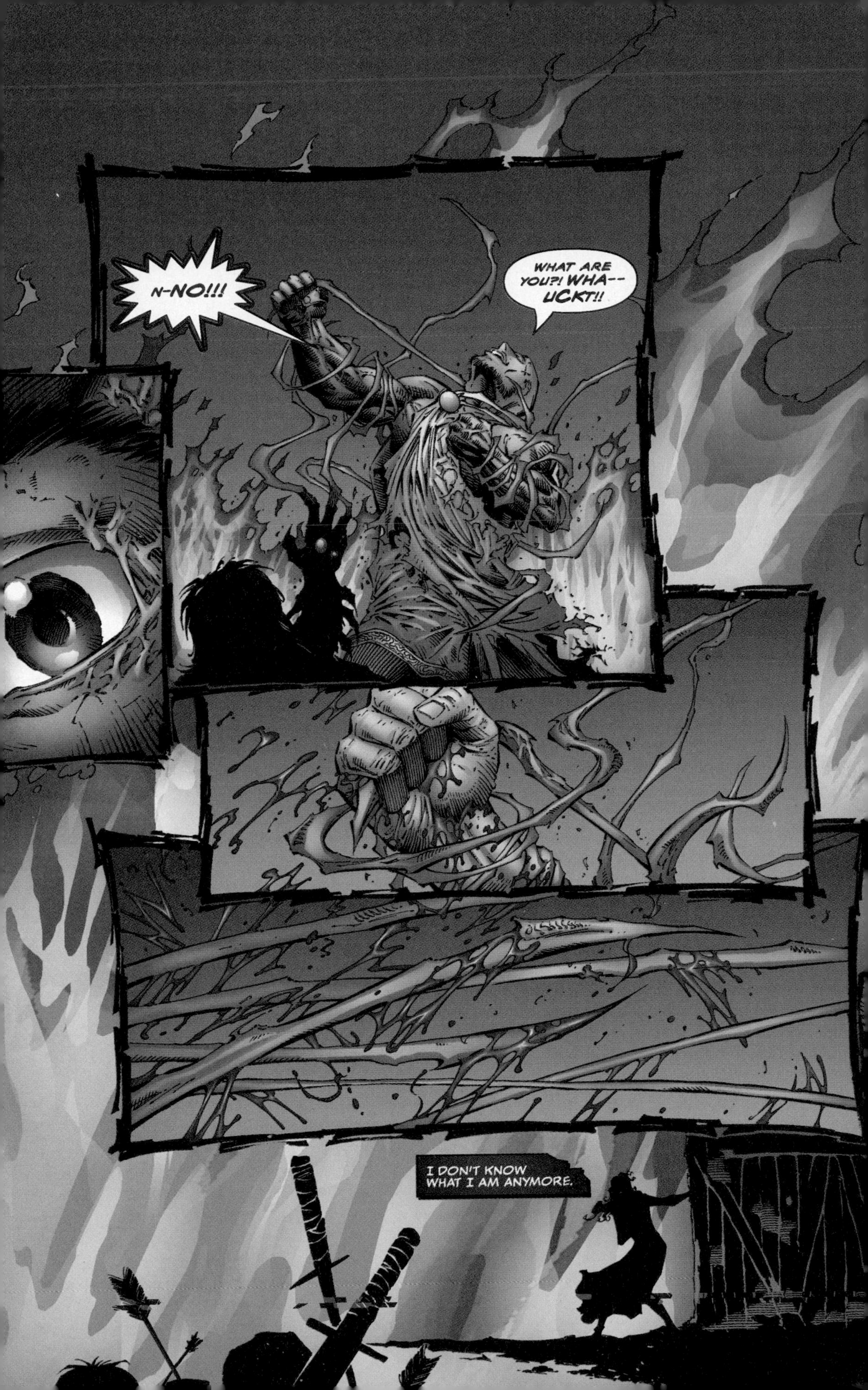
N-NO!!!
WHAT ARE YOU?! WHA-- UCKT!!
I DON'T KNOW WHAT I AM ANYMORE.

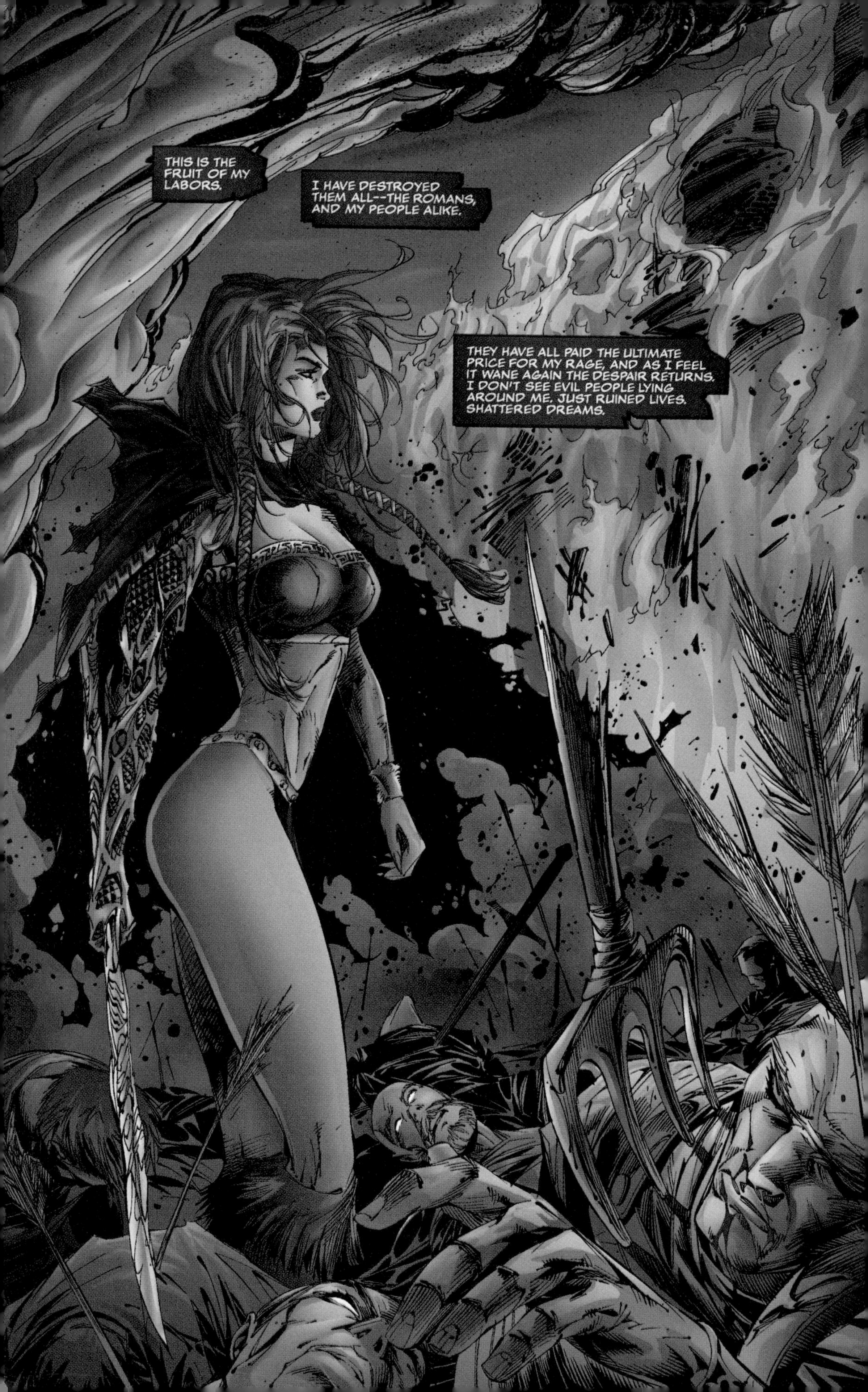
THIS IS THE FRUIT OF MY LABORS.
I HAVE DESTROYED THEM ALL--THE ROMANS, AND MY PEOPLE ALIKE.
THEY HAVE ALL PAID THE ULTIMATE PRICE FOR MY RAGE, AND AS I FEEL IT WANE AGAIN THE DESPAIR RETURNS. I DON'T SEE EVIL PEOPLE LYING AROUND ME, JUST RUINED LIVES. SHATTERED DREAMS.

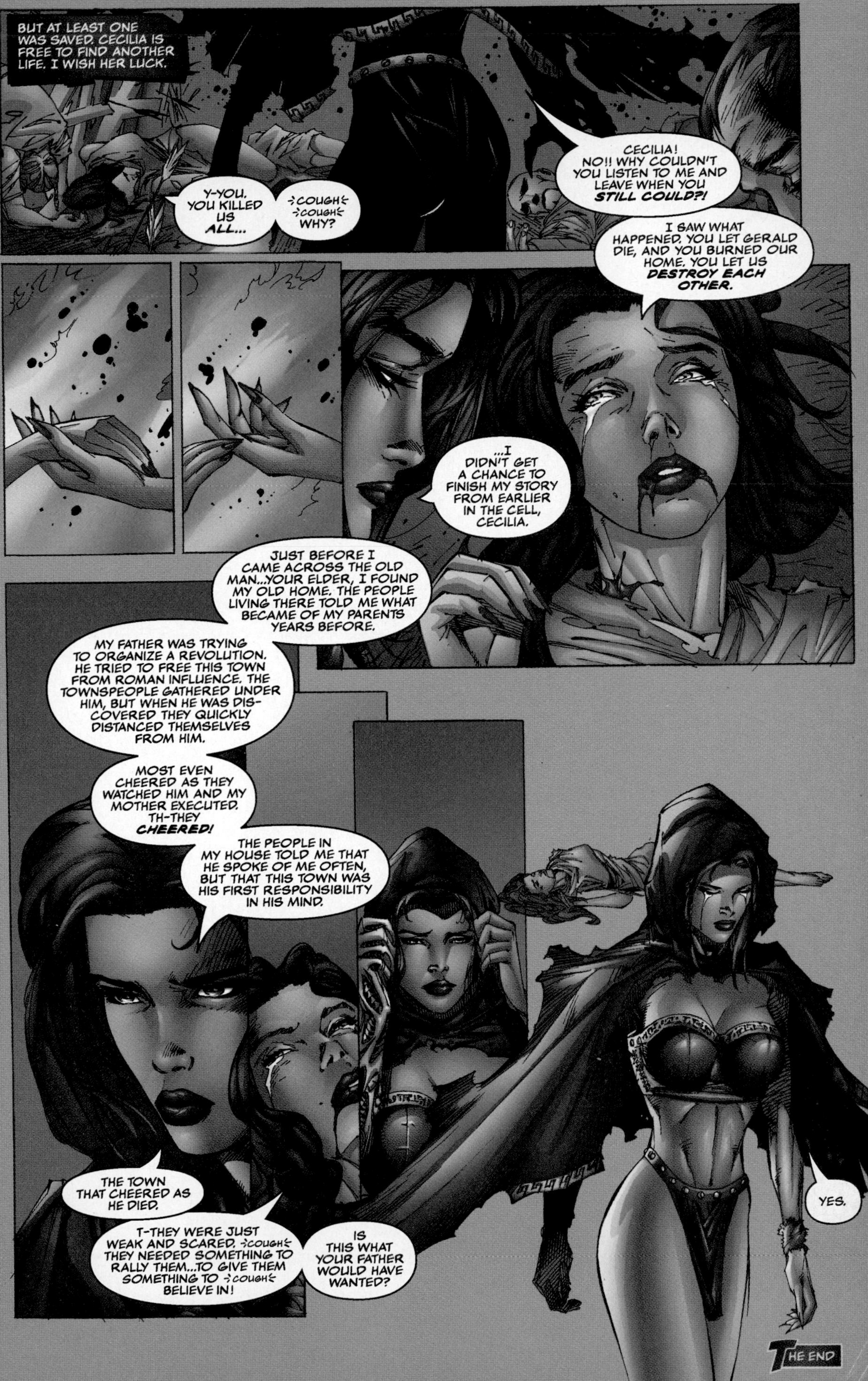
BUT AT LEAST ONE WAS SAVED. CECILIA IS FREE TO FIND ANOTHER LIFE. I WISH HER LUCK.
Y-YOU. YOU KILLED US ALL...
COUGH *COUGH* WHY?
CECILIA! NO!! WHY COULDN'T YOU LISTEN TO ME AND LEAVE WHEN YOU STILL COULD?!
I SAW WHAT HAPPENED. YOU LET GERALD DIE, AND YOU BURNED OUR HOME. YOU LET US DESTROY EACH OTHER.
...I DIDN'T GET A CHANCE TO FINISH MY STORY FROM EARLIER IN THE CELL, CECILIA.
JUST BEFORE I CAME ACROSS THE OLD MAN...YOUR ELDER, I FOUND MY OLD HOME. THE PEOPLE LIVING THERE TOLD ME WHAT BECAME OF MY PARENTS YEARS BEFORE.
MY FATHER WAS TRYING TO ORGANIZE A REVOLUTION. HE TRIED TO FREE THIS TOWN FROM ROMAN INFLUENCE. THE TOWNSPEOPLE GATHERED UNDER HIM, BUT WHEN HE WAS DISCOVERED THEY QUICKLY DISTANCED THEMSELVES FROM HIM.
MOST EVEN CHEERED AS THEY WATCHED HIM AND MY MOTHER EXECUTED. TH-THEY CHEERED!
THE PEOPLE IN MY HOUSE TOLD ME THAT HE SPOKE OF ME OFTEN, BUT THAT THIS TOWN WAS HIS FIRST RESPONSIBILITY IN HIS MIND.
THE TOWN THAT CHEERED AS HE DIED.
T-THEY WERE JUST WEAK AND SCARED. *COUGH* THEY NEEDED SOMETHING TO RALLY THEM...TO GIVE THEM SOMETHING TO *COUGH* BELIEVE IN!
IS THIS WHAT YOUR FATHER WOULD HAVE WANTED?
YES.
THE END

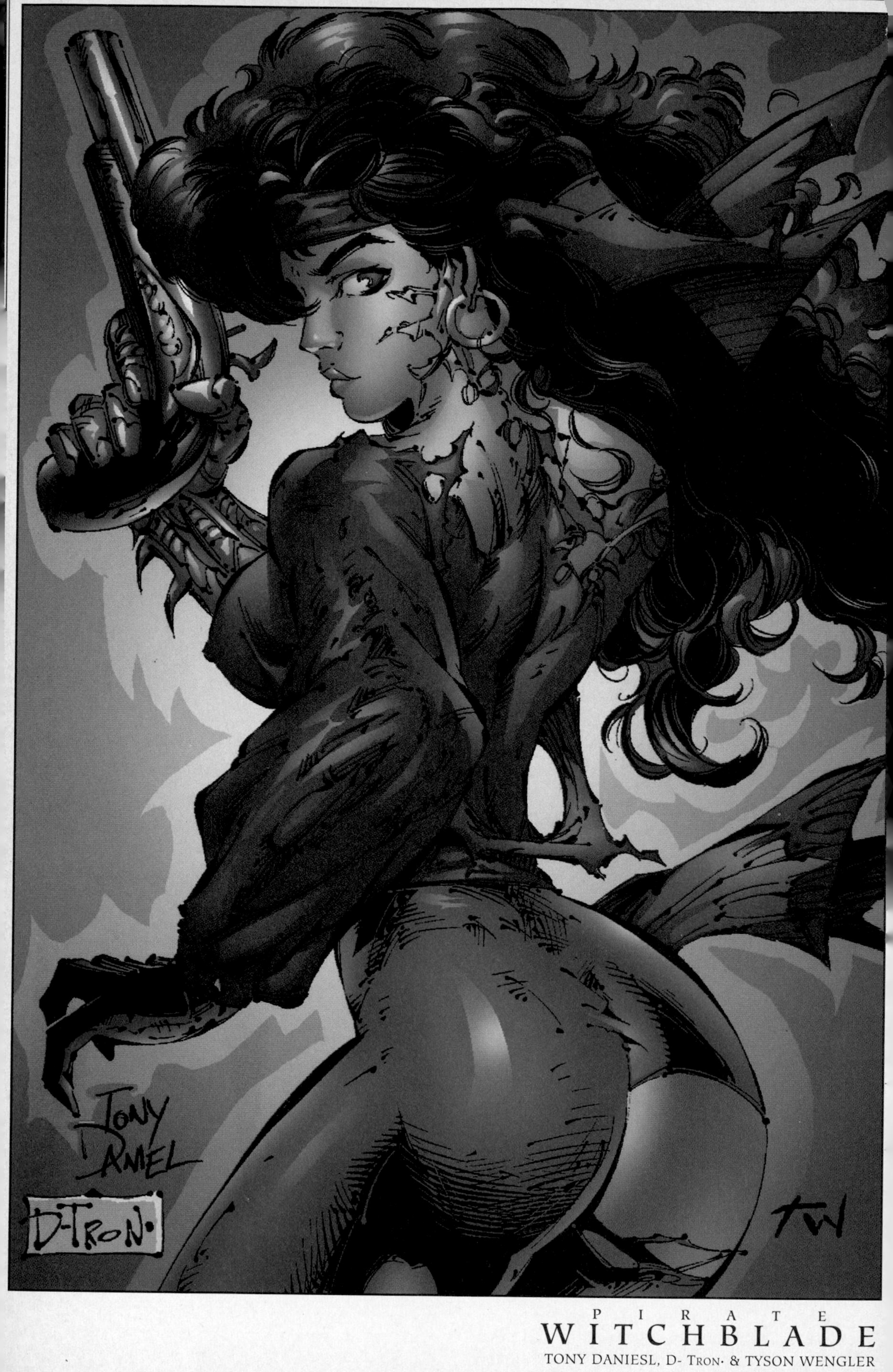
TONY DANIEL
D-TRON•
TW

P I R A T E
WITCHBLADE
TONY DANIESL, D- Tron• & TYSON WENGLER

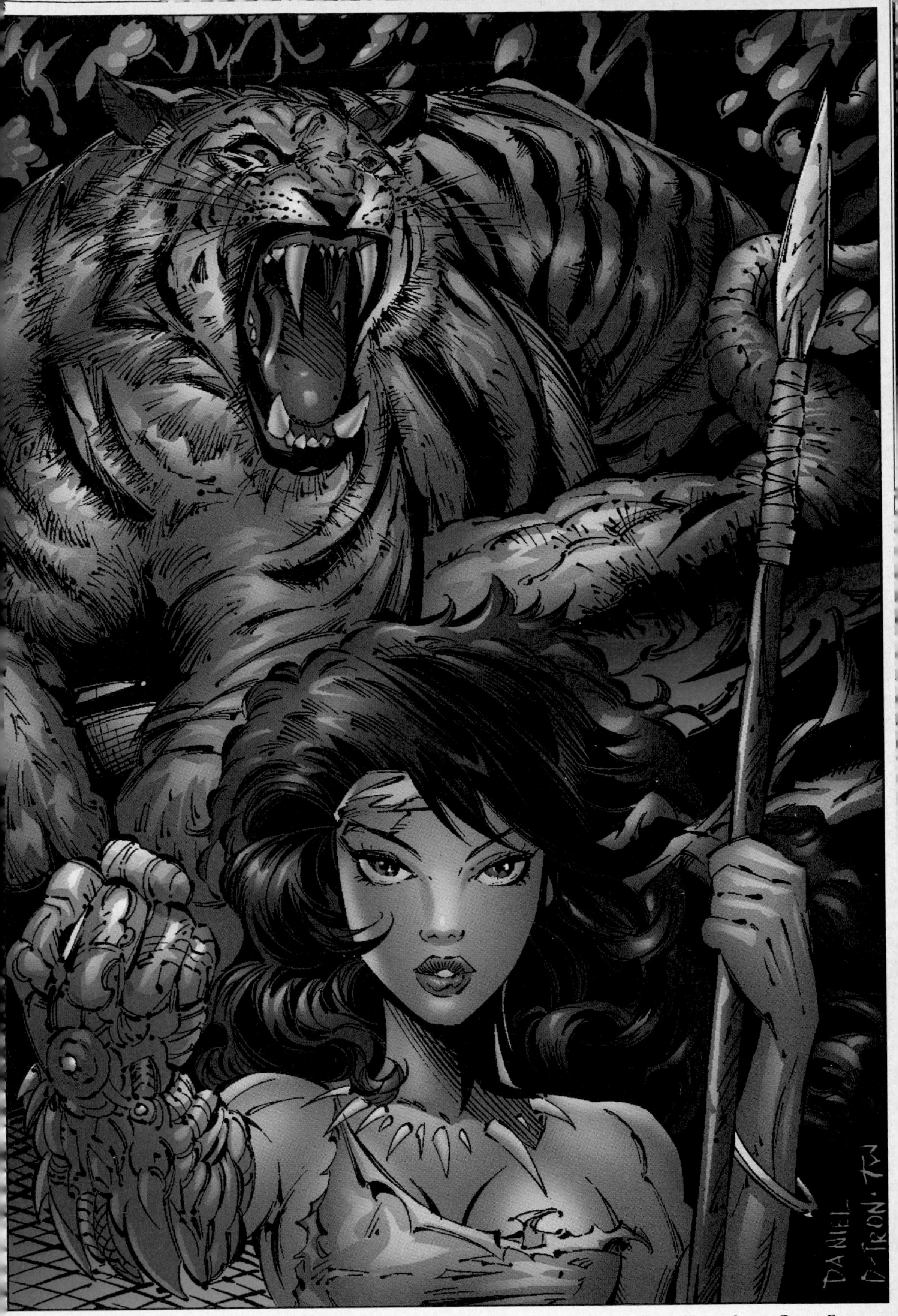
DANIEL.
D-TRON · TW

S A V A G E
WITCHBLADE
TONY DANIESL, D- TRON· & TYSON WENGLER

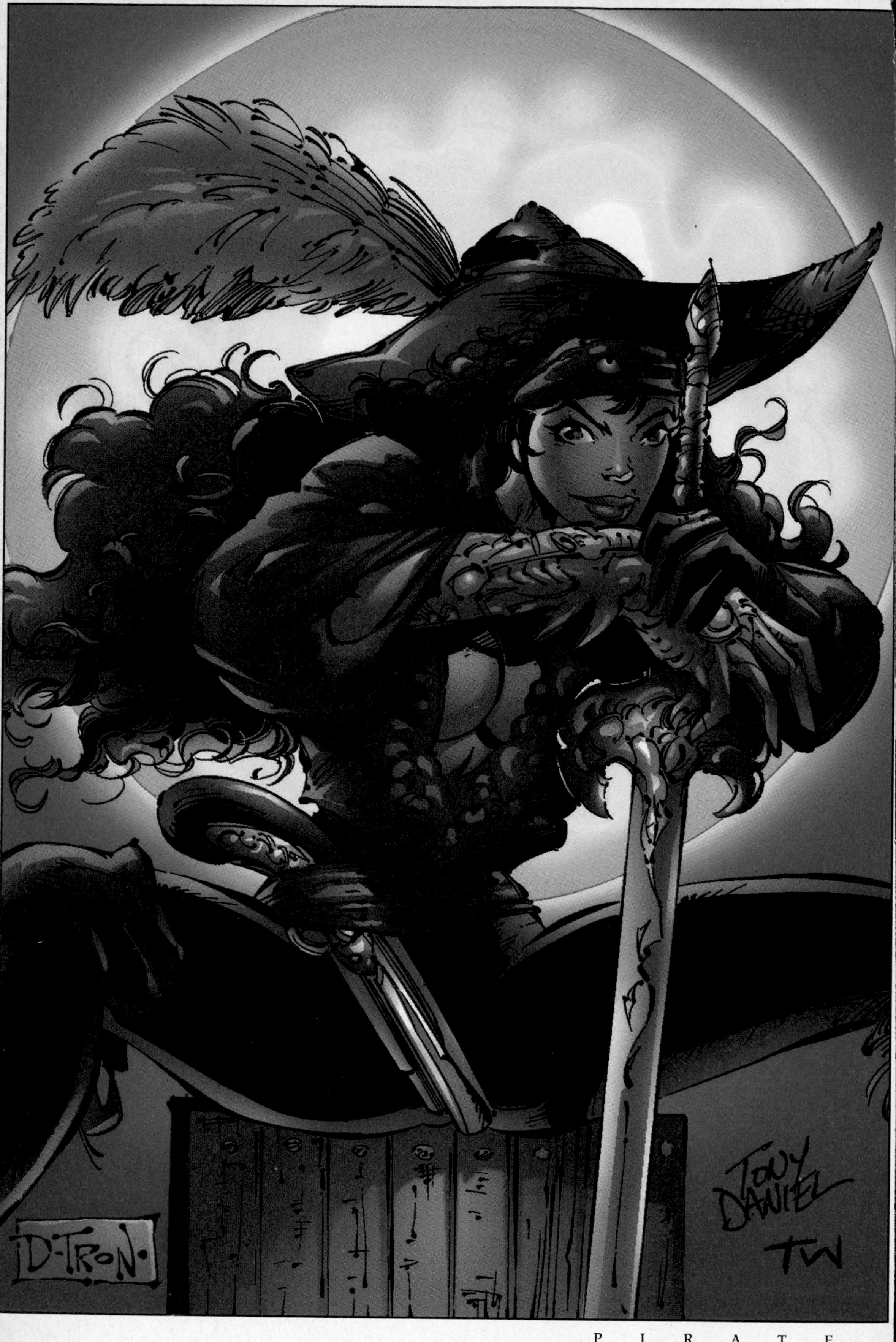
D-TRON
TONY DANIEL
TW

P I R A T E
WITCHBLADE
TONY DANIESL, D- TRON· & TYSON WENGLER

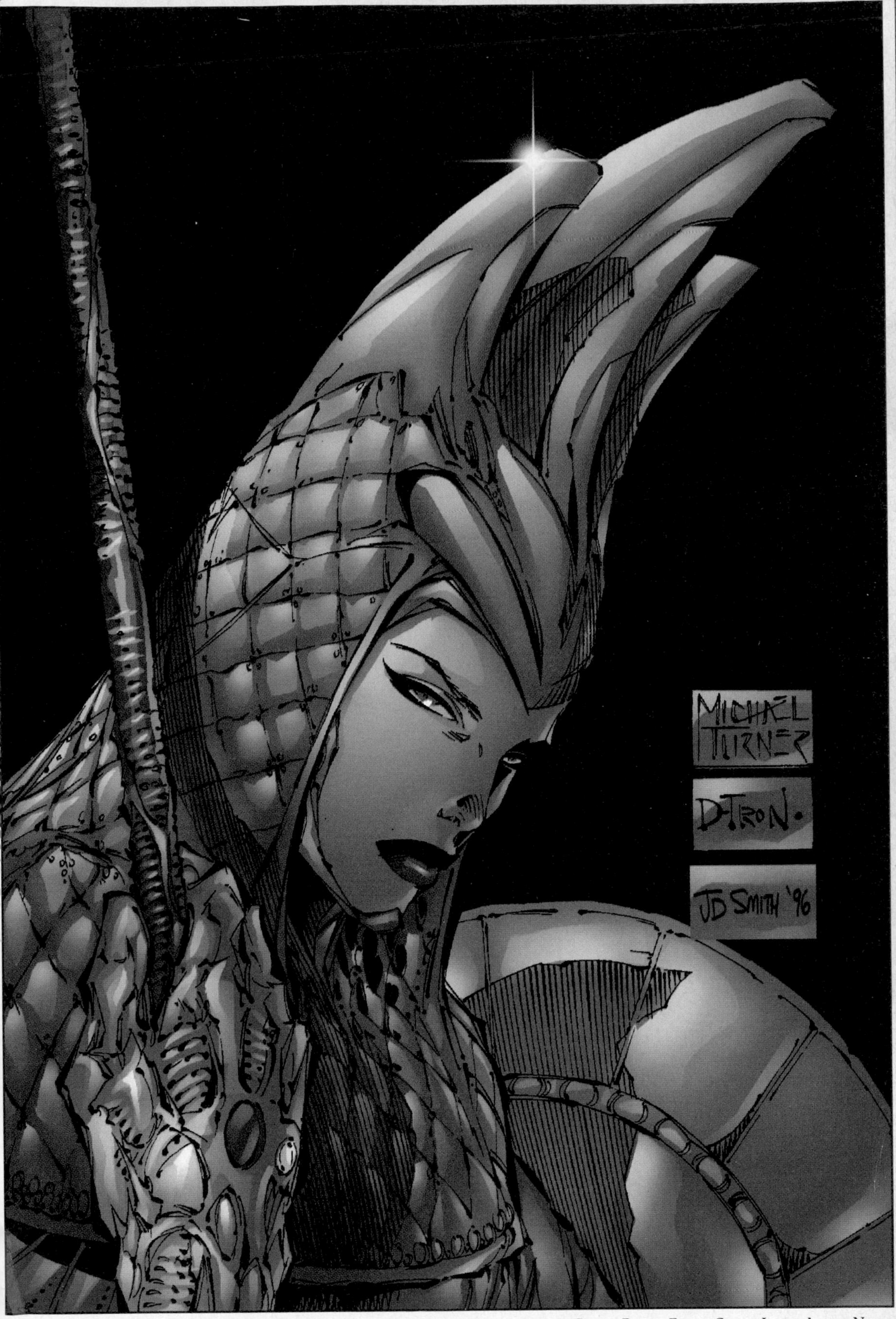
MICHAEL TURNER
D-TRON.
JD SMITH '96

GRECIAN
WITCHBLADE
MICHAEL TURNER, D- TRON· & JONATHAN D. SMITH